Rerun
Nation

Rerun Nation

How Repeats Invented American Television

DEREK KOMPARE

Routledge
New York • London

Published in 2005 by
Routledge
270 Madison Avenue
New York, NY 10016

Published in Great Britain by
Routledge
2 Park Square
Milton Park, Abingdon
Oxon OX14 4RN, U.K.

Routledge is an imprint of the Taylor & Francis Group.

Printed in the United States of America on acid free paper.

Library of Congress Cataloging-in-Publication Data
Kompare, Derek, 1969-
    Rerun nation : how repeats invented American television / by Derek Kompare.
        p. cm.
    Include bibliographical references and index.
    ISBN 0-415-97054-7 (hb: alk. paper) – ISBN 0-415-97055-5 (pb: alk. paper)
    1. Television reruns–United States.   2. Television broadcasting–United States–History.   I. Title.
PN1992.8.R47K66 2004
791.45'6–dc22   2004017248

Table of Contents

To Sally, for sharing the ride,
and to Benjamin, for joining it

Introduction and Acknowledgments

I grew up in the 1970s, a time that has been retrospectively constructed as one of the high water marks of television in the United States. Self-consciously "relevant" situation comedies like *All In The Family*, *The Mary Tyler Moore Show*, and *M*A*S*H*, and variously witty, violent, and camp police dramas like *Columbo*, *The Rookies*, and *Starsky and Hutch* dominated network prime time. While I was certainly cognizant of such programs at the time (and was even allowed to watch some of them), I was far more familiar with the programs that aired earlier in the day, in that tantalizing block of the schedule I knew as "after school." From about 3 pm to 5:30 pm (when Walter Cronkite would reliably materialize on our nineteen-inch Zenith), the independent and network-affiliated stations that we received presented an array of programs and characters transported from recent and distant years. *Gilligan's Island*. *Star Trek*. *The Beverly Hillbillies*. *Bewitched*. *The Little Rascals*. *Rocky and Bullwinkle*. *The Three Stooges*. *Tom and Jerry*. *The Brady Bunch*. Some of these programs were in color, while others were in black and white. Some seemed to be almost like the "present," while others were clearly from far, far in the past.

As I grew a bit older, I began to take more notice of the differences between these shows, and learned to connect them to particular times (e.g., Jethro = 1960s; Spanky = 1930s). I also became captivated by particular series, like *The Dick Van Dyke Show*, *Star Trek*, and *The Twilight Zone*, and diligently watched them every day in order to insure I had seen every episode, and, more importantly, could locate each episode in its historical place. Long before the Internet, I voraciously consumed published episode guides in books and magazines, and recognized how the television series I enjoyed were products of a creative industry, originally conceived and produced at particular times in the past. I connected Rod Serling's smoking and Rob Petrie's skinny ties to a mythical monochrome 1960s of morality plays, office hijinks, and cocktails, where the threat of horrifying apocalypse lay behind every one-liner and suburban dinner party. These reruns encapsulated a cultural past that I had not personally experienced more effectively than any other book or film I encountered. In presenting such programs, television functioned for me—and for many others, as I was soon to find out—as a window on to the past, literally a time machine.

I am now growing old in the 2000s, during a time of apparent televisual plenty. Not only does my set receive over 200 channels (via Direct Broadcast Satellite); I can also access television via a digital Personal Video Recorder, a DVD player, and, the old standby, a VCR. In addition, I can transfer television, in the form of various digital file formats, to my computer (or the Internet), for further archiving, editing, or playback possibilities.[1] Nevertheless, I still recognize "television"—not only the actual set, but the cultural and industrial institution—as a time machine, albeit it in a broader manner. Television asks us as viewers to unwind in its presence, or to bottle it up for later enjoyment. Well before that moment, however, television asks advertisers to buy this very time, exchanging it for access to hypothetical consumers.[2] And before *that* moment, television asks networks and stations to purchase time in the form of programming, in order to attract the advertisers, who hope the programs attract consumers. Time, in short, is the institution of television's primary product. Television, I have learned in these inter-vening years, is not a window onto the past, somehow "open" to let the past in. Rather, it is an engine that produces and reproduces time. The commodity of time flows through daily schedules, syndication contracts, DVD box sets, and the same old shows that I enjoyed a quarter-century ago. Moreover, while this time is certainly made up of hypothetical futures and more concrete presents, it also substantially constructed out of recycled time, that is, "bottled" time sold and repeated again and again. In short, reruns.

This is a book about the history of reruns on American television. More specifically, it is a cultural and industrial history, tracing how reruns developed as a particular practice in the business of television in the United States, and how they have shaped our experiences of television, and understanding of the recent past. My primary question is quite simple: why reruns? Why has television in this country consistently presented, indeed, has relied upon, so many of its past texts? Look beyond the network schedules—which have been well represented in historical studies of television—to the schedules of local television stations—which have not—and you will find a televisual mélange of present and past. Whether originally produced for theatrical release or made for television, extant films and videotapes have always dominated American television. Even during the 1920s and 1930s, when commercial television was only speculative, experimental broadcasters relied more on existing films than they did on live performances.[3] In the late 1940s, old films from Hollywood and Britain regularly appeared on the new medium. Within a few years, filmed programs that had been made for television were beginning to be repeated. As television became a dominant national institution in the 1950s and 1960s, these repeats became standard programming fare on every station, continually presenting and representing "the past" as an interminable array of feature films, short subjects, cartoons, newsreel clips, and cancelled network series. During the 1970s and 1980s, this repetition became tacitly acknowledged as an historical source, helping foster the national memory of television via the construction of a "television heritage." Since that point, reruns have become one of the primary products of television, fueling unprecedented industrial synergies and corporate branding, while becoming ensconced in American popular culture, and fostering experiences and practices of television structured around continual repetition.[4]

Despite this overwhelming repetition, television's ontology, its "essence," is still said to reside in its "liveness": its ability to transmit events as they happen to millions of receivers all across the nation or even world. This presumption has continued despite the fact that very few events on television are actually "live" in the classical sense; almost all are prerecorded and edited. "Liveness" in this capacity thus refers to the simultaneous national experience of a new program, even if it is only the premiere of a new (filmed and edited) episode of *Friends* or *ER*. The decisive shift towards reality-oriented event programming on the networks in the early 2000s (e.g., *Survivor, The Bachelor, American Idol*) would seem to bolster this sensibility, as such series function primarily as serialized narratives, routinely deliver large national audiences on their only national run, and are generally not repeated. However, what if this liveness assumption is wrong? What if television is not the ideal conduit for "live," new events, but is instead a machine of repetition, geared toward the constant recirculation of recorded, already-seen events? As Philip Auslander points out, the very concept of "liveness" has only existed as long as there have been "mediatized" alternatives, ranging from photography in the nineteenth century to the latest digital imaging today. "The very concept of live performance presupposes that of reproduction," he writes, "[the] live can exist only *within* an economy of reproduction."[5] I argue in this study that, despite frequent iterations of liveness (or pseudo-liveness), repetition is actually the primary structuring factor of commercial television in the United States. The promise of continual exploitation offered by televisual repetition—"bottled time"—has fostered a cultural and industrial television system fueled by reruns, even of reality programs.

Although the television rerun has only existed since the mid-1950s, Auslander's broader concept of an "economy of reproduction" has a much longer history. Repeated cultural forms have had a decisive structuring effect on the production and experience of culture for thousands of years, dating back before recorded history.[6] However, the histories and forms I am most concerned with date back a little over two hundred years, to the beginning of *industrialized cultural repetition*.

Beginning in the late eighteenth century, cultural forms ranging from books to sheet music to illustrations were produced and distributed on a massive scale as capitalist commodities. Fueled by new technologies, economic reorganization, and the rapidly evolving legal principle of copyright, once discrete and relatively limited cultural forms expanded throughout American society over the nineteenth century, shaping new national cultures, and solidifying the concept of the cultural commodity.[7] Moreover, by the end of the nineteenth century, individual texts within these forms were already regularly reprinted and recirculated over time, and even adapted into other cultural forms. Since then, new technologies of inscription (photography, cinematography, audio and video recording, digitization) and transmission (radio and television broadcasting, cable and satellite broadcasting, computer networks) have extended the range of commodified cultural forms, and the experience of industrialized cultural repetition. Nineteenth century novels are still reprinted in new versions, while twenty-first century pop music and films are regularly downloaded and catalogued on portable digital media players.

In exploring the various forms and practices of repetition, however, it is important to disentangle (though not entirely separate) questions of cultural production, textuality, and reception. Although media forms are certainly assembled as cultural artifacts, and are ultimately read, listened to, viewed, or interacted with by people (i.e., individual social and psychological subjects), industrialized cultural repetition is primarily an issue of cultural *production*, that is, how media texts are conceptualized, organized, produced, and distributed by media institutions (and individuals within those institutions). Accordingly, my focus in this book is on the material practices of media institutions; i.e., what is generally referred to as "the industry." Too often in media studies, the industry is treated as only the source of media texts, as if all the important and interesting stuff only happens in the finished textual product or its reception. On the other side of the same token, the industry is equally often seen as the be-all of media analysis, implying that a breakdown of a firm's corporate holdings somehow explains the meanings of their practices and products. I believe that the industry is neither merely a source nor merely a blueprint, but is rather a complex site of production, in the broadest sense of the word. To be sure, industries produce "products," in the usual sense of objects or services in commodity form. Indeed, as I will argue throughout, television programs (and reruns) certainly function as particular kinds of cultural products in a capitalist economy. However, industries also produce cultural and social practices, skills, sensibilities, and ideologies. Accordingly, while the issue of allocative control (i.e., the "money reason," as one of my industry-veteran colleagues puts it) is certainly critical towards understanding what goes in "the industry," it is not the full account of cultural production. Operational concerns—how particular forms and practices develop and promulgate within a particular institution or across an industry—provide a much clearer picture of the development of industrial forms, standards, and other "rules."[8]

The primary practice of cultural production investigated in this study is syndication, the sale of national (or even global) media texts to local outlets. Syndication began in the late nineteenth century during the expansion of newspaper and magazine publishing, and repeated particular cultural texts—e.g., comic strips, opinion columns, serialized fiction—on a national scale via local venues. Despite the much-promoted construction of broadcasting as a centralized national medium throughout the twentieth century, syndication continued unabated on both radio and television.[9] Although it has thus always been a significant part of the industry and culture of broadcasting in the United States, it has remained largely unexplored by broadcast historians. Typical accounts of television in the United States explore the medium primarily at the level of the nation, although in almost every case, the "nation" is understood only through the institution of the network, or more precisely, through network prime-time programming (and to a slightly lesser extent, daytime drama). While this conception of television has generated, and continues to raise, important insights and analyses of television texts, institutions, and audiences, it has also tended to reify a sense of the "TV nation" as limited to network programming.

However, syndicated programming is also national in scope, but it is also decidedly *not* network-based. Indeed, a conceptual gap dating back to the first decade of commercial radio broadcasting has always separated syndicated from network fare, particularly within the broadcasting industry. This gap has stemmed from the fact that syndicated programs are sold directly to stations on an ad hoc basis, rather than transmitted simultaneously across a national network. While network series are ostensibly vetted at the highest levels of television, syndicated programs are "peddled" on a station-to-station basis. This difference has fostered a sense of syndication as second-class national programming: either not "up" to network standards, or, in the case of off-network syndication, regarded as an aftermarket of hand-me-downs. This perception has also been fueled by industrial and critical attitudes towards particular program genres, audiences, and dayparts. While prime-time network programming is regarded as "mainstream" (incorporating a spectrum running from the acceptably banal to the engagingly cosmopolitan), syndicated programming is seen as somehow exterior to this mainstream. Its audiences are typically historically regarded as too feminine, too young, too old, too poor, too ethnic, too provincial, or too crude for a mainstream, network sensibility. Its programming is too sentimental, too tawdry, or too infantilizing, and is relegated, quite literally, to the "fringes" of television: too early or too late for prime-time, or, on independent stations, located "off the grid" of the networks.

Accordingly, it is not surprising that, while studies of syndication are common in media policy and economic work, they are rare in the critical/ cultural and historical field of television studies. William Boddy's important *Fifties Television: The Industry and its Critics*, published in 1990, has been virtually the only major book-length historical work that significantly incorporates issues of syndication into a study of the development of US television. Similarly, but less comprehensively, Phil Williams' 1994 *Journal of Popular Film and Television* article "Feeding Off The Past: The Evolution of the Television Rerun," has been the only published historical analysis of television reruns *per se* in humanities-based television studies. A 1999 double issue of the *Quarterly Review of Film and Video*, edited by Mark Williams, also featured accounts of syndication among its articles on regional and local television. While these works have been important and influential (to varying degrees), the issue of the development of syndicated reruns as an industry and culture largely still remains.

In addition to the lack of material study of reruns (and of syndication in general), because of the localized and ephemeral nature of broadcast texts and the broadcasting industry, the primary materials of this history have, to a great degree, been lost in space and time, dispersed in specific localities, and/or depleted through corporate upheaval, legal redaction, acts of god, or sheer neglect. While I have drawn from corporate and legal records wherever possible (especially in regards to NBC), the majority of information for this study has come from industry trade journals, and in particular the industry's primary journal, *Broadcasting*. Established in 1931, *Broadcasting* has been the radio and television industry's most prominent site of information, promotion, and debate. Editorially, it has unswervingly promoted the commercial organization of broadcasting, what it referred to in its first issue (and consistently thereafter) as the "American system" of broadcasting.[10] While *Broadcasting* is thus clearly a significant component of the media establishment, this does not necessarily mean that its pages speak with one voice. As discussed above, the "industry" has never been a monolith. Throughout *Broadcasting*'s run, groups and individuals from across the broadcasting business and policy worlds have dissected, debated, and debunked every aspect of media textuality and practice. Even industry-directed advertisements for stations, programs, and services in its pages suggest how particular texts and practices were promoted in divergent ways at particular times. *Broadcasting* and other trade publications have thus functioned as important intellectual spaces in the industry, fostering discussions and shaping concepts and practices that have impacted broadcasting in the United States, and around the world.

Rerun Nation is organized in chronological order, although the complexity of certain moments and practices necessitate some overlapping. Particular themes ranging from syndication's relationship to national memory to the legal restructuring of the industry around back-end exploitation resonate throughout. The first chapter traces the beginnings of modern industrialized repetition to the late eighteenth century, as key technologies, and accompanying industrial, commercial, and legal practices, contributed to the spread of "mass" cultures during the subsequent century. Creative works were not only made available on a wider basis during this period; they were also constantly *re*-produced, *re*-distributed, and *re*-consumed, staying in the culture, instead of disappearing. The *regime of repetition*—a dominant economic, legal, and cultural logic that determined the production and reproduction of culture—formed from several forces at this point. This opening chapter considers how the practices and principles of repetition—ranging from the standardization of genre and form to the reproduction and adaptation of popular texts—broadly functioned in the nascent industrialized culture of the late nineteenth and early twentieth centuries, with attention particularly paid to models circulated in the publishing, music, and film industries.

By the time radio broadcasting became commercially viable in the 1920s, all the key elements of the regime of repetition were in place, except for one: the broadcasting (and rebroadcasting) of recordings over the airwaves. Radio broadcasting was dominated by commercial and governmental interests who championed an ideal of live programming from the 1920s to 1940s, as the cultural discourse of "liveness" prevailed against the seemingly more practical principle of recording performances for later broadcasts and for posterity. However, during the same period, the recording was still regarded as a legitimate form of broadcasting in the everyday practices of local radio stations. As a physical commodity, the recording was both a cultural text and an economic asset that could be accessed and redistributed at will. Chapter 2 explores how recordings flourished on radio in the 1930s and 1940s due largely to independent syndicators like Frederick R. Ziv, and the World Broadcasting Service, who each successfully sold their recorded programs directly to sponsors and local stations. By the late 1940s, after advances in both the technology and the culture of recording, and acceptance by the dominant networks, the recording had become the dominant mode of radio broadcasting.

Even after recordings had come to rule radio, however, the concept of "reruns" had still not been fully legitimated. In the late 1940s, the familiar tension between live and recorded programming resurfaced in the nascent television medium, once again pitting national dictates against local pragmatics. Film, the only available recording medium for television until the early 1960s, quickly and quietly became the standard form of programming at the local level, where the utility of recorded programs was greatest. Syndicators and minor Hollywood studios leased hundreds of titles to stations across the country, selling them the rights to broadcast films not only once but multiple times. Many television executives, advertisers, and audience researchers were dubious of the economics of television film production and distribution. However, by the mid-1950s, ratings evidence affirmed the practice: repeats were successful in attracting not only the rapidly growing "new" television audience, but also viewers who had already seen the original broadcasts. Hence, *reruns*, as they now began to be called, became a staple form of local-originated programming. Chapter 3 examines how the developing aesthetics and business practices of television enabled reruns to become a fully accepted cultural, economic, and legal broadcasting practice.

By the early 1960s, reruns were established as an everyday part of the television schedule on local stations nationwide. Nevertheless, as the culture and industry of television was still very much developing at this time, so was the function of repetition within television. Accordingly, reruns developed into a significant form of capital across the industry. As the economic significance of reruns to program distributors and local stations grew, the syndication trade formalized and expanded through the 1960s. A wave of UHF-band independent stations came on the air in the largest markets, and organizations like NATPE formed to facilitate the program trade. However, the decade also produced scathing accounts of network power, reports that, by 1970, ultimately culminated in the two most sweeping FCC regulations in television history: the Prime Time Access Rule (PTAR), and the Financial Interest and Syndication Rules (fin-syn). While each rule scaled back the role that the networks could play in national (and international) program distribution, the industry's overall reliance on repetition continued to expand. Chapter 4 traces how the rerun functioned as the nexus of these debates and practices during the 1960s and 1970s.

In addition to their growing industrial significance, reruns also constituted a critical part of a rising cultural interest in the recent American past in the 1970s, and became the foundation for the *television heritage*: activated memories of television that were elided with broader memories of the postwar era. Throughout the 1970s and 1980s, television's past was cited as a source of American cultural heritage on many different fronts. Legitimate cultural institutions, including the Smithsonian and the new Museum of Television and Radio, canonized particular television creators, characters, and series. Mainstream books and articles remembered early television. Humanities-based academic television studies emerged as a viable field of study. Television fans organized their appreciation of several different series into clubs, conventions, and publications. Chapter 5 explores how reruns moved beyond the economic impact of repetition, and contributed to the shaping of postsixties nostalgia and popular memory.

The emerging television heritage, in turn, also impacted the business of television in significant ways. Since the early 1970s, shifting regulatory regimes and erratic business cycles have produced a turbulent programming environment on television. Off-network syndication flourished during this period, aiding the rise of nonnetwork firms such as MTM, Viacom, and Metromedia. The television heritage boosted the cultural profile of past programs, which in turn raised their marketability. The industry-wide bust of the late 1980s ultimately accelerated this process, as it generated a variety of significant, interrelated economic trends which continued throughout the rest of the century: a larger reliance on first-run, nonfiction programming; the growth of advertising barter; and the massive consolidation of the media industry, linking content libraries and distribution channels to an unprecedented degree. Chapter 6 argues that an unswerving belief in the power of televisual repetition has served as the fundamental logic that has tied together the cultural, economic, and legal regimes of off-network syndication since the mid-1970s.

By the 1980s, though, broadcast fare was only part of television, as cable networks, relying on libraries of repeated programming like feature films and off-network reruns, further enhanced the experience of televisual repetition. Since then, dozens of specialized channels, such as Nick At Nite, TV Land, and the Sci-Fi Channel, have taken the principle of repetition to a new level of intensity. These channels function as television *boutiques*, focusing on particular audiences and genres, and providing not only rerun programming but an entire formal iconography and ethos geared towards a particular television brand. Chapter 7 examines how cable channels, including, in particular, Viacom's Nick At Nite and TV Land, developed this "boutique" model of televisual repetition, creating highly stylized spaces for showcasing past television programs.

While broadcast and cable reruns have certainly fueled the television heritage, the rise of home video since the 1970s has added an additional element to the regime of repetition: the ability of viewers to *acquire* permanent copies of the television heritage on tape or disk. However, economic and legal concerns have shaped how these technologies and practices have developed in the home. While a viable system of releasing feature films on home video was in place by the mid 1980s, the particular cultural and economic aspects of television have challenged both the distribution and acquisition of television series on home video. The rapid rise of DVD in the late 1990s and early 2000s sparked a revolution in the status of television on home video, as entire seasons and series were packaged in box sets designed for consumer acquisition. The final chapter of *Rerun Nation* traces how the practices of home video have both reinforced and challenged the established modes of repetition, as television moves from the broadcast schedule to the video shelf.

Beyond home video, the transition to digital media is arguably the most significant issue facing media producers, distributors, scholars, and users in the current decade. Significant cultural, industrial, and legal issues, ranging from cacophonous megachannel media systems to Internet file sharing, have challenged and shaped the established practices of repetition. The conclusion to *Rerun Nation* speculates about the ultimate fate of twentieth century televisual repetition in twenty-first century media systems.

Rerun Nation would not have been possible without the intellectual and spiritual support of many people and organizations.

This project was conceived during my graduate study in the Media and Cultural Studies division of the University of Wisconsin-Madison Communication Arts Department. I am grateful for the program's support and guidance during its initial phase. Julie D'Acci was a particularly strong influence on this book (and its author), and I will always value her intellect, wit, and support. I would also like to thank Michele Hilmes, John Fiske, David Bordwell, Tino Balio, Vance Kepley, and Nietzchka Keene, and visiting scholars William Boddy and Eileen Meehan for their continued interest and support.

My student colleagues at UW were, and remain, model scholars and friends. I am grateful for their community during and after our studies, but would like to extend particular thanks to Doug Battema, Ron Becker, Kim Bjarkman, Norma Coates, Jennifer Fuller, Dorinda Hartmann, Michael Kackman, Donald Meckiffe, Jason Mittell, Matthew Murray, Tasha Oren, Lisa Parks, Paul Ramaeker, Chris Smith, Jeff Smith, and Pauline Zvejnieks, for their insights and commiserations. Developing a project with several parallel concerns, Daniel Marcus has been a particularly unceasing source of inspiration and thought, and I am especially grateful for his friendship.

I have also benefited immensely from the community of scholars in Television Studies, through the Society for Cinema and Media Studies and other venues. Henry Jenkins has been a constant source of encouragement throughout this endeavor, and I am thankful in particular for his attention to this book in 2002–2003. Several others have provided direct or indirect encouragement in preparing this study, and I appreciate their work, comments, and discussions: Michael Curtin, Mary Desjardins, Mary Beth Haralovich, James Schwoch, Mimi White, and Mark Williams.

The faculty and students of the Radio-Television-Film Department at Texas Christian University were also supportive during this project's writing. I would like to single out Richard Allen for his ongoing curiosity and insights about reruns, Patricia Kirk for her impeccable office assistance, and Roger Cooper for his energy and wit. Several of my students also helped keep this project moving with their interest and passion for television; I am appreciative in particular of Jason Davis, Adam Faust, Scott Hinze, and Ashley Hungerford.

My editor at Routledge, Matthew Byrnie, was a model of efficiency, encouragement, and patience. I am grateful to him and his assistants for their skill and assistance in bringing this book to you.

Tim Anderson has been a ready source of discussion, distraction, and dynamism. His energies and challenges propelled me at particularly sticky points, again proving to me that he is not only a first-rate media scholar; he is a hell of a friend.

I would also like to thank my parents, Ed and Maria Kompare, for humoring, and nurturing, their son's long interest in television, and my in-laws Larry and Betty Tritschler for their constant interest and encouragement.

Finally, only one other person has had to live with this project through its many meanderings, and I remain in awe of her constant love, support, patience and humor.

Notes

1. Moreover, once in this form, I can manipulate it in any way I want to. Its time need not function as it did on television, but can be "cut," "grabbed," "sampled," and "PhotoShopped." For more on the malleability of digital media, see Lev Manovich, *The Language of New Media* (Cambridge, MA: MIT Press, 2001), 27–48, 115–175.

2. We consumers in front of our sets are not hypothetical. However, the consumers represented in statistical data generated largely by the A. C. Nielsen Company, the only consumers the television industry is interested in, most certainly are. See Eileen Meehan, "Why We Don't Count: The Commodity Audience," in Patricia Mellencamp, ed., *Logics of Television* (Bloomington: Indiana University Press, 1990), 117–137.

3. Joseph H. Udelson, *The Great Television Race: A History of the American Television Industry, 1925–1941* (Tuscaloosa: University of Alabama Press, 1982), 24–27.

4. As of this writing (early 2004), premium and basic cable channels routinely run episodes of their series dozens of times over months and years, personal video recorders (PVRs) like TiVo hold one hundred hours of recorded television, and season box sets of television series on DVD are the fastest-growing segment of the home video industry.

5. Philip Auslander, *Liveness: Performance in a Mediatized Culture* (New York: Routledge, 1999), 51.

6. Harold A. Innis, *Empire and Communications* (Toronto: University of Toronto Press, 1972).

7. See John Guillory, *Cultural Capital: The Problem of Literary Canon Formation* (Chicago: University of Chicago Press, 1993), on the historical and theoretical roots of aesthetics and political economy in the seventeenth and eighteenth centuries, especially pp. 306–326.

8. The work of Keith Negus has been particularly helpful to me in locating the production of culture among the interactions of cultural workers and institutions. See especially his *Music Genres and Corporate Cultures* (New York: Routledge, 1999).

9. Indeed, one of the most popular, influential, and controversial programs in network radio history, *Amos 'n' Andy*, originated as the prerecorded, syndicated program *Sam 'n' Henry* in 1928.

10. From the premiere editorial, dated 15 October 1931:

   > *Broadcasting* makes it [sic] bow firm in its belief in the American system of radio. With all its youthful faults, Radio by the American Plan still expresses a certain genius of the American people—the genius of free enterprise.... To the American system of free, competitive and self-sustaining radio enterprise, this new publication, accordingly, is dedicated.

   "We Make Our Bow," editorial, *Broadcasting*, 15 October 1931, p. 18.

1

Industrializing Culture: The Regime of Repetition in the United States, 1790–1920

> Characterized less and less, then, by its organization into two distinct realms, that of manufacture and that of distribution, the nineteenth-century economy slowly began to take on the appearance of a single system of endless circulation.[1]

Historians have long addressed the importance of industrialization to the nascent United States of America in the nineteenth century. Americans were a socially disparate people, spread over an immense, wilderness-filled space, yet national cultures were still effectively promulgated over the Republic's first century. While significant points of conflict simmered and boiled over at critical junctures (e.g., the moral and political standoffs that culminated in the Civil War, the ongoing war between capital and labor, the virtual extermination of the continent's original inhabitants, and the anxieties over immigration), a particular image of "America" still coalesced during this period, an image repeated in millions of mass-produced, mass-distributed cultural commodities ranging from dinnerware to sheet music. This image centered largely on the dyad of home and frontier: the reproduction of domesticity on alien terrain. "America," as circulated through this mass-produced image, was a nation of (white) settlers building communities and sharing in the bonds of Home and Property. The simplicity of this image amplified its appeal, both in the United States and abroad (to actual or would-be immigrants), and its industrialized production seemed to offer voluminous evidence of its veracity. See, it suggested, America really is about turning the wilderness into home, reproducing the familial (and the familiar) in a New World. It is striking that this image, its visibility exponentially amplified through industrial repetition, prophecies the comforting characters, settings, and narratives of so many twentieth-century television reruns.

This opening chapter is concerned with the industrial and cultural roots of television reruns in nineteenth and early twentieth century mass-produced culture. Although, as Chapter 3 will examine, reruns appeared to be a novel concept to the television industry of the 1950s, the cultural, industrial, and legal frameworks of such mediated repetition were laid throughout the previous 150 years. Over the course of the nineteenth and early twentieth centuries, secular culture, particularly in the United States, became truly "mass" in scale for the first time in human history, propelled by industrial capitalism, high technology, and tumultuous social shifts (e.g., the Civil War; the emancipation of slaves; waves of immigration; rapid urban growth; rising intellectual challenges to capitalism; the standardization of formal education; and the formation of industrialized working, middle, and upper classes). These factors, and others, helped shape repetition as a major principle of the industrial production of culture; that is, as a set of widely-held perceptions and practices that sustained the cultural presence of mass-produced cultural products, or returned them to the culture, instead of allowing them to fade into obscurity. Industrial repetition became a taken-for-granted approach to cultural production over the nineteenth and into the twentieth centuries, a way of thinking that stabilized particular cultural genres, forms, styles, and themes, and marginalized alternative modes of cultural production.

The very idea of culture was industrialized to an unprecedented degree during this period. In addition to the burgeoning commercial trade in mass-produced cultural objects, key social institutions increasingly adopted an industrial approach to the production of cultured citizens, utilizing modern practices of standardization, discrimination, and reproduction. For example, the concept of a "great books"-oriented English curriculum was promulgated in American secondary education in the last quarter of the nineteenth century largely as a form of social distinction: a mechanism with which to police access to the elite colleges.[2] The publishers who manufactured various "libraries" of "great books" facilitated this goal: all the "necessary" works of English literature made available in a standardized commodity form, sometimes complete with matching shelves. This highly organized social reproduction had largely been achieved through the mass reproduction of culture. Despite the noise and fleeting significance generally attributed to mass-produced culture by most of its critics over the past two centuries, the massive scale of its system of production has fostered a cultural terrain in which particular texts, genres, and themes have a longer and broader presence in the popular consciousness than was previously possible.

Culture became a form of renewable economic and cultural capital in the nineteenth and early twentieth centuries, a status reached through the confluence of technological, legal, economic, and cultural forces. Three decisive factors stand out in this history. First, new technologies were developed and adapted to emerging forms of commodity production. Various printing technologies (e.g., stereotyping) greatly facilitated the extended commodification of existing works, reducing the labor and time required for reproduction. At the same time, the railroad enabled a broader, timelier geographical distribution of products, a key factor in the development and maintenance of a national culture across the expanse of the United States. Second, the complex and dynamic legal principle of copyright formalized the economic value of the cultural work, solidifying its status as capital, and assuaging the fears of entrepreneurial cultural producers and reproducers. Articles, stories, books, illustrations, musical compositions, films and audio recordings were all granted copyright protection in the United States by 1909, protecting their owners from piracy, and facilitating their proprietary reproduction. Third, the creation and expansion of markets for cultural works, and the development of new, reproducible forms and practices to serve them, greatly shaped the experience of industrialized culture for millions of readers, viewers, and listeners. Taken together, these forces had naturalized the products of industrialized cultural repetition by the early twentieth century.

These technologies and practices of repetition developed in the industrialization of two broad media forms between the 1790s and 1920s: print media (book publishing, music publishing, and newspaper content syndication), and audiovisual media (audio recording and film). While the works produced by these industries differed in significant ways, they shared key technologies; legal protections; production, distribution, and consumption practices; and even some aesthetic principles. Most critically, each industry was radically altered by industrialized cultural repetition: by successfully managing the mass reproduction and circulation of cultural works over space and time. I will explore these industries in a rough chronological order in this chapter (in keeping with the rest of the book), but divided into the broad areas of print and audiovisual media. They are separated here in order to distinguish the impact of each on the immediate cultural terrain of the twentieth century.

Since this is a book about television, the overview of earlier cultural production presented here is, by necessity, brief. More thorough investigations, from scholars more adept than I, can be found in the works I have consulted. This limited foray is only intended to broadly explore how the material and conceptual practices of mass, industrialized culture coalesced between the 1790s and 1920s, enabling the regime of repetition, and, ultimately, the culture and industry of television reruns.

Print Media

The eighteenth century ended not only with epochal political revolutions in Europe and North America, but also with the equally critical acceleration of industrialized capitalism. The nineteenth century would see the culmination of each of these processes, and their application to the production of culture. New modes of production (involving both the organization of labor and the impact of new technologies), new economic and legal concepts (statutory copyright protection, royalties, trade associations, etc.), new markets for commodities (not only larger numbers, but greater cultural, geographical, and social diversity), and new methods of marketing developed during this period. Economic historian Alfred P. Chandler notes that these innovations fueled the shift of the American economy away from single-owner enterprises and towards modern managerial capitalism, as "the visible hand of management replaced the invisible hand of market forces where and when new technology and expanded markets permitted a historically unprecedented high volume and speed of materials through the processes of production and distribution."[3]

All of these changes factored into the development of the publishing industry,[4] which grew from an intellectually substantial, if culturally and socially limited, creative and political endeavor, to become the center of mass-produced cultural expression. From its European inception in the fifteenth century through most of the eighteenth century, publishing had been a time-consuming, expensive process with little profit for publishers and authors. Indeed, authors themselves still typically paid most of the production costs of publication in the 1790s.[5] However, changes in the organization and technologies of printing prompted an expansion of the scope of the publishing industry in the nineteenth century. As Ronald J. Zboray notes in his study of antebellum publishing in the United States, publication production began to be reorganized away from skills-intensive artisanal modes and toward more rationalized modes oriented around new technologies, "a reorganization that for the most part destroyed traditional work rhythms and relationships."[6] While labor was displaced because of these changes (and not for the last time), publishers reaped the benefits of much more efficient production processes, enabling faster production, and more standardized copies.

The most critical new production components were new forms of type that not only streamlined the printing process, but also represented fixed capital for their owners. With the right type, publications could be more easily reprinted, reducing or eliminating the labor necessary for resetting text on the press. Less expensive but more durable metal typefaces first became available to U.S. music publishers in the 1790s, greatly facilitating the production of "songsters," widely popular and affordable collections of songs (lyrics and, in some cases, musical notation). Andrew and Daniel Wright's *The American Musical Miscellany*, a three-hundred-page collection of 111 songs, was published in 1798 with this new type; by 1825, over 400 such songsters had been published (often in several editions) in the United States.[7] While such typefaces helped standardize the look and production of published works, an arguably more significant process was developed during the 1830s and 1840s whereby entire typesets could be preserved on sets of metal plates (instead of as collections of individual letters). We are familiar with the term for this process today—stereotyping—and its contemporary meaning stems from its earlier utility, i.e., as a shortcut to textual production. Prior to this time, books, articles, and musical compositions only generally existed through one print run, and had to be completely reassembled for subsequent production; stereotyping enabled publishers to preserve entire typesets for later reproduction. Accordingly, the stereotype plates themselves thus became significant physical assets: commodities sought and acquired by nineteenth-century publishers in much the same way rights to extant media properties are bought and sold today. As Russell Sanjek states in his history of the U.S. music industry, by the 1850s, "[a] publisher's true financial worth was best judged by the number of plates he owned, and they were the most important element in the acquisition of a music house going out of business or in the disposition of an estate left by a music publisher."[8]

While stereotyping made the reproduction of text more efficient, lithography facilitated the reproduction of illustrations. In early lithography, images were indelibly drawn on a slab of limestone, which was then used to press highly detailed copies, fostering the trade in mass-produced illustrations as decorative prints, book illustrations, and sheet music covers. Like the printed word or musical composition, these reproduced images helped promote particular, standardized visions of American life to more, and more geographically dispersed, readers, fostering a national cultural identity. The famous Currier & Ives illustrations of pastoral rural life were particularly popular in this regard during the mid-nineteenth century, and were among the first iconic images of America mass produced and mass distributed as commodities.[9]

The adaptation of steam power to the actual printing process (in faster, larger-capacity presses) accelerated the reproductive capacity of typesets and lithographs. Similarly, another key steam-based technology, the railroad, greatly standardized, accelerated, and expanded the distribution of cultural works across the continent. According to Chandler, the effect on commerce was revolutionary. Even by 1840, railroads already built had the capacity to carry more than 50 times the freight per mile than established canals.[10] The railroad's impact on the print trade was particularly profound. Railroads not only shipped publications to otherwise distant markets in an efficient and timely fashion; they also prompted new spaces for the consumption of publications (in train stations and on trains), and boosted the distribution of new, mass-oriented literary forms designed for quicker consumption, including magazines, story-papers, and dime novels. Since these forms were mass-produced for a national audience, they contributed to a broadening and standardization of U.S. print culture. As Zboray states, "[railroad] development transformed the nature of community life for readers and oriented them outward to the national culture and away from local exigencies."[11] Moreover, as Chandler argues, the speed of the railroad helped prompt the synchronization of the world's time zones, thus enhancing regional and international trade, and the industry itself offered a model of modern corporate organization, with middle managers replacing direct top-down decision-making, which soon spread to other industries, including publishing.[12]

By the mid-nineteenth century, the United States had the largest, most diverse, and most geographically dispersed literate population in the world. Book publishing had developed as a mass-market industry sooner than in any other nation. While the new technologies of production and distribution fed a growing demand for publications throughout the nation, they also fostered new organizations of labor and capital. Accordingly, concern over the control of these works, as reproducible economic assets, grew in step with the industries themselves.

Copyright, as it is codified officially in U.S. legal code, is rooted in British legal principles, and particularly in the Copyright Act of 1710 (i.e., the "Statute of Anne"). While copyright has often been described as a legal mechanism to protect the author/creator of a work, legal historian David Saunders argues that the justification of the 1710 law was primarily economic, originating not with authors, but with printers and book-sellers, who were able to claim the exclusive legal ownership of works they produced.[13] The statute further codified an earlier practice (the registration of works in the Stationer's Office), and described the exclusivity of copyright for copyright holders (the *legal owners*, as opposed to the actual creators of works). The act also set time limits on this exclusivity: an initial 14 years, plus a possible second 14 years while the original copyright holder was still living. While particular aspects of the statute, and the question of an author's "natural" rights to their work (regardless of its legal ownership under copyright law), would still be disputed throughout the eighteenth and nineteenth centuries in British courts, this original law and its application greatly influenced the shapers of the first U.S. copyright laws. Indeed, copyright is one of the very first legal principles of the United States, enshrined in Article I, Section 8 of the Constitution as a means to advance knowledge in the new society ("to promote the Progress of Science and useful Arts, by securing for limited times to Authors and Inventors the exclusive Right to their respective Writings and Discoveries"). This intent was elaborated in the first U.S. Copyright Act (1790), focused as it was on "useful" works, as Saunders argues.[14]

As the markets for cultural commodities expanded in the nineteenth century, so too did the provisions of copyright law. These legislative changes, always the result of intensive and contentious lobbying from multiple interests (creators, publishers, labor, merchants, etc.) consistently addressed two key principles of the law: the duration of copyright, and the designation and remuneration of various copyright holders.[15] The legal category of "authorship" was refined over time to curb the piracy of patents and publications, fostering a system of exclusive rights holders and licensees, whereby rights could be transferred or distributed to different owners on a permanent or temporary basis. Significantly, however, the U.S. statutes only initially applied to the works of U.S. citizens; foreign publications were not protected until the 1891 revision. Accordingly, American publishers routinely poached British works for decades. While British authors and publishers were not happy with this situation, American publishers were able to produce massive amounts of noncopyrighted British works, fueling the early expansion of publication readership and retailing.[16] Despite this issue, copyright law moved towards a conception of authorship as proprietorship, a legal precedent that would be significant for subsequent media forms, as later chapters will detail.

With these legal reconceptions of cultural work increasingly in place, by the 1850s, writers began to work less as solitary creators and more as company employees, "[writing] quickly, regularly, and according to the specifications of another," according to Janice Radway.[17] These so-called "hack" writers worked diligently to fill the pages of the burgeoning story-paper and (later) dime-novel industries, often with no individual credit; their work would instead go out under a publisher's brand.[18] Thus, the publisher (and, increasingly, the editor) assumed the role of a manager of a cultural factory, treating works more for their fit into the firm's (and the industry's) "list," "catalog," or identity, rather than their individual virtues. As Radway notes, this was the beginning of the industrialization of cultural producers: "corporate, prosthetically augmented, creative agent[s] whose capacity to produce reading material was significantly expanded by social cooperation and by systematic integration into a carefully managed and controlled, mechanically assisted system."[19] Together, the new modes of production and distribution, and the increasingly extensive property rights protected by copyright law (and policed by zealous new publishing trade organizations), fostered an economic environment in which publishers could produce and distribute on a massive scale, and reap unprecedented profits. However, impressive as the increase in scale may be, it does not alone explain the changing forms of print culture in the nineteenth century. That is, how did *particular* forms and genres develop, and become entrenched in the culture? The answer to this question lies in the cultural functions of industrial repetition: the codification, canonization, and exploitation of popular creators (authors and composers), forms, and genres.

The rise of professional writers at this time indicates how the publishing industry was changing publishing culture, producing a conceptual split, during the last half of the nineteenth century, between "serious" and "popular" publications. The more publications become available—in cheaper editions, and to wider publics—the less exclusive literacy became. Accordingly, cultural elites feared the corruption of cultural values, or at least the values that they favored. Inexpensive, widely distributed forms of literary fiction like story-papers and dime novels were a particular target of their ire. From the elites' perspective, these cheap books were produced only for profit, and provided emotional excitement in stock narratives; they thus held no redeeming literary value. "Commercial" books such as these were designed for a market-based ephemerality, appearing and disappearing as profits and tastes dictated, and taking full advantage of the flexibility afforded by the new modes of production and distribution, and the accompanying new markets for cultural goods. By contrast, cultural gatekeepers reified the "literary" book as a more traditional (and thus, more "worthy") text *and* cultural object, often valued as much for its physical qualities as for its intellectual content.

As Radway notes, the new, "commercial" press was premised upon the repetition of its products in space and time. While "literary books" were ostensibly meant to be singular and timeless, "[the commercial] system of cultural production conceived of publication as an endless process of circulation or cultural recycling, as a reformulation and ever-widening distribution of previously existing material."[20] Accordingly, commercial book, newspaper, and music publishers all found that careful investment in and marketing of particular, easily recognizable concepts (including the celebrity value of particular authors and composers) paid off with long-term benefits. As a physical capital investment, electroplated stereotyping encouraged publishers to develop and maintain relationships with popular authors and composers, in order to subsume them under their imprint, list, catalog, or brand, and fully exploit their copyrights. A popular creator (or even corporate creator-persona) could be effectively marketed as a distinct personality, drawing consumers in to previous works as well as new ones.[21] Accordingly, stipulations for the publication of future books became prevalent in author–publisher contracts by the late nineteenth century.[22] However, even self-consciously "literary" firms also promoted this sense of an author's (or even publisher's) "personality," often via the books themselves as aesthetic objects. Michael Kearns argues that Herman Melville's mid-nineteenth-century author persona was shaped by the design and promotion of Wiley & Putnam's editions of his works (particularly in their "Library of American Books" of the 1840s and 50s) as desirable tangible objects: "[The publishers] had a definite idea of the buying public's different horizons and pecuniary motive for situating a given work within one or several of those horizons. Their decisions helped create the author 'Herman Melville' by providing readers with expectations about the value, significance, and genre of this author's early productions."[23] Similarly, particularly shrewd publishers sold the same titles in several different versions, appealing to different readers, for completely different reasons. By 1860, for example, many publishers were already offering "deluxe" versions of particular titles, with more elaborate binding, covers, and endpapers. Although ostensibly marketed as literary texts, these versions functioned primarily as decorative objects in upper middle-class homes.[24]

The elaborated marketing of books from the mid-nineteenth century forward exemplifies the contradictory motives of industrialized cultural production, factors that would continue to shape culture into the age of television in the next century. Publishing firms required a constant supply of new material in order to attract customer interest and develop new audiences. However, as the expanding markets for culture, and the complex legal construction of copyright indicate, the repetition of existing cultural products also became a fiscally lucrative enterprise at this time. These twin virtues of disposability and recyclability seem paradoxical, but they stand at the heart of the changing culture of the nineteenth century, and would only gain in significance in the twentieth. Cultural works were increasingly ephemeral (in an increasingly crowded market), and yet relied heavily upon repeated forms, themes, and content. Accordingly, publishers sought ways to foster repetition over time, extending the cultural lives, and financial worth, of their texts and authors. The existing and emergent cultural institutions of education and public culture provided an effective means by which particular books, authors, composers, genres, and even forms could be linked with particular cultural values. Thus, the forces of cultural codification facilitated the design of industrialized repetition.

Nowhere was this more apparent than in education, which helped shape canons and syllabi throughout the last quarter of the nineteenth century. As a major public institution, education determines the viable boundaries of knowledge and culture in a society. Both the music and literary industries marketed their wares via this ostensible virtue, using the support of schools and individual educators for cultural validation as well as profit. Music educators and students constituted the primary market for extant songs, scores, and folios throughout the nineteenth century, as domestic piano sales surged, and musicianship became a standard component of a middle-class upbringing.[25] Similarly, book publishers joined with schools and libraries to promote "classic" literature as a form of self-betterment. As public libraries increased in number and scope, a new system of literary organization, designed by Melvil Dewey, was introduced in 1876 for the express purpose of promoting readership rather than merely storing books. As Radway claims, this was a further step towards more "reader-driven" books: "Books in his system were assumed to be in dialogue with one another; readers were conceptualized as people with prior goals and topical interests; and the business of knowledge production itself was conceived as an infinitely expanding, always progressing enterprise."[26] Along the way, particular books were promoted as more important to the cultivation of readers. N. N. Feltes notes how this period saw the publication of several "100 Best Books" lists, in both Britain and the United States. Such lists, generated by critics and academics, and published in journals and newspapers, "[completed] the fetishization of 'the classic',," according to Feltes.[27] By the first decades of the twentieth century, the conception of the literary canon as a form of "instrumental" cultural production had become the de facto mode of the education system, with the acquisition of classic works seen as a ticket to the Ivy League. Indeed, Collier's Harvard Classics Library, first produced in the 1910s, and comprised of works selected by longtime Harvard University president Charles W. Eliot, was the physical manifestation of exactly such an elite *habitus*, and was sold complete with a five-foot bookshelf.[28]

Established commercial publications also were connected to developing cultural concerns, and even to nostalgia. Sometimes a mass-produced text could become so identified with a particular sensibility as to not only sell well for its publisher over many years, but also take on a mythical function through continual recirculation and "versioning," or the repetition of the text in different forms (e.g., theatrical, cinematic, iconographic, etc.). As Michelle Moylan demonstrates in her study of the cultural functions of Helen Hunt Jackson's popular 1884 novel *Ramona*, the continual reinterpretations of such texts adds multiple, material layers of signification to its textuality, such that "when that interpretation becomes otherwise dominant, future readers must contend with it—they may choose to read with or against it, but that meaning is difficult to ignore."[29] In the case of *Ramona*, such reinterpretations ranged from theatrical and (later) cinematic versions to an entire cottage industry of "mission nostalgia" centered on the Southern California town that took the novel's name. Along the way, these versions have transformed the original novel's critique of the European settlers' treatment of Native Americans into a pastoral narrative of forbidden romance.[30] The text of *Ramona* is thus still repeated, but in myriad, contradictory forms.

In his study of Tin Pan Alley, Nicholas Tawa claims similar tendencies of reinterpretation were accelerating the music publishing industry, particularly from the 1880s onward, as popular music publishers zealously obtained and promoted songs to capture the buying public's shifting tastes. Like the popular music industry of today, these firms generally sought to minimize risks by replicating already-successful styles and themes. If particular songs failed in the marketplace, the most successful firms were always ready to promote new or old titles more attuned to the zeitgeist. According to Tawa, these song publishers had to be "fusionists, assimilating different cultural tendencies, responding to any cultural drift of the moment," or rather their perceptions of "cultural drift."[31] Such tactics have been common among cultural producers since this time, as old texts and forms are adapted and repeated time and again.

Print culture by the early twentieth century was diverse and "modern," in the sense of having a variety of viable forms for a wide array of readers and users. At the same time, however, it was also broadly familiar, as literary and musical genre conventions, as well as specific works, were reified by cultures and economies of repetition. Editions of Stowe, Longfellow, and Jackson were regularly circulated, in many different versions, throughout society, and the notoriety of their prose and narratives extended well beyond the bounds of the books themselves, into many other repeated media forms. Similarly, Stephen Foster's songs, most of which were not particularly popular during his lifetime, were now considered American standards. Countless other mass disseminated works by thousands of lesser known, even anonymous, creators had helped reinforce particular forms, genres, and themes in American popular culture. Their work adhered to formulas crafted for commercial success shaped over decades of economically, geographically, and socially expanding readerships. While such homogenization has been among the primary targets of most cultural critics over the years, its achievement, in a society as disparate as the United States in the nineteenth century, is certainly noteworthy.[32] Mass commercial publishing, whether of literature or music, helped construct a national culture of familiar themes, genres, figures, and individual works. Print culture, in the forms of books, newspapers, magazines, and sheet music, became part of the everyday, shared American cultural experience, a status reinforced through other cultural venues and social institutions (e.g., formal education, the theater, public libraries, religious organizations, rail travel, etc.), and continued in the new media technologies of the new century.

Audiovisual Media

While print culture remained dominant well into the twentieth century, dazzling new mechanical media forms developed parallel economic, legal, and cultural systems, all premised on repetition. Commercial motion picture production and exhibition formally began in the mid-1890s, following many years of experimentation with mechanized photography. Like still photography, lithography, and print before it, motion picture photography facilitated the physical reproduction of visual works, as copies were easily produced from masters. The 1890s also saw the introduction of the commercial audio recording and playback industry, after nearly two decades of experimentation and scuttled uses. Audio recording and playback technologies have always been a crucial technological and cultural companion to cinema, even prior to the coming of sound, a fact most film histories fail to acknowledge. From the beginning, each audiovisual medium shared mechanical components, engineers, financial backers, manufacturers, marketing strategies, consumers, and even physical spaces. Mutoscopes and kinetoscopes sat side-by-side with pianolas and phonographs as coin-operated techno-logical marvels in the amusement parlors of the 1890s and 1900s, in much the same way DVDs and CDs occupied adjacent shelves in the large retailers of the 1990s and 2000s. While it would take several years for these new technologies to find a stable place in the culture and economy, their ability to transform existing cultural forms into mechanically reproduced media was apparent from the beginning.

The content of early film drew from a wide variety of existing forms popular at the turn of the twentieth century, including short stories, novels, songs, public events, vaudeville performances, dioramas, magic lantern shows, and theatrical drama. Attributes of all of these were recycled to varying degrees on film, but translated to the new languages of cinema. As basic film theory argues, the capturing of an event through a camera changes the perception of the event represented. Nevertheless, in crafting the production practices and semiotic codes of cinema during its first 20 to 30 years, filmmakers adapted representational devices from other media forms well familiar to turn of the century audiences. For example, as Ben Brewster and Lea Jacobs explore in their study of theatrical influence on early film style, cinematic narrative was primarily conceived in 1900–10 fictional film production in terms of quasi-static dramatic "situations": moments of narrative action suitable for "pictorial" staging as tableaus. Plays and films alike were thus designed around the concept of *tableaux vivants*, as "a series of pictorially repre-sentable moments."[33] As Brewster and Jacobs note, with *tableaux vivants*, cinema was offering a repetition of established formal structures: "[It] is precisely their stereotypical nature that makes them useful as an aid in plot construction. Invention becomes a matter of combining preexisting situations, of motivating them and . . . making them acceptable to a contemporary audience if they are likely to be found 'unacceptable'."[34]

However, even while "combining preexisting situations," film style still evolved in particular ways, shaped largely by the rapidly shifting economics of the early film industry. Tom Gunning traces in his study of D.W. Griffith's Biograph films how the narrative-driven "story film" emerged as a popular and lucrative genre in the Nickelodeon era (circa 1904–09) to draw a more middle-class, "respectable" audience to theaters, displacing the earlier "cinema of attractions" along the way. Griffith's cinematic innovations (what Gunning collectively refers to as the "narrator system") helped solidify and standardize film as a unique form of storytelling, i.e., as another means of promulgating familiar narratives and situations.[35] Indeed, as Douglas Gomery shows, the repeated cinematic adaptations of classic literary works (many of which were available for public domain use; i.e., outside of potentially expensive copyright restrictions) during this period were designed precisely to capitalize on their familiarity with this particular audience class.[36] Established stories and situations were regularly reproduced in cinematic form, adding another layer of significance to their presence in the culture, and reaffirming nodes of what would later be called "middlebrow" culture.[37]

While the narrative mode, with its attendant recycling of forms and stories, was clearly dominant, individual films still did not have a long market lifespan. Indeed, due to the intensity of demand and attendance at this time, films generally had a run of a week or less at nickelodeons. Most exhibitors changed films *daily* by the late 1900s, according to Gunning, forcing studios to release over a dozen new reels each week.[38] Like the Vaudeville performances that co-existed with it in popular culture and often on the same bill, cinema's early mode of repetition was thus based more on spatial, than temporal, exploitation: i.e., getting the same films out to as many theaters as possible. A film was considered a short-term investment, with almost all of the returns coming upon its initial release. While "older" films (measured in months rather than years) were sometimes available for exhibition at discounted rates, the financial engine of the industry remained on novelty: i.e., first-run texts.

In the wake of the shift to narrative, film stabilized as a standard form of mass entertainment, and major interests sought to exert control over the industry. While the Motion Picture Patent Company (MPPC) regulated film production, distribution, and exhibition for a few years, the subsequent development of the Hollywood-based, vertically-integrated studio system out of companies resistant to the MPPC further solidified an American cinematic culture closely modeled after the burgeoning consumer culture of standardized products and experiences.[39] Moreover, the economics of the "run-clearance-zone" system developed by the most elaborated studios ultimately built cinematic repetition into the system, through the "aftermarket" of discount theaters. By the peak of the Hollywood era in the 1930s and 1940s, films would typically run in progressively less expensive theaters over the course of many months, with a dozen or more stops along the way in the largest cities. While this system did not factor in film revivals (the exhibition of a film several years after its initial release) in any meaningful way, it did provide the studios with the material means to extend the market viability of their products, and gave viewers the ability to watch a film multiple times over an extended period.[40]

While film developed as a medium for mass exhibition (i.e., outside the home), audio technology expanded from public arcades to private drawing rooms at the turn of the century, in the form of player pianos and variations of the Edison phonograph. These technologies provided another kind of cultural repetition, offering recordings of popular songs already available in print. Piano rolls, the perforated scrolls that drove player pianos, were the first widely popular form of recorded music, made available for purchase as individual songs or in collections. At the same time, audio recordings of performances were also mass-produced and distributed on phonograph cylinders and disks for domestic use. Just as fixed forms of reproducible text represented long-term capital for nineteenth century publishers, audio recordings became the foundation for an increasingly lucrative consumer cultural industry in the twentieth century.

Like print before it, these new forms were also brought under copyright law. Sales of recording hardware and software boomed in the first decade of the twentieth century, with the number of disks and cylinders produced expanding tenfold; 27.5 million were manufactured in 1909 alone.[41] Composers and publishers, however, had no fixed means by which they could be compensated for the recording of their compositions under the current copyright law. Although the right to compensation was added to the public performance statute in the 1891 copyright revision, it did not clearly apply to the new technologies, which fixed performances in a static form. However, after a controversy involving monopoly allegations against the Aeolian Company, the dominant manufacturer of player pianos and piano rolls, the major copyright revision of 1909 established the first restrictions on "mechanical reproduction," and mandated the collection of royalties on the sale of every piano roll or phonograph disk or cylinder. From that point forward, music publications have been legally connected to their recordings as well as their performances. Indeed, since the rise of format radio in the early 1950s, most of the profits in the music publishing industry have long come from such royalties, rather than from sheet music sales.[42]

Early recording firms sought to identify and exploit emerging trends, as well as draw extensively from past texts where possible. Since the target audience of most record labels was middle-class homes, these goals coincided most of the time. All three major record companies of the 1900s and 1910s (Columbia, Edison, and Victor) launched "high culture" labels featuring not only classical and operatic performances, but renditions of popular songs from the past century. These songs were familiar to the audience, but performed anew by popular stage artists. Each of the majors utilized this strategy in order to maximize sales. Indeed, the first million-selling audio recording on the Victor Company's Red Seal label was of Stephen Foster's "Old Folks At Home" performed by one of the era's most popular singers, Alma Gluck.

Rerun Nation 1920

By the 1920s, the essential cultural, economic, and legal parameters of the regime of repetition were set. American popular culture was mass-produced, mass-distributed, and mass-consumed, via increasingly standardized forms, genres, and venues. People in Boston could read the same books and see the same films as people in San Diego. Moreover, 1920s readers, listeners, and viewers were often enjoying texts (or versions thereof) originally produced years or even decades previously. While the long-term value of particular films and audio recordings was not yet as evident as it was with literary properties, and would not develop into a stable source of cultural and financial capital until much later in the century, the cultural and economic value of copyright was well-established. Texts were recognized as legal objects, i.e., as property. Moreover, industrialized cultural production had become a critical component of the modern capitalist nation-state. Indeed, the reified images, icons, iterations, and ideas circulated by the engines of repetition served to sustain and expand critical ideals of nationhood and identity in a world otherwise straining under immense changes. Industrialized repetition offered precisely the kind of mediated "imagined communities" described by historian Benedict Anderson, ready-made worlds that fostered a dazzling, universal, and secular *lingua franca*.[43]

By coincidence, the years 1926–28 marked a particular culmination of these forces, with the introduction of three major media institutions. The Book-of-the-Month Club offered an instrumental, concrete form of literary culture, one attuned to domestic schedules and middlebrow aspirations, rather than notions of timeless quality.[44] Simultaneously, the film industry honored its own in 1928 with the first Academy Awards, setting in motion an annual tradition, forging a canon of cinematic art, and priming a ready source of cinematic repetition for the future. Finally, as will be addressed in the next chapter, the National Broadcasting Company (NBC) was formed out of the warring partners of the Radio Corporation of America (RCA), presenting the ultimate achievement in spatial repetition: nationwide radio broadcasting. However, even the stentorian rhetoric of "live" radio promoted by NBC could not supplant the model of industrial textual repetition already in motion. Indeed, as the next chapter will explore, repetition was already a significant component in the industrial and cultural logic of radio broadcasting before NBC reached the air.

Notes

1. Janice Radway, *A Feeling For Books: The Book-of-the-Month Club, Literary Taste, and Middle-Class Desire* (Chapel Hill, NC: University of North Carolina, 1997), 131.

2. Radway describes how Collier's "Harvard Classics Library" was developed with precisely this goal in mind; See *A Feeling For Books*, 146–147.

3. Alfred P. Chandler, *The Visible Hand: The Managerial Revolution in American Business* (Cambridge, MA: Harvard University, 1977), 12.

4. For the sake of clarity in this chapter, the publishing industry refers not only to book and magazine publishers, but also to music publishers, whose wares

were also produced on paper with ink, and sold to culturally literate consumers.

5. Russell Sanjek, *American Popular Music and Its Business: The First Four Hundred Years (Vol. 2, 1790–1909)* (New York: Oxford University Press, 1988), 4–5.

6. Ronald J. Zboray, "The Ironies of Technological Innovation," in Cathy N. Davidson, ed., *Reading In America* (Baltimore: Johns Hopkins, 1989), 182–186.

7. Sanjek, *American Popular Music and Its Business*, 21. As suggested by the title of the Wrights' highly popular book, such collections helped frame the experience of popular music in the US at this time.

8. Sanjek, *American Popular Music and Its Business*, 35; see also Zboray, "The Ironies of Technological Innovation," 188.

9. Sanjek, *American Popular Music and Its Business*, 36–38, 42–43.

10. Chandler, *The Visible Hand*, 86.

11. Zboray, "The Ironies of Technological Innovation," 193. Zboray also notes that this cultural growth was concentrated, not surprisingly, along railroad lines. Thus, the urban, industrialized, rail-thick Northeast saw the bulk of the development of a national culture, relative to the more rural South and West (192).

12. Chandler, *The Visible Hand*, 81–187.

13. David Saunders, *Authorship And Copyright* (New York: Routledge, 1992), 51–57.

14. Saunders, *Authorship and Copyright*, 155.

15. As with the British 1710 Act, the duration of copyright in the original 1790 statute was 14 years from the date of the work's creation, plus a possible extension of another 14 years, continuing the principle of exclusive exploitation. Over the course of the next century, both the duration and extension had doubled in length. During the twentieth century, as mass-produced creative works took on a larger economic profile, legislation continued to extend this period. The last extension, the Sonny Bono Copyright Term Extension Act (1998), amounted to the life of the author plus 70 years.

16. Some US firms made remunerative arrangements with British publishers that would allow them a first opportunity at particularly sought publications, if not actual exclusivity.

17. Radway, *A Feeling For Books*, 132.

18. Radway, *A Feeling For Books*, 133.

19. Radway, *A Feeling For Books*, 133.

20. Radway, *A Feeling For Books*, 135.

21. Zboray, "The Ironies of Technological Innovation," 189.

22. N. N. Feltes, *Literary Capital and the Late Victorian Novel* (Madison: University of Wisconsin, 1993), 25–26.

23. Michael Kearns, "The Material Melville: Shaping Readers' Horizons," in Michele Moylan and Lane Stiles, eds., *Reading Books: Essays on the Material Text and Literature in America* (Amherst: University of Massachussetts Press, 1996), 53.

24. See Radway, *A Feeling For Books*, 147–151; Zboray, "The Ironies of Technological Innovation," 190. Books are arguably even more aestheticized objects in our era, with later twentieth-century changes in production and marketing emphasizing covers in particular. This embodiment of cultural value in the appearance of the textual object would eventually reach the realm of television reruns, in the marketing of DVD box sets in the 2000s (see Chapter 8).

25. Sanjek, *American Popular Music and Its Business*, 39–49, 347–348.

26. Radway, *A Feeling For Books*, 137.

27. Feltes, *Literary Capital*, 41–48.

28. See Radway, *A Feeling For Books*, 146–147.

29. Michele Moylan, "Materiality as Performance: The Forming of Helen Hunt Jackson's Ramona," in Moylan and Lane Stiles, eds., *Reading Books: Essays on the Material Text and Literature in America* (Amherst: University of Massachussetts Press, 1996), 225.

30. See Moylan, "Materiality as Performance," 231–242.

31. Nicholas E. Tawa, *The Way to Tin Pan Alley: American Popular Song, 1866–1910* (New York: Schirmer Books, 1990), 38–40.

32. See Saunders, *Authorship and Copyright*, 163–164.

33. Ben Brewster and Lea Jacobs, *Theatre To Cinema: Stage Pictorialism and the Early Feature Film* (New York: Oxford University Press, 1997), 19–22.

34. Brewster and Jacobs, *Theatre To Cinema*, 23.

35. Tom Gunning, *D.W. Griffith and the Origins of American Narrative Film: The Early Years at Biograph* (Urbana, IL: University of Illinois, 1991).

36. Douglas Gomery, *Shared Pleasures: A History of Movie Presentation in the United States* (Madison: University of Wisconsin, 1992), 31.

37. Indeed, as Radway argues, middlebrow culture solidified during the first decades of the twentieth century largely via the merger of different cultural forms and planes: "The middlebrow was formed...as a category, by processes of literary and cultural mixing whereby forms and values associated with one form of cultural production were wed to forms and values usually connected with another. ... [T]he scandal of the middlebrow was a function of its failure to maintain the fences cordoning off culture from commerce, the sacred from the profane, and the low from the high." Industrialized popular forms like literature, drama, and cinema were instrumental in this process. See *A Feeling For Books*, 150–152.

38. Gunning, *D.W. Griffith*, 60, 86–87.

39. See Gomery, *Shared Pleasures*, 34–56.

40. The question of whether, and to what extent, cinemagoers of the 1930s and 1940s took advantage of such opportunities is certainly intriguing, but beyond the purview of this book.

41. Sanjek, *American Popular Music and Its Business*, 388.

42. As Geoffrey P. Hull writes, "A century of technological innovation and evolution and the concomitant change in copyright laws . . . has turned an industry that once created and marketed products into a copyright industry that primarily licenses others to utilize its properties." *The Recording Industry* (Boston: Allyn and Bacon, 1998), 48.

43. Benedict Anderson, *Imagined Communities* (New York: Verso, 1983).

44. See Radway, *A Feeling For Books*, for historical and cultural analysis of The Book of the Month Club.

2
Transcribed Adventures: Radio and the Recording

> To most rural listeners, and, for that matter, to most city dwellers a radio program takes on no flesh and blood aspects. To them a broadcast performance can never be other than a remote quantity. So your listener is but little interested in whether live, breathing persons pour it into a mike, for instant use, or whether they engrave it in wax for future reference.[1]

According to most broadcasting histories, the seminal moment in the development of radio as a mass communications medium occurred in the fall of 1920, when Frank Conrad, an engineer at Westinghouse, began transmitting programming from his jury-rigged "station" on the roof of his workplace. While radio had functioned as a point-to-point medium (and concomitant industry) for over 20 years, and amateur operators not so different from Conrad were already technically "broadcasting" (i.e., transmitting their signals over long distances with the intent that unknown others would receive them), it was Conrad's operation that most publicly ushered in what we recognize today as not only broadcasting, but *commercial* broadcasting. Westinghouse, after all, soon furnished Conrad with better equipment, facilities, and even personnel in order to utilize the station, christened KDKA, as a form of advertising, to promote the sales of their radio equipment.

From this quasi-mythical origin, the dominant model of broadcasting in the United States was organized almost entirely around its ostensible technical properties (themselves a truncation of existing two-way radio technology) rather than its content. The decisive fact of broadcasting then remains the same now: that multitudes of people could be reached simultaneously with the same programming. Whether they were reached by a newscast, soap opera, baseball game, cooking show, dance band, superhero adventure, or murder mystery was, by contrast, a secondary concern. This does not mean that content per se was and has been *un*important, but rather that the primary business of U.S. broadcasting was broadcasting, i.e., transmitting a signal that the consuming public received. Regardless of the content of that signal, the radio industry promised listeners (and, more to the point, advertisers) a distinct cultural experience, based on a rarefied physical presence, rather than a commodified copy, as with other, older cultural forms (e.g., publishing and film). In other words, if you tuned into NBC on Tuesday night, you would hear Jack Benny. Not a cheap copy of Jack Benny, nor a mere photographic image, but *Jack Benny*, in person, via your radio speakers. This "live," commercially-directed presence ("brought to you by Jell-O") functioned as a primary nexus of the "American system" of broadcasting: the organization of radio into a for-profit, one-way, hear-it-now national communications medium. As Michele Hilmes notes, the logic of this system was not only commercial; radio had a significant role in the construction and elaboration of American identity during one of the nation's most trying periods.[2] However, by the end of the 1920s, less than a decade after Conrad's station had ostensibly inaugurated the Age of Broadcasting, the idealized vision of this "American" system of unique, live broadcasts was already being seriously challenged by its aural opposite: the recording.

This chapter concerns the transition of radio from a live to recorded medium, a shift that set the stage for television's similar move in the 1950s. As the previous chapter showed, by the early twentieth century, culture was already mass-oriented, industrialized, and commodified. Physically extant cultural objects ranging from prints to poems were bought, sold, traded, copied, collected, adapted, and commercially reproduced. Phonograph records were among these objects by the time radio technology began to spread in the 1910s and 1920s, and amateurs and professionals alike were already regularly broadcasting them, despite the emerging dominant industrial, cultural, and legal orientation of the medium towards live programming. As the national network-based American system took hold, recordings were simply more convenient and affordable for stations seeking to fill empty schedules and sell local sponsorships. Moreover, in addition to standard, domestic phonograph records, entire programs were being recorded by the end of the 1920s, or rather *pre*-recorded, in the form of electrical transcriptions, produced for later playback rather than live transmission. While the independent firms that produced these high-fidelity recordings, such as the World Broadcasting Service and the Frederick W. Ziv Company, agreed with the major networks that radio was premised upon reaching audiences, they disagreed about the means to do so. Instead, they bypassed the idea of liveness entirely, selling their programs directly to radio stations and advertisers on an ad hoc basis. The networks' vision of radio was national and simultaneous; the transcription companies' was local (or regional) and asynchronous. However, as the use of transcriptions and records expanded and became more accepted, even the networks eventually embraced the logic of recording by the late 1940s. Along the way, critical debates about the industrial, legal, and cultural status of broadcasting recordings occurred in the pages of *Broadcasting*, at the annual National Association of Broadcasters' convention, in Federal agency hearings, and in hundreds of meetings nationwide between stations, advertisers, and talent. The very forms of broadcasting were taking shape in these evolving discussions and practices, resulting in decisions and standards that would affect not only radio, but continue into television several years later.

By the end of the 1940s, industrialized repetition had become standard practice on radio, as recordings were the dominant program source, with live material reduced to an increasingly marginal status. However, even though these programs existed in tangible forms (i.e., as transcription disks), and even though recorded music on radio was becoming a massively repeated national standard (via the development of formats and the postwar resurgence of the record industry), reruns, as we would recognize them today, were still largely an alien concept. While thousands of older episodes of programs physically existed on transcription disks, they were rarely ever heard again on radio. The development of repetition on radio from the 1920s through 1940s was thus concerned more with the principle of fixing program material in mutable, transportable forms, forms that represented fixed capital, but were in practice only *potentially* repeatable. Regardless, the eventual dominance of this principle fostered a technical, cultural, legal, and industrial environment in which extant texts were eventually repeated, although it would take a new medium, and new priorities, to establish this practice in American culture.

Before exploring the uses of recording on radio, it is worthwhile to briefly consider how this medium repeated so much of the culture that preceded it. Like publishing and film, radio drew forms, genres, and texts from familiar cultural sources. While each of these forms had to be adapted to an aural medium, they all retained enough of their original elements to constitute a form of repetition. That is, when *Lux Radio Theater* presented "Dark Victory," for example, they were presenting it primarily as an adaptation of the film, rather than as a distinct radio production. Comic strips were a ready source of radio material, since they already provided known characters and situations, and were followed by millions daily. Several popular strips became long-running radio serials at this time, including *Little Orphan Annie*, *Superman*, and *Tarzan*. These adaptations indicate how repetition continually evolves with new industrial, cultural, legal, and technological forms and practices. Indeed, the owners of existing cultural properties typically seek out these new avenues, as the two main newspaper feature syndicates, King and United, did in the mid-1930s in soliciting the radio rights to their popular comic strips and columns.[3] Thus, even though radio was certainly a "new" technology and cultural form, and even though the dominant model of broadcasting was premised upon liveness and simultaneous presence, as a medium it was as reliant upon established industrialized cultural forms as the audio recording and film industries had been a generation earlier.

Live vs. Recorded

In the earliest predictions of broadcasting, the conventional wisdom held that the new technology would provide only live events beamed directly to the home: live theater, music, sporting events, and public affairs. Radio and television would ideally "bring the world home," as it happened, providing simultaneous cultural and social experiences on a previously unimaginable scale. In contrast, the idea that broadcasting would also transmit recordings of past events and performances was reluctantly acknowledged but generally delegitimated by most major radio critics and developers, who viewed the practice as inferior when compared to the ideal of live programming. Nevertheless, while the dominant broadcasting philosophy promoted the ostensibly superior quality of live events—i.e., their unique "excitement" and "energy"—recordings of musical, comedy, and dramatic performances quietly became a staple form of programming on almost every radio station nationwide.

As detailed by Michael Jay Biel in his 1977 dissertation, recordings had been used in experimental radio broadcasts throughout the first decades of the twentieth century.[4] For ostensible broadcasters more interested in the act than the content of transmission, recordings were a reliable programming form. They always required less trouble and expense than live broadcasts, as instead of actual on-air talent, all one needed was a phonograph and some disks. Accordingly, early radio amateurs often shared recorded music and readings over the airwaves straight from the horns of their Victrolas. Largely due to the relative ease of this set-up, the dominant interests in broadcasting (and largest proponents of the discourses of "liveness") associated the use of recordings with "amateurism," stigmatizing all uses of recordings in commercial broadcasting throughout the 1920s and 1930s. The broadcasting establishment generally considered recordings to be "cheap" and "inferior" when compared to the more expensive, more difficult, and thus more culturally "worthy" live performances. In addition, this dominant aesthetic of "liveness" aspired to the ethos of presence, as seen in the theater and in public events. This concept of presence was further inflected with upper-middle-class aesthetics and mannerisms, particularly in broadcasting's first decade. Indeed, as the photographs of early professional broadcasting operations reveal, this rhetoric of high-class aesthetics (or at least fidelity and "authenticity") even extended to studio décor and the talent's wardrobe, despite the fact that these visual factors would be inconsequential to listeners.

1922 regulations from the Commerce Department—which regulated the use of the airwaves until the establishment of the Federal Radio Commission (FRC) in 1927—reinforced this stigma, reserving the more attractive "class B" radio frequencies to "stations that could meet more stringent technical and programming requirements"; this included the complete prohibition of "mechanically operated instruments," i.e., phonographs.[5] Moreover, even in the more elaborate broadcasting environment that had developed by the late 1920s, FRC rules still considered recordings to be something less than standard broadcasting. FRC General Order 78 mandated the identification of recordings just prior to their broadcast, and at 15-minute intervals during the length of the program. These regulations soon became entrenched in the developing industry, and live broadcasting became the standard of the "American" system.

Beyond this explicit government regulation, many of the largest and most powerful stations—including the networks' owned-and-operated stations, known as "O & Os"—adopted strict no-recording policies of their own, further legitimating the philosophy of "liveness."[6] Biel lists many reasons for the dominant interests' bias against recordings in radio, such as the belief that recordings lacked "quality" and "excitement," or, worse, that they "cheated" audiences out of the "genuine" experience of broadcasting.[7] However, the key argument against the use of recordings had little do to with these arbitrary aesthetic distinctions. Rather, it was the belief that recordings would destroy the economic rationale for the networks' expensive landline interconnection system.[8] The system of leased AT & T telephone lines was the effectual nervous system of the networks, physically extending their reach across the continent, and making possible the fundamental operating principle of network broadcasting: simultaneous, nationwide dissemination of programming. Only the major networks could offer such timely, live, coast-to-coast access on a regular basis. Under this philosophy, live broadcasting was thus the only conceivable legitimate form of radio; recordings were considered a pale substitute.

The expense and difficulty of live program production, and networking, were thus thought to be worthwhile investments for the networks and their flagship stations. This stance was in turn facilitated by the network-affiliate relationship that developed as the networks expanded in the 1930s. Under the "option time" provision of a standard affiliation agreement, a station agreed to grant the network the exclusive rights to particular blocks of time throughout the broadcast day, ceding local interests to the national address of the network.[9] "Interconnected" stations, physically connected to the network via the leased telephone lines, served as an instantaneous outlet for network programming. Thus, a program that originated in New York was broadcast simultaneously on affiliates nationwide. In order to support the mammoth undertaking of this system, the networks generally required national sponsors to purchase time across the entire network rather than in specific markets. These additional markets, known as "must buys," frustrated smaller regional and local advertisers, who were forced to buy time over all of NBC, for example, rather than only in the Northeast, or the New York City market.

Electrical transcriptions—specially-recorded, high-fidelity sixteen-inch phonograph disks—presented a particularly challenging counter-philosophy to the dominant network-based model, one which completely disconnected program production, distribution and exhibition, and offered producers, sponsors, and local stations considerable flexibility. Even before the networks had formally started broadcasting, transcriptions were already being syndicated—i.e., sold on an ad hoc basis to individual stations—nationwide. In 1927, at the very beginning of network broadcasting, radio promoter Edgar H. Felix sagely predicted the recording's eventual superiority, writing that transcriptions would replace "the fleeting radio performance of today."[10] The success of transcription syndication proved that effective radio could be scheduled locally, and that ad hoc, transcription-based "networks" (identical programming, but different schedules, sponsors, and stations) were a viable alternative to the dominant networks. Programs could be recorded well in advance, resulting in more comfortable working conditions and the ability to correct errors.[11] Sponsors could target specific markets and times rather than take the all-or-nothing deal offered by the networks. Local stations could program a transcription at their discretion, instead of relinquishing control to the New York network feed. In addition, transcription production offered independent producers—rather than only networks, sponsors, or ad agencies—a relatively open market in which to develop programs. Unlike typical network programs, which were owned, produced by, and identified with a major sponsor in conjunction with an advertising agency, transcribed series were generally produced "open-ended," without specific sponsors, leaving appropriate silent breaks for live or recorded commercials to be inserted. Most importantly, the transcribed program existed not only as a potential broadcast event, but also as a physical set of disk recordings; once produced, these programs could (at least theoretically) be used and reused many times over. Transcriptions were thus to radio what film would be for television: recordings designed primarily for immediate programming flexibility, and only secondarily for multiple uses.

Transcriptions also offered local advertisers and stations the promise of national quality at local prices. As Storm Whaley, the General Manager of KUOA in Siloam Springs, Arkansas wrote in *Broadcasting* in 1937, "the greatest of stars, the smoothest of productions, the most forceful commercial appeal and the best of entertainment becomes as readily available to the smallest station as to the greatest at real economy."[12] Whaley's comments indicate how the merger of national and local modes of address was more balanced through syndication than with network interconnection. While network programs were, at this time, only available with network strings attached (e.g., option time, loss of advertising fees, etc.), transcriptions facilitated an alternative model of broadcasting that placed national culture under local control. Syndicated programs thus "belonged" to their local stations, advertisers, and communities in a somewhat dialectical manner in which network programs did not. This distinction between broadcast and syndicated texts (and contexts) would continue into television.

Together, the open sponsorship and mere physical existence of transcription disks allowed for their circulation in different markets under the auspices of different sponsors. Transcribed programs were thus not limited to a particular scheduled time or place, and could run sporadically throughout the country over a period of months or even years.[13] Thus, while a network broadcast was singular and ephemeral, a transcription was multiple, endlessly reproducible. However, although many series in circulation were often quite old as a result, they were not marketed as "reruns." Instead, in a manner similar to the studio-era Hollywood film distribution system discussed in Chapter 1, a disk series might start in larger markets, move to medium markets, and finally end up, vastly discounted, in the smallest markets many years after its initial release. The rights to many series were transferred from owner to owner over the years, and while these programs' proven ability to draw audiences was cited in reports and advertising, their "classic" status was generally not.[14]

Regardless of the growing use of transcriptions, however, they still met with great resistance from the dominant radio interests. Transcription providers and users alike had to promote this form of programming against this bias, despite the great success of some notable programs, including *Sam 'n' Henry*, the first incarnation of *Amos 'n' Andy*, that was transcribed and syndicated out of WMAQ in Chicago in 1928–1929.[15] Their promotion efforts exemplify how changes in cultural systems are often the long-term result of active persuasion. That is, forces in the industry (and the culture, more generally) have to be won over to the new practice or media form. Support for the new form could come quickly, or might take years to build, requiring multiple strategies. Regardless of the particular form these discourses took at this time, however, they focused on closing the perceptual gap between live and recorded programming. This wasn't so much a gap in the listeners' perception, but rather a gap of the industry's (and, to an extent, the government's) perception of that perception. That is, transcription advocates had to work uphill against the biases built into the so-called "American system" of broadcasting, biases that were often couched in particular visions of "the public interest" advanced by the dominant commercial interests.[16]

World Broadcasting Service was arguably the most prominent independent transcription producer and distributor of the 1930s, airing dozens of programs in markets nationwide. Despite this track record, however, they had to struggle to locate transcriptions within the terms dictated by the hegemonic forces in radio. Those terms necessitated a careful "middle ground" between the network ideal of liveness and the devalued amateur use of phonograph records. Transcriptions were unlike either of these forms, but had to be inserted between them in industrial and public discourses. That is, a transcription was positioned as a unique product *almost* "as good as live." World's ad campaigns in *Broadcasting* throughout this period, aimed at advertisers, agencies, and stations, emphasized their recordings' various advantages along these lines. A 1931 ad touted World's use of Western Electric sound engineering and promised "indescribably clear" sounds "silhouetted brilliantly as on a stream of ether."[17] However, a 1932 ad from the same campaign was aimed at economics more than aesthetics, and pointed out transcriptions' inherent flexibility over network time.[18] World matched this ad presence by taking a lead role in the promotion of transcriptions at a regulatory level, and aimed to convince the government to repeal Rule 176, the FCC's continuation of the FRC's General Order 78 (see below).

While regular full-page ad copy in the industry's primary trade journal was certainly useful publicity, testimony from clients (advertising agencies and broadcast stations) arguably contributed more to the general acceptance of transcriptions by the end of the 1930s. Several surveys and voluntary testimonials were featured in *Broadcasting* and distributed directly to interested parties during this period, helping promote the legitimacy of transcribed programming to skeptical advertisers, ad agents, and station managers. A 1932 survey of stations commissioned by the Batten, Barton, Durstine, and Osborn ad agency found transcriptions had steadily increased in volume and quality since 1929, and argued that the alleged listener opposition to recordings that the networks always hypothesized was actually a phantom presence: "fan mail from various sections of the country indicates that the prejudice to transcription programs as 'canned music' has been largely overcome by the superior quality and careful recording of the regular sponsored programs."[19] Later that year, a more independent study, by Professor Barry Golden of the Wharton School at Penn, found that a clear majority of stations and advertisers were favorable towards transcriptions, citing their lower costs and programming flexibility.[20] Similarly, stations and advertising agencies reported an increasing acceptance of transcriptions among their clients at this time.[21]

Radio engineers also contributed to these efforts, mostly by testifying to transcriptions' superior sound quality vs. regular phonograph records in order to dispel the stigma of earlier recording standards. J. R. Poppele, the chief engineer at WOR in Newark, pointed out that transcriptions were electrically, rather than mechanically recorded, with top-notch Western Electric technology, resulting in a cleaner, higher-fidelity sound. Presaging later media theory, he also made the prescient yet heretical argument that "the direct broadcast is not flesh and blood any more than the recorded."[22] More comprehensively, a group of fourteen engineers, led by Alfred N. Goldsmith, the former General Engineer of NBC's parent company, the Radio Corporation of American (RCA), and member of the National Advisory Council on Radio in Education, noted the increasing quality and utility of transcriptions in a 1934 report, and generated a list of eight distinct advantages of transcriptions, focusing on their greater flexibility in scheduling.[23]

By the mid-1930s, transcriptions had achieved a relatively solid place in U.S. broadcasting. Even prominent top-level stations had begun to program transcriptions, including Chicago's WGN (the last station in their market to accept transcriptions), and several of NBC's O & O's.[24] However, these were still gradual moves towards the overall acceptance of recorded programming on radio. The stigma still lingered in dominant practice and government regulation. However, the election of Franklin D. Roosevelt on a platform of massive government action to stem the Depression presented transcription advocates with an opportunity to reshape regulations in their favor. FRC Rule 176, which mandated the announcement of recordings prior to their broadcast, was their primary target.

Rule 176

Federal Radio Commission Rule 176 was a formalization of the earlier General Order 78, and required the identification of recordings on the air immediately before their broadcast. Its continued existence in the 1930s, despite the growing acceptance of transcriptions, indicates how entrenched the division between live and recorded programming (and the character of the "American" system) had become at an industrial and regulatory level. Again, while there was nothing intrinsically "live" about radio broadcasting, the live form had become the hegemonic standard of regulation, advertising, and most station and network practice. By 1933, several forces aligned to attempt to change, or ideally eliminate, Rule 176, and thus end the open segregation of live and recorded programming.

World Broadcasting System led the charge against Rule 176. The rule had hit them particularly hard due to their new "library" service, which provided a large collection of short programs (up to 15 minutes in length) to stations on an ad hoc basis. Rule 176 stipulated the announcement prior to each recording, meaning that a typical library presentation might be interrupted several times in the space of an hour. World acquired the legal counsel of Ira H. Robinson, a former FRC commissioner, who contacted the new commission within the first few weeks of the Roosevelt administration. In his letter, in keeping with the ongoing campaign to legitimize transcriptions, Robinson explicitly separated transcriptions from other recordings. He suggested retaining Rule 176, but removing transcriptions from its requirements. That way, transcriptions could better develop as a legitimate business and broadcast form:

> The change which I am asking will be beneficial to the public interest in that it will encourage the use of transcriptions by advertisers and stations not now using them because stigmatized in a class with mere ordinary phonograph records; advertisers being fearful that the public do not appreciate phonograph records and stations being fearful that their credit before the Commission is harmed by the use of anything but live talent.[25]

Building from this argument, at that fall's National Association of Broadcasters' convention, several station managers successfully lobbied for a resolution calling for the elimination or alteration of Rule 176. The text of the resolution cited both the growing acceptance of transcriptions, and the harm that Rule 176 caused stations.[26]

While the interest on this issue remained strong, and World filed a formal petition to clarify Rule 176 for transcriptions in 1934, the revamped environment of the 1934 Federal Communications Act (and with it, the new Federal Communications Commission) delayed formal hearings on Rule 176 (which was retained under FCC radio regulations) until June of 1935. A parade of industry representatives presented testimony supporting and opposing any changes in Rule 176. Their comments indicate how transcriptions in particular, and recordings in general, were seen by the various major powers in radio. Among the most prominent opponents of the change was the American Federation of Musicians (AFM), the performance union that was concurrently engaged in a protracted battle against the use of recordings on radio. They saw recordings as a serious threat to their profession, not only on radio but also in other venues, and sought to maintain the live status quo as much as possible.[27] World defended transcriptions on the AFM's grounds, contending that increased transcription recording had increased the employment of musicians, and had raised their pay scale (and royalty collection) relative to phonograph records. Accordingly, World suggested the union's ire would be better focused on the phonograph companies and the networks, rather than on transcription companies.

CBS, despite widely utilizing transcriptions on its affiliates and O & O's, also opposed any change to Rule 176 on the grounds that, if recordings went unannounced, the public would be deceived. This notion of public "deception" was particularly resonant in the dominant model of U.S. broadcasting at this time, as rising concerns over false advertising claims were prompting industry and federal attention. By lumping transcriptions in with other "deceptive practices," CBS was attempting to locate itself on the traditional high ground of live network radio. For its part, NBC sought a slightly more conciliatory solution, agreeing with CBS that the announcement be maintained, but that the term "electrical transcription" be replaced with "recorded program." This solution softened the language, but still preserved the distinction of live programming. On the other side of the hearing, individual independent stations, a coalition of advertising agencies, and the NAB all supported World's perspective, arguing that transcriptions had become invaluable to local broadcasters and advertisers, and were helping non-network broadcasting thrive. The NAB even claimed that transcriptions were the *only* form of programming keeping stations profitable, an argument that would continue to resound in debates over television syndication in subsequent decades.[28]

The FCC announced their decision in February 1936. The Commission admitted that the current rule was too vague, and had resulted in more violations than any other broadcasting rule on the books. Nonetheless, they decided to retain Rule 176, but reword it, adding language to distinguish transcriptions and phonographs, and requiring announcements at the beginning and ending of programs, and at 15-minute intervals during a recorded program, rather than after every single recording presented. While they accepted the premise that recordings were increasingly vital to broadcasting, they still sought to maintain the stated distinction between recordings and live programming. Typically, their opinion couched this distinction in the dominant terms of public responsibility:

> There is no doubt but that the listener's interest is enhanced by the knowledge that the artist is performing simultaneously with the reception in the home. Likewise it is most important to guarantee the continuance of such appearances both from the standpoint of the public and from the standpoint of continuing the gainful employment of the artists who have contributed so much to the art of broadcasting. Indeed radio broadcasting would lose much of its appear to the public if the rendition of live talent programs is in any way curbed.

While the interference and stigma of Rule 176 was diminished with the ruling, the FCC would still clearly consider transcriptions second-class programs. The notion that listeners somehow had a more "enhanced" experience by being reassured of a program's live origination was already a dubious assertion in 1936, but well within the *de facto* understanding of broadcasting. Live programming would retain its distinctive status, and the "American" system would continue virtually undiminished.

However, despite this setback, the transcription market continued to grow. A few years later, the Commission would reconsider the entire question of distinction between live and recorded programming. A section near the back of the 1940 *Report on Chain Broadcasting*, the investigation into alleged monopolistic practices at the top networks, suggested that transcriptions could be every bit as worthy as radio as live programs, pointing out that "electrical transcriptions invite careful rehearsing, and permit great perfection of programs."[29] The report noted that transcriptions were a nearly $5 million business in 1938, and that the business was dominated by a handful of firms. One of them was World, but the largest distributor of transcriptions by this point was actually NBC, the network that continued to champion live broadcasting, but had started to profit directly from transcriptions.

Double Standard at the Networks

In his study of NBC's contradictory practices concerning transcription syndication, Alexander Russo notes that the main goal of the dominant model of broadcasting in the United States—the "American" system of privately owned, advertiser-supported, live network radio—was to protect its very dominance, by delegitimating any alternative forms of broadcasting. In NBC's case, this had involved not only supporting versions of the recording announcement rule, but also warning the public (and ostensible sponsors) about the inferiority of recordings, as they did in a 1929 promotional book.[30] In the mid-1930s, with Rule 176 still in place, and transcriptions thus put "in their place," the networks' system of interconnected, simultaneous broadcasts continued to define mainstream radio among advertising executives, the broadcast press, and regular listeners alike. Despite this dominance, however, the market in syndicated recordings had become much too large and lucrative for the networks to completely ignore. As Biel notes, "once the idea of syndication was developed, the percentage of stations equipped to play recorded programs was always larger than the number of stations affiliated with a network."[31] In fact, this gap was even larger than network puffery would admit. As Russo points out, large parts of the West and South did not have primary network affiliates, leaving millions of listeners outside of the mainstream of the network's "national" address.[32] The networks knew this, and saw how, through transcriptions, ad hoc "networks," such as World's, were extending beyond the physical limits of their interconnected affiliates to reach these stations in the hinterlands. While both major networks began to pursue transcription production in distribution as an adjunct to their live networking at this time, NBC was more aggressive in its development of transcriptions.[33]

As early as 1929, RCA's General Engineer Alfred N. Goldsmith, who would ultimately advocate transcriptions in the 1930s (see above), wrote a letter to NBC President M.H. Aylesworth advocating the use of recordings, and recommend that the corporation's energies should be focused on not on "wire connection," but on syndication, including sales of existing programs to local stations and the general public.[34] Aylesworth and other NBC executives balked, and maintained their vision of network-based, live broadcasting. While the network did open local service bureaus in particular O & O's in 1932, in the hope of drumming up local sponsors in particularly large markets, they were still generally hostile to mixing recordings and radio. In September 1933, however, World commenced their transcription library service, which offered subscribing stations and advertisers up to 8 hours of daily recorded programming, all scheduled according to a station's needs.[35] World's programming was suddenly available at a greater rate than NBC's, and with increasing talent and production values. Moreover, it was programming that local stations could sell to local sponsors, unlike the sustaining programs that made up most of NBC's schedule at this time.[36] Accordingly, after a few months of internal debate, NBC began their very own transcription service in the spring of 1934.

At that point, the primary task of the NBC Recordings Division was the network's response to World's threat: their own library service, *Thesaurus*, which consisted of fare similar to World's service: short musical selections, educational and documentary reports, and a few brief dramatic programs. Like many other programs available at the time, *Thesaurus* was offered to stations as an archive of discs available for unlimited use by a station within the duration of the contract.[37] NBC went the extra mile in promoting their service as part of their network vision, providing an archive system and even scripts for continuity announcements. Even so, the service was initially limited to NBC O & O's or affiliates; if NBC had to enter the transcription business, it was not going to provide programming for its competitors.[38]

Thesaurus consisted of transcription-only programming; none of it was, or would be, transmitted over NBC's main networks. However, during World War II, the networks began to utilize recordings of their network programs to provide thousands of hours of network-level programming for distribution to military personnel overseas via the Armed Forces Radio Service (AFRS), a system of military radio stations which repeated U.S. network programming. Although separated both physically and culturally from mainstream commercial network operations, the successful use of transcriptions on AFRS indicated that recordings could be successfully used on a regular basis without compromising network principles of "quality." Nevertheless, NBC maintained its strict ban on network use of transcriptions until the late 1940s. The ban was finally broken on network radio in increments: first at the O & Os, then in some daytime programs, and finally in prime time. By that point, radio talent, led by major stars such as Bing Crosby, had successfully lobbied for recordings to be used in prime-time programming, at least to eliminate the second live performance for the Western time zones.[39]

Thus, the networks were able to maintain two contradictory philosophies throughout the 1930s and 1940s: live programs on their publicly visible, network broadcasts, and recorded programs through lower prestige scheduling on local and government stations.[40] This uneasy dichotomy would be reproduced in network television in the 1940s and 1950s, when film would offer a similar challenge to live broadcasting.

Labor and the Recording

While producers, packagers, stations, and even networks benefited from recordings, radio laborers (performers and technicians) were more ambivalent. The recording process was certainly more convenient in the short term—e.g., to time shift an earlier live broadcast for the West Coast—but the existence of the recording after its initial broadcast potentially threatened the livelihood of all radio artists, as it could reduce radio's continual need for live performers. For years, while the owners of both transcription and phonograph recordings reaped the profits of continued recirculation, radio performers received little compensation. The American Society of Composers and Performers (ASCAP) had established a royalty system through provisions in the 1909 Copyright Act, which allowed their membership to collect fees for each broadcast of a song or performance in their purview. When the fees escalated throughout the 1930s, however—due to the expansion of the radio industry—the broadcast networks and record companies balked, and ultimately formed their own music licensing agency, Broadcast Music, Incorporated (BMI), in 1939. Over the next few years, the two organizations would engage in several battles, boycotts, and subsequent legal decisions, but both would ultimately acquiesce to a Justice Department consent decree that stabilized the royalty situation between them.

In addition to music, other repeatable program forms prompted the pursuit of "residuals": royalty fees for repeat performances or airings. Although the market in full-length program reruns was virtually nonexistent in the late 1930s, commercial spots were beginning to be recorded and repeated on an increasingly regular basis, with little or no additional compensation for performers. The newly-formed American Federation of Radio Artists (AFRA) sought to correct this situation. In early 1939, AFRA obtained a major agreement with independent radio producers and advertising agencies, the AFRA Code of Fair Practice, which established repeat fees of roughly 50% for a variety of program genres.[41] Two years later, as transcriptions became more prevalent, a revision of the code shrewdly insured a system to track residuals owed to recording artists via transcriptions or any "electrical reproductions now or hereafter devised."[42] Similarly, the AFM, under the leadership of James C. Petrillo, strove for compensation for their members via a long ban on the use of recordings in radio in the mid-1940s, and a similar limit on the use of recorded film music on television.

Labor historians Lois Gray and Ronald Seeber argue that technological changes such as the recording always have a profound effect on labor in the arts, entertainment, and electronic media industries, consistently challenging job security in a field already plagued with high unemployment rates.[43] As culture in general moved from the live and ephemeral to the recorded and recyclical, the principle of residual payments was the key victory for these and other labor organizations, and became a standard point of negotiation in all subsequent guild and union contracts in the U.S. media industries. The television boom of the 1950s would solidify the regime of repetition, bring hundreds of old theatrical films to the new medium, merge the television and film industries, and continually keep the unions on guard for their livelihoods.

Standardized Repetition on Radio

By the late 1940s, radio transcriptions had become the standard form of broadcasting. While many major programs were still aired live, the majority were recorded. The networks had not only ultimately capitulated to the logic of recording; they had embraced it. Moreover, other firms had extended the logic and reach of repetition. One of the most prominent nonnetwork syndicators at this time was the Frederick W. Ziv Company, a Cincinnati-based program packager that had originated in the 1930s as a radio advertising agency. Ziv had built a network-like reputation for programming through several shrewd principles: exploiting "presold" properties by acquiring the radio rights to established characters and texts; pursuing Hollywood-level talent wherever possible; and making program sales and promotion the firm's top priority in every market.[44] Ziv himself was perhaps the most ardent supporter of syndicated transcriptions in radio at this time, creating and distributing series that often ran on more stations than comparable network programming. In a *Variety* overview of radio in 1947, he boasted that "it's only natural to want to produce the finest programs possible...and it's only natural for listeners to want to hear the best program possible. The best—the finest—programs today are broadcast by transcription."[45]

Like the publishers and early film producers, Ziv relied upon the repetition of established cultural figures and texts, but to a greater extent than most other transcription firms. The company obtained the radio (and subsequently television) rights to literary characters such as the Cisco Kid and Boston Blackie, and produced condensed radio versions of well-known literary classics in the anthology series *Favorite Story*. Similarly, Ziv drew open established talent, in the somewhat unlikely form of Hollywood stars (including Ronald Colman, Adolphe Menjou, Humphrey Bogart, and Lauren Bacall), whose participation in series radio was virtually unprecedented, as the live networks had rarely been able to attract such stars to series work.[46] In addition, Ziv pioneered the practice of textual repetition on radio by obtaining and recirculating older transcribed series, including a few that had originally run on the networks. These were not explicitly marketed as reruns, however, and were instead repackaged, usually with new titles and/or formats. For example, the company acquired the rights to *Skippy Hollywood Theatre of the Air* in 1951, which was retitled *Movietown Radio Theatre* for syndication.[47] Ziv's industrial practices at this time indicate that while cultural recycling was an active philosophy, outright repetition—explicitly promoting a series as an "old favorite" or "classic"—was not. The reuse of existing programs as reruns—on both radio and television—would only begin on television in the 1950s, and Ziv would be on hand to promote it when it did.

Even though the particular practice of rerun repetition was not an explicit consideration in the use of recordings on radio, the potential for such repetition would exist as long as the recordings themselves did. As early as the late 1930s, transcribed programs were dusted off and readied for the market again.[48] More significantly, the very existence of transcriptions from this era began to fuel the nostalgia for (and marketing of) "old-time radio" (aka "OTR") in the 1960s. Without the technology of recording, and particularly electrical transcriptions, 1930s and 1940s radio could only be reconstructed from written accounts and fading memories. Instead, this era of radio has become a legitimate—albeit quite marginal—form of American popular culture in the years since. Thus, industrialized textual repetition was eventually utilized for radio, enabling the "radio heritage": a construction of an aural "Golden Age" roughly stretching from Black Monday to V-J Day.

That said, it is significant that this perception only became possible in the age of *television*, not only because a new technology tends to create feelings of nostalgia for an old one, but because the concept of rerun repetition—at least as far as full-length, fictional entertainment programs were concerned—had first been standardized on TV, rather than radio. Throughout the 1940s and 1950s, a resurgent "American" system of television, dominated by the same few firms, would pitch live programming against the recording again. The eventual outcome by 1960 was an industry based not only on the recording, but, increasingly, on the rerun.

Notes

1. Scott Howe Bowen, qtd in "Opposition to Disk Broadcasts Fading," *Broadcasting*, 1 April 1932, p. 10.

2. Michele Hilmes, *Radio Voices: American Broadcasting, 1922–1952* (Minneapolis: University of Minnesota Press, 1997), 1–33.

3. "Newspaper Syndicates Offering Comic Strips and Other Features to Radio," *Broadcasting*, 1 January 1936, pp. 8+.

4. Michael Jay Biel, "The Making and Use of Recordings in Broadcasting Before 1936" (Ph.D. diss., Northwestern University, 1977), 208–227.

5. Qtd. in Biel, "The Making and Use of Recordings," 232.

6. Biel, "The Making and Use of Recordings," 233.

7. Biel, "The Making and Use of Recordings," 595–598.

8. Biel, "The Making and Use of Recordings," 600.

9. Though option time was a standard operating principle from the beginning of the network era into the first decade of television, the FCC banned the practice in May 1963. Affiliates were uncomfortable about network option time throughout this entire era, though as William Boddy points out, in the vast majority of cases, local stations were too reliant on their network affiliations to complain too loudly about the practice. William Boddy, *Fifties Television: The Industry and its Critics* (Urbana: University of Illinois Press, 1990), 119–121.

10. Qtd. in Biel, "The Making and Use of Recordings," 382.

11. Since transcriptions were recorded exclusively on disk until the 1950s development of magnetic tape, precise editing was still impossible. If a mistake was made, it was necessary to re-record the entire program.

12. Storm Whaley, "General Adoption of Transcriptions By Public Claimed," *Broadcasting*, 1 March 1937, p. 65.

13. As live network series often boasted of their timeliness, transcribed series were sold on their time*less*ness. Broadcast live, and only once, fictional network series generally strove to remain timely, making references to contemporary figures, places, and events. In contrast, transcribed series, hoping to stay viable for years, followed the opposite principle, avoiding references to recent events in order to keep the programs from dating too quickly. Biel cites this as one reason why westerns and fantasy narratives dominated transcription production. Biel, "The Making and Use of Recordings," 515.

14. See, for example, Advertisement, Walter Biddick Company, *Broadcasting*, 15 August 1936, p. 47. A rare example of a radio series being marketed as a rerun took place in 1938 in Los Angeles, when Scholts Advertising Service ran *The Air Adventures of Jimmie Allen* from the beginning. The series' four-year run had ended in 1936, but Scholts' new sponsor successfully cultivated a new child audience from a repeat program. See Tom Scholts, "Recorded Re-Run of Jimmy Allen on Coast Is Success," *Broadcasting*, 15 March 1938, p. 28.

15. Melvin Patrick Ely, *The Adventures of Amos N Andy* (New York: Free Press, 1991), 53–56; Michele Hilmes, *Hollywood and Broadcasting: From Radio to Cable* (Urbana: University of Illinois Press, 1990), 144.

16. See Hilmes, *Radio Voices*, 6–10.

17. "On A Stream of Ether Floating," Advertisement, World Broadcasting System, Inc., *Broadcasting*, 1 November 1931, p. 21.

18. "YOU can build your own broadcasting chain," Advertisement, World Broadcasting System, Inc., *Broadcasting*, 15 March 1932, p. 4.

19. "Disk Program Nearly Trebled in 1930; Five Distinct Advantages of Use Cited," *Broadcasting*, 15 February 1932, p. 8.

20. Barry Golden, "Some Views on Electrical Transcriptions," *Broadcasting*, 1 September 1932, p. 7.

21. Percy B. Brown, letter, *Broadcasting*, 1 March 1932, p. 30; "Prospects for Electrical Transcription Business Held Very Good by Agencies," *Broadcasting*, 1 September 1932, p. 6.

22. J.R. Poppele, "Some Practical Facts About Transcriptions," *Broadcasting*, 15 October 1932, pp. 7+.

23. Interestingly, among these advantages (ranked number seven) was the "possibility of repetition of important programs at a later date." "Appraisal of Transcriptions," *Broadcasting*, 15 June 1934, p. 20.

24. The restrictions were only lifted during particular broadcast hours in each case; evenings were still reserved for live programming at that time. Typically, NBC also retained the full "disk ban" at their flagship stations WEAF and WJZ. "*Broadcasting* Ban on Disk Programs is Lifted," *Broadcasting*, 1 May 1932, p. 6; "Pro-Recordings," *Broadcasting*, 1 September 1932, p. 7.

25. Ira H. Robinson, letter to Federal Radio Commission, April 12, 1933, qtd. in "Ask Change in Disc Broadcast Order," *Broadcasting*, 1 June 1933, p. 6.

26. "Texts of Resolutions Adopted by NAB Convention," *Broadcasting*, 15 October 1933, p. 6. The full text of the resolution:

> Whereas, the use of the electrical transcription method of broadcasting programs is generally accepted by both stations and by listeners, and has become an important economic factor in the operation of broadcasting stations, and Whereas, there is definite evidence of serious loss in income to stations because of existing requirements that electrical transcription programs must be so announced, and Whereas, there has been sufficient progress in the manufacture of electrical transcription programs that the reproduction of the majority of such programs is now generally considered as excellent, and Whereas, the broadcasting industry would be greatly benefited by the removal of existing restrictions, therefore, be it Resolved, that the NAB hereby respectfully urges the Federal Radio Commission to alter the existing regulations requiring that electrically transcribed programs made especially for broadcasting be so announced, so that such a transcription may be announced merely as a production of the concern making such transcription.

27. A 1933 memo to the FRC opposing World's petition to relax Rule 176 bluntly stated these sentiments: "This entire resolution is but a demand to relieve one slight restriction upon machines in order that they may produce more profits to their owners and reduce more men to penury." "Musicians Protest NAB Disk Request," *Broadcasting*, 1 November 1933, p. 8.

28. "Change in Disc Announcement Is Considered at FCC Hearing," *Broadcasting*, 1 July 1935, pp. 12+.

29. Qtd in "Monopoly Report Urges FCC Kill Disc Announcement Rule," *Broadcasting*, 1 July 1940, pp. 18+.

30. Alexander Russo, "'Choosing Between Expediency and Refusing to See The Light of Competition': Liveness, Sound-On-Disc Recording, and the Economics of Network Broadcasting," *The Velvet Light Trap* 54 (Fall 2004).

31. Biel, "The Making and Use of Recordings," 417.

32. Russo, "Choosing Between Expediency."

33. Biel, "The Making and Use of Recordings," 696–722.

34. Biel, "The Making and Use of Recordings," 722. Similarly, Goldsmith also predicted that recordings would supplant live broadcasts on television as well.

35. "New Disk Service Offered by World," *Broadcasting*, 1 September 1933, p. 8.

36. Russo, "Choosing Between Expediency."

37. National Broadcasting Company, "NBC Electrical Transcription Service: Its Growth and Volume," 11 May 1937, ts., NBC Collection, Wisconsin State Historical Society, Box 92c, Folder 44.

38. "NBC Offers Discs To Local Sponsors," *Broadcasting*, 1 July 1934, p. 20.

39. "CBS Heave-Ho on 'Live' Coast Repeats Cue to NBC Relaxing Its Disk Ban," *Variety*, 18 June 1947, p. 24; Jack Gould, "The News of Radio," *New York Times* 13 June 1947, p. 40; "Radio and Television," *New York Times* 4 February 1949, p. 46; Rita Morley Harvey, *Those Wonderful, Terrible Years: George Heller and the American Federation of Television and Radio Artists* (Carbondale, IL: Southern Illinois University Press, 1996), 40. NBC was particularly reticent to allow transcriptions on its network programs, and only acquiesced after *Truth or Consequences* host Ralph Edwards convinced the network that a remount for the West Coast was becoming too problematic. " 'T or C' 1st Program to Break Ban by NBC on Disking Coast Repeats," *Variety*, 30 June 1947, p. 31.

40. Even so, there was some concern within NBC during this period that *Thesaurus* in particular could be used in direct competition with NBC network programs. John F. Royal, memo to Lloyd Egner, 4 January 1937, ts., NBC Collection, Wisconsin State Historical Society, Box 92c, Folder 44.

41. Harvey, *Those Wonderful, Terrible Years*, 31.

42. Qtd. in Harvey, *Those Wonderful, Terrible Years*, 39.

43. Lois S. Gray and Ronald L. Seeber, "Introduction," *Under The Stars: Essays on Labor Relations in Arts and Entertainment*, Gray and Seeber, eds. (Ithaca, NY: Cornell University Press, 1996), 2–6.

44. For an exhaustive account of the company, see Morleen Getz Rouse, "A History of the F.W. Ziv Radio and Television Syndication Companies: 1930–1960" (Ph.D. diss., University of Michigan, 1976).

45. Frederick W. Ziv, "Doin' what comes naturally—by transcription," *Variety*, 9 July 1947, 35.

46. Rouse 92–98; "Open-End Game," *Time*, 28 April 1947, p. 66. Colman and Menjou were the respective radio and television hosts of *Favorite Story*, while Bogart and Bacall performed in the 1950 radio series *Bold Venture*, an adventure series reminiscent of their film *Key Largo*. The only major network series that regularly used Hollywood stars was the *Lux Radio*

Theater, a Hollywood-originating anthology series which adapted popular Hollywood films to radio using familiar stars. See Hilmes, *Hollywood and Broadcasting*, 78–115.

47. Rouse, "A History of the F.W. Ziv Radio and Television Syndication Companies," 44, 69–70, 148–150.

48. See, for example, an advertisement for the Walter Biddick Company, *Broadcasting*, 15 August 1936, p. 47; Tom Scholts, "Recorded Re-Run of Jimmy Allen on Coast Is Success," *Broadcasting*, 15 March 1938, p. 28.

3
(R): Film on Early Television

Several attempts have been made to exhume film "oldies" from the vaults of Hollywood and put them on the air. This practice is definitely a complete misfire unless aired with the object of showing the photographic technique of former days.[1]

One of the primary reasons for the transition of radio not only to recordings, but to specialized "formats," was not its programming per se, but rather the concomitant development of a new broadcasting medium: television. The dominant interests in radio broadcasting—the national broadcast networks—were keenly developing television throughout the 1930s and 1940s. Though publicized and legally designated as "experimentation," the television broadcasts of this period were not only exercises in electrical engineering; they were also attempts to gauge the public efficacy of various forms of programming, including extant motion picture film. Although commercial broadcasting would not commence until 1945, the networks focused public attention on an imminent system of live transmission while more covertly exploring the business of television film distribution.

Speculation and Experimentation

Recordings on radio had gained legitimacy by the end of the 1940s, but their use on the emerging television medium was far from certain. The earlier aesthetic and economic debates about the validity of live vs. recorded programs were repeated nearly verbatim. In the early years of television broadcasting, film was the televisual equivalent of the electrical transcription: the only available source of existing, previously recorded material. As a consequence of these limitations, the suggested program forms for television were built upon two preexisting models: network radio broadcasting—which itself had largely been built upon Vaudeville and the legitimate theater—and Hollywood cinema. From the very beginning of television, film technology and the film industry would factor heavily in its development. For example, the experimental television broadcasts of the 1920s often utilized existing films as a simple means to test visual resolution. The earliest American television experimenter, Charles Francis Jenkins—an inventor of crucial motion picture technology dating back to the 1880s—produced short, silent "silhouette films" for his short-wave television broadcasts in the mid-1920s.[2] The major Hollywood film studios observed these and other developments with interest—and even some participation—throughout the experimental period of the 1920s through mid-1940s.[3]

The FCC allowed only experimental, noncommercial television broadcasting in the 1930s, because the technological standards of television were still unsettled.[4] Even though the faint, sporadic broadcasts were clearly "experimental," and were seen by almost nobody, television developers sought to enchant both the general public and potential advertisers through these publicized trials. Throughout the false starts of the 1930s, when staged demonstrations and their concomitant publicity constantly reiterated the idea that television was "just around the corner," major forces in radio broadcasting began to develop their television programming plans. Would the live, interconnected network be carried over from radio, or would a "wireless," asynchronous network of film syndication be more economical? The major networks and minor interests—such as the California-based Don Lee network—all utilized both live performances and films in their experimental television broadcasts. While the former programs consistently achieved greater notoriety for their innovation in bringing live, visual events to the home, the latter were also programmed with interest, for if film proved both technically feasible and popular, old cinematic titles could conceivably be recycled for a new, lucrative market on television.

As early as 1934, executives at both NBC and RCA—then already mired in debate about the use of recordings in radio—began to plan for television. An internal report from February of that year indicates an interest in pursuing the broadcasting of film, and displays prophetic vision, boldly stating that "it is clear from the operating standpoint alone, transmission from film will have such great advantages that probably 80 to 90% of the programs will be of this nature." Accordingly, the report goes on to advocate a system of film distribution rather than a more expensive system of physical interconnection.[5] In 1938, NBC made television history by broadcasting the first full-length feature film shown on television—the then-current *The Return of the Scarlet Pimpernel*—over experimental station W2XBS in New York.[6] Many other films were similarly broadcast on NBC television throughout the late 1930s and early 1940s, including British features, American B-pictures from minor studios, government documentaries, travelogues and musical shorts.[7] Given the tiny screen size of RCA's televisions, which measured eight inches diagonally, NBC's primary concern was to test the visual quality of their televised images.[8] However, they were also clearly interested in film's viability as a programming source, and measured audience response accordingly. A survey of two thousand visitors to NBC's television exhibition at the 1939 New York World's Fair found Motion Pictures to be the fifth-most popular programming form, rating less than Stage Plays, Musicals, Sports, and News Events, but more than Education, Fashion, War News, Political Talks, and Parlor Games.[9]

NBC was particularly concerned about the age of the films it was showing; the proven audience acceptance of older material was still more than a decade away. In a May 1940 memo to programming director Thomas Hutchinson, NBC vice-president Edward Hungerford was anxious to reach a deal with Monogram Pictures to rebroadcast some of their more recent films: "Since most of our present pictures are at least five years old, this would indeed be an improvement, and would eliminate a lot of criticism which we now get on the old pictures by reason of costume change in ladies' dress." A year later, in a letter to E.A. Alexander of the Philco Radio-Television Corporation discussing recent films broadcast on NBC, Hungerford lamented the films' "costume trouble": "you were undoubtedly amused...to note just how much women's fashions have changed since 1933 or '34. It is unfortunate for both of us that our largest potential supply of pictures seems to peak up during these years." As this correspondence indicates, the use of older films was only pursued at this time through necessity—they were often the only films available—rather than exploiting their archival value.[10] The idea that viewers might actually enjoy seeing older films did not seem to occur to television developers at this time. For example, in his 1942 book *The Future of Television*, broadcasting booster Orrin E. Dunlap noted that

> New York and London telecasters report that films rank third in popularity polls. No doubt this is because old pictures have been shown, generally of five or ten years' vintage, with costumes outmoded and a number of the stars long since dead.[11]

These experimental film broadcasts were always secondary to the goal of establishing a national, live television network, however. Despite evidence of some internal debate about the issue, neither NBC nor CBS ultimately hesitated to follow the model established by radio broadcasting, and developed a physical network of interconnected stations. Live interconnection had served them well in their dominance of radio, and they saw no compelling reason why television should not follow the same route. No system of ad hoc program syndication could match their potential simultaneous audience or control of the airwaves. Accordingly, the bulk of resources went into facilitating quality, coast-to-coast, live television broadcasting. However, as they had done eventually with transcriptions on radio, the networks realized that they could still participate in the recording-based economy *without* abandoning the principle of live broadcasting. Thus, while they spun the lofty rhetoric of live, nationwide communication to the FCC and sympathetic critics and journalists in the 1940s, they also explored the television film trade.

Film and the Networks in the 1940s

The first legitimate, if still somewhat limited, commercial television boom arrived in 1947–48, with stations already on the air in the largest cities, and several more on the way across the country. However, this system was still far from the networks' goal of nationwide interconnection. True network interconnection, via new, higher bandwidth coaxial cable technology, was limited at first to a few cities on the east coast; the majority of network affiliates had no way of obtaining a live program feed from New York, and had to draw extensively from two other sources of programming: local live production, and syndicated films.[12] Accordingly, despite their pursuit of an interconnected system, the networks saw a parallel opportunity in film syndication that was too great to ignore. However, their heavy investment in live broadcasting had spread resources thin, and the costs of constructing a film production plant from scratch were too prohibitive. Moreover, had the facilities even been available at that point, the fact that the budget of the average B-film was still significantly higher than the average live television production kept the networks firmly tied to the latter. Still, many inside and outside the networks believed that the shift to filmed programming was inevitable, and that, regardless of the short-term costs, the networks should invest in film production not only for network use, but, perhaps more importantly, for syndication to local stations. As television developer and former NBC programming director Thomas Hutchinson wrote in 1946,

> We are going to be able to do things on film for television that cannot possibly be done live and the fact that a program on film is available to a station manager where and when he wants it is going to be tremendously important to the industry.[13]

The first years of commercial television (1945–48), just prior to the FCC's freeze on new television broadcast licenses, were marked by network indecision on the film question. Nowhere was this more apparent than at NBC, which had always acted as the self-proclaimed champion of live broadcasting in radio, and would continue to do so in television.

Many within the network felt that if the network were to continue on top in the new medium, film had to be seriously pursued. In a 1947 letter to John F. Royal, the NBC Vice President for Television, Hollywood bureau chief Sidney N. Strotz worried that the network's indecision in this area would cost it in the long run:

> To me it is a sad commentary that a company such as ours, which is seriously interested in going into television, can't provide money to look forward to what the needs of the trade are going to be within the next few years. There is no question in my mind but that a syndicated series of film properly prepared for television . . . is going to be in terrific demand and any investment we or anybody else makes now will pay big dividends in the future.[14]

Others at NBC felt the same way. Russ Johnston headed the Film Division from 1947 through 1949, during which time he helped oversee NBC's entry into the film syndication market via the acquisition of broadcasting rights to existing films and the licensing of independently-produced films made expressly for television syndication. Johnston repeatedly advocated the expansion of NBC's film operations not only for syndication, but for network use as well. He made a concerted effort to change their limited policy during his tenure, but was ultimately unsuccessful. In late 1949, he appealed directly to NBC President Sylvester "Pat" Weaver for more film development. In a memo from August 1949, Johnston averred that while the costs of live programming had gone up, new techniques had brought the costs of film down. He also listed several of television's "ills" which could be cured by film programs: time zone differentials, program quality, program reuse, and—most importantly—profits.[15] Three months later— just before resigning in disgust—he made a last-ditch effort to persuade Weaver. In a report baldly titled "An Insurance Policy for NBC Television: Film Network and Programming," Johnston again outlined the advantages of film over live, and declared unequivocally that NBC was doomed if it followed its current radio-network based model.[16]

Despite the networks' declared dedication to live programming, the time differences across the continent still presented a considerable obstacle to network legitimacy, as it had with radio. A program sent out live from network headquarters in New York at 9 p.m. Eastern Time *could* go out live in Los Angeles at 6 p.m. Pacific Time, but that would disrupt the West coast schedules and would likely miss its biggest audience. Like the relatively limited use of the transcription in early 1940s network radio, the stop-gap method utilized to bridge liveness and recordings on network television was the kinescope. Kinescopes were 16mm films of television broadcasts produced by running a film camera in front of a special television monitor. Prior to the development of videotape in the late 1950s, kinescopes were the only way to preserve television broadcasts. The networks utilized this technique mostly to record a few select programs for sponsors' screenings and internal reference, to time-shift New York-originating programs for airing on the West coast, and to provide a delayed, "bicycled" network feed to noninterconnected affiliates.[17] The kinescope was the first form of recorded television. Since it had the least interconnected affiliates, the Du Mont network was the primary user of this technology; it had even developed the technique, calling it the "tele-transcription."[18] Kinescope distribution was also explored as a back door into television film syndication, and some network and locally-produced series were distributed as first-run and rerun programming in this format.[19] Nonetheless, despite technical attempts to improve their visual quality, they were always considered the poor stepchildren of live television and film. However, just as with transcriptions on radio, kinescopes remain the only record of hundreds of hours of early television broadcasting, and many have subsequently remained in the television heritage as "vintage" reruns.[20]

Nonnetwork Film on 1950s Television

> Almost anything, recorded on film, would make good television programming, provided it could be used enough times to amortize the original cost. ... Why not record each studio show, or, for that matter, every program![21]

After the license freeze ended with the FCC's Sixth Report and Order in 1952, new television stations flooded onto the airwaves. By 1958 there were over 500 stations on the air; a five-fold increase from the last year of the freeze. Similarly, television sets became a fixture in a majority of American homes over the same period. In 1950, television was in 9% of households; by the end of the decade, it was in nearly 86%.[22] In short, television became a major cultural institution in the 1950s. Accordingly, all of these new stations and viewers presented a major market for programming; a real one this time, instead of the more limited "boomlet" at the end of the 1940s. Although television remained in principle a "live" medium, the sheer demand for programming on local stations still necessitated the use of film. This demand would be met from two sources: recirculated theatrical film, and films specifically made for television distribution—i.e., "telefilms," or, in *Variety*'s argot, "vidpix." While the networks tentatively dabbled in telefilm distribution during the late 1940s and early 1950s, other firms had more definite plans to provide recorded programming for the new medium. Accordingly, like the transcriptions on 1930s radio, the majority of filmed programming on television at this time had *not* passed through network origination, and was instead syndicated directly to local sponsors and/or stations. Televisual repetition—as opposed to merely recording—was thus initially fostered by theatrical film and first-run syndication distributors, who helped legitimate film-based, locally-originated-but-nationally-distributed, repeatable television programming.

Theatrical Film on 1950s Television

Most of the film broadcast on television at this time was not produced originally for television, but consisted of older theatrical films. As the

1950s proceeded, these old Hollywood titles—primarily feature films, but also animated and live-action comedy shorts—took up an increasing percentage of available broadcast time, arriving on television at a greater rate than the newer telefilms. Virtually all of the material released to television distribution in the 1950s was produced prior to August 1, 1948, as per the major studios' labor agreement with the Screen Actors' Guild (SAG), which prevented more recent films from appearing on television pending a revision of the agreement governing the distribution of residuals owed talent from the repetition of films in which they appeared. As the decade wore on, this meant that older films represented the bulk of available material. During the 1940s, the major discourses producing the concept of "television" usually distinguished it from Hollywood cinema.[23] However, as stations actually went into operation, and films began to be commercially distributed and viewed, the perception of televised film began to change. As several historians have traced, the amount of films available for television use early in the 1950s was a trickle, dominated by smaller studios like Eagle-Lion, and independent producers like Alexander Korda.[24] By the end of the decade it was a torrent, with every major studio releasing nearly all of their libraries to television distribution. Long before that point, however, the daily scheduling of old theatrical films was standard practice at nearly every television station, contributing not only to the industry's reliance on recorded material *per se*, but also to the prevalence of televisual repetition, and the concomitant recycling of American popular culture.

In the late 1940s, nonnetwork time on local stations was dominated by the B-films of minor studios, and particularly by westerns. Even though these films were hardly considered quality Hollywood properties, they were wildly successful on television.[25] According to William Lafferty, however, from the major studios' perspective at the beginning of the 1950s, it was still not clear whether television presented a more profitable home for their past product than the theatrical reissue market.[26] In addition, as Michele Hilmes details, the studios also sought to construct their own television system—via experiments in pay and theater television—as an alternative to the networks and local stations.[27] By the middle of the decade, however, a myriad of court decisions, the virtual evaporation of the theatrical reissue market, and the television boom had convinced the majors to exploit their libraries on television.[28] Led by the sale of the RKO film library to C & C Television Corporation in December 1955, the majors soon followed suit. As Lafferty notes, "in 1956 alone, as a direct result of the major studios finally releasing product to television, almost 3000 features entered television distribution—two-thirds of the number released in all previous years."[29] Blocks of features and shorts from every major studio were acquired by a variety of speculators and distributors throughout this period, with a number of notable films receiving their television debuts, including Warner Bros's *Looney Tunes* and *Merrie Melodies* cartoons, and Universal's horror series.[30] By the end of 1957, almost all of the major studios had released the majority of their pre-1948 material to television, often by entering into lucrative agreements giving them a stake in the television business. For example, in 1956 Twentieth Century-Fox struck a deal with National Telefilm Associates (NTA) that released 450 of their features to television in exchange for half ownership of NTA and its proposed film-based ad hoc network.[31]

Despite the general lack of post-1948 films on the market for several more years, the theatrical films released to television in the mid-1950s were strong performers on local TV, proving that older, seemingly obsolete titles and stars could gain new audiences and reenter popular culture. Gordon Gray, the station manager of New York's WOR, claimed that his station "literally climbed out of the red into the black, from a no-rating status to a top-rated status, via cans of feature films."[32] Thus, televisual repetition was established with 1950s TV audiences via theatrical film, and encouraged by its constant scheduling on daily broadcast schedules, often with titles from as much as a generation earlier. The acceptance of these films was most apparent with the repackaged 1930s and 1940s animated and comedy shorts, which found an appreciative new generation of viewers in Baby Boom children. In 1956, Associated Artists Productions (AAP) acquired the rights to hundreds of Popeye and Looney Tunes cartoons from their respective studios (Paramount and Warner Bros). These shorts—some of which were over 20 years old at this time—were extraordinarily successful within only a few months, and soon became standard television fare.[33] Similarly, Interstate Television's revival of Hal Roach Studios' "Our Gang" series at the same time was equally successful, with the Depression-era shorts leading the ratings amongst child viewers nationwide in 1956; the bemused former child stars were even lured out of retirement into public appearances.[34] Los Angeles independent station KTTV even reproduced the spirit of the "cliffhangers" of the 1930s and 1940s by scheduling an afternoon block of adventure serials from those decades in 1957, though *Broadcasting* noted that "today's children" only had to wait 24 hours—instead of a whole week—to find out the fate of their heroes.[35] Old Hollywood stars and characters, such as Bela Lugosi, Boris Karloff, Shirley Temple, William "Hopalong Cassidy" Boyd, Laurel and Hardy, The Three Stooges, Bugs Bunny, Heckle and Jeckle, Woody Woodpecker, and others became staples of rerun television virtually overnight, and would remain so for decades. This new presence could only have enhanced the "legend" of "old Hollywood" already taking shape in the 1950s, as older films were imbued with the patina of nostalgia by virtue of their continual appearance (and reappearance) on the "new" medium of television.[36]

First-Run Telefilm Syndication

Theatrical film represented the largest amount of recorded material presented on television in the 1950s. At the same time, however, telefilms were also regularly aired on local stations. While theatrical film had partially established the principle of recirculation on television—i.e., that material produced for one medium could be successfully replayed on another—telefilm series insured that television's own generic forms, stars, and titles could become just as familiar and repeatable with audiences.

With so many stations coming on the air, and average station broadcast time expanding past 100 weekly hours, the prospects for a viable syndication market for first-run telefilms increased sharply; network programs, local live production, and theatrical films would not be able to fill all the time on all the stations. Television programming had only been a speculative game in the 1940s, but it soon became a critical concern in the film, broadcasting and advertising industries, as "film vs. live" debates raged in the pages of trade journals and the lay press alike, repeating the arguments over transcriptions in the 1930s. While proponents of live television continually repeated their contention that live events held a certain "excitement" and "spontaneity" that film lacked, telefilm producers claimed that films were more flexible and more profitable in the long run, due to their extended amortization via reruns.[37] A January 1952 editorial in *Broadcasting* on the differences between the beginnings of the radio and television industries noted that "[in] television, the filmed program corresponding to the radio transcription has been standard from the beginning, and promises to occupy even a greater share of program time than it does now."[38] Sponsors and ad agencies, the real powers-that-be in television programming at this time, were themselves divided about the issue. A Levoy Poll of over 700 executives from agencies, sponsors, and stations conducted in late 1952 found that 60% preferred live programs.[39] However, at the opening of the Advertising Club of Los Angeles in December of that year, Nat Wolff, the head of radio and television production at the Young & Rubicam advertising agency, announced his firm's preference for telefilm packages. Speaking at the same event, Klaus Landsberg, the vice-president of Paramount TV Productions, and general manager of Paramount-owned independent station KTLA, boasted that "video films" would be "the death knell" of networks, as they would practically negate the advantage of network interconnection.[40] John L. Sinn, President of Ziv Television, the television subsidiary of the major radio syndicator, evoked similar sentiments in defending film programs. Arguing that film insured the survival of "local and regional levels" of the new industry, he wrote that

> with film—and only with film—hundreds of stations and thousands of advertising agencies and sponsors will be able to secure high quality

programming....For these stations, agencies and sponsors, film is an economic must. Without it, television is only for a handful of the nation's largest advertisers.[41]

These comments indicate that the live vs. film debate was also becoming a euphemism for the battle lines being drawn between the network and local station. As it had in radio, the recorded program enabled local interests to procure national properties on their terms. Whether in the form of theatrical film or telefilm, film programming was already regarded as an essential component of a local television schedule.

Although contentious opinions about the advantages and disadvantages of either format abounded throughout the 1950s, the critical numbers— i.e., ratings and profits—were beginning to stack up in favor of syndicated film. In a May 1953 editorial, *Broadcasting* speculated that network dominance might even be eroding in the face of syndication, noting that there were more syndicators' exhibits at the annual National Association of Radio and Television Broadcasters (NARTB) trade show, and that even the network's film divisions were pitching themselves against network programs.[42] *Variety* noted a "bullish, 'go film' attitude" at the same convention.[43] As early as July of 1953, 25% of the programming at interconnected network affiliates, including the network O & O's, consisted of syndicated programming, including both theatrical films and telefilms. Noninterconnected affiliates used such film more than half of the time, and nonaffiliated stations over 60%.[44] Moreover, with the license freeze barely thawed, syndicated film had already outpaced local live production for good.[45] Thus, despite the principle of liveness and local origination still encouraged by FCC regulations, local stations became primary outlets for nationally-distributed film programming almost as soon as television became a viable broadcasting medium. Syndicated film usurped most time on local schedules, time that would have otherwise gone to live, local productions.

Moreover, most of the remaining live productions on local television were actually frames for the presentation of recycled films. Weekday morning and afternoon children's series, Sunday afternoon features, and Friday night horror films would generally be hosted live from the station's studio (often by the same person in multiple roles), and would occasionally feature guests, studio audiences, and even ironic commentary (well before *Mystery Science Theater 3000*). While these programs generally offered a vital local connection (even if only to particular sponsors or community groups), they only existed at all because of their symbiotic relationship to syndicated film. Local live production was thus already largely dependent on televisual repetition by the mid-1950s.

Although theatrical films dominated the syndication market at this point, telefilm distribution increased throughout the decade. Because prime-time network fare had been almost entirely live until about 1954, the majority of telefilm series in syndication in the early to mid-1950s were not off-network, but produced for first-run syndication by independent firms and the nascent television production arms of Hollywood studios. Accordingly, the period of 1952–56 has been called first-run syndication's "Golden Age" by historian William Boddy, as telefilm packagers and producers like Vitapix, United Television Programs (UTP), Screen Gems, MCA, Flamingo, Ziv, and others—as well as the three networks' film divisions—thrived for a few years producing new programming for local stations.[46]

One reason for the success of first-run syndication in this era was its attention to the newborn postfreeze stations in the smaller markets. Unlike the relatively impersonal network-affiliate relationship in which the network gained the bulk of public glory (and advertising gold), film distributors geared their sales to individual stations and/or advertisers, sending armies of salesmen nationwide to peddle their wares. Telefilm syndication of this sort often acted in lieu of network service in some markets.[47] Clamoring for affiliates in larger markets, where most viewers and TV sets were concentrated, the networks sometimes bypassed smaller cities. However, because film syndicators had little to lose from pursuing these small markets, they stepped in where networks feared to tread. A May 1954 profile of station KMID in Midland, Texas in *Broadcasting* reported that the station had sought network affiliation, but that the set count in the area was too low for the networks to be interested. Using syndicated film programs—driven by a mix of local and national advertising—and an aggressive promotional campaign, the station signed up several local advertisers to help promote both their station and the medium of television. After four months of this campaign, set ownership in the Midland area shot up from around 500 to over 32,000.[48] According to station manager S.A. Grayson, the appeal of film programs to local advertisers was the key factor in building their station's audience.[49] Telefilm also helped nonnetwork stations become viable competitors in larger, multistation markets. Independent station KTTV in Los Angeles built itself on the brokering of syndicated film packages across the West, and also pioneered the broadcasting of off-network, prime-time programs in its daytime schedule.[50] Similarly, independent stations such as WPIX in New York and WGN in Chicago consistently acquired the most desirable first-run telefilm and theatrical film packages in their markets in large part because they could offer more prime-time hours relative to the network affiliates.

One of the most successful telefilm syndicators was a veteran of the radio trade, the Frederick W. Ziv Company. Ziv produced some of the most popular series in first-run syndication in the 1950s, including *Highway Patrol*, *I Led Three Lives*, and *Science Fiction Theatre*. *Variety* even referred to them in 1953 as "one of the major broadcast phenomena of the decade."[51] As they had in radio, Ziv focused its television efforts on the recycling of existing properties. This principle was never clearer than in the production of two of its earliest series, *Yesterday's Newsreel* and *Sports Album*. Assembled from various stock footage acquired in purchases of major film libraries in the mid-1940s—all linked together with appropriate voiceover narration and music—the programs were the first on television to exploit past film material primarily on the basis of its apparent age.[52] Continuing the recycling principle, Ziv brought several successful radio series to television early in the 1950s, including *Favorite Story*, *Boston Blackie*, *Mr. District Attorney*, and the immensely successful *Cisco Kid*.[53] Ziv successfully forged a nationwide television presence entirely through local syndication, despite having none of its programs on network schedules (until its *West Point* was aired by CBS in 1956). While its programs were visibly produced on the cheap when compared to anything aired by the networks, they were consistently among the top-rated series in first-run syndication, attracting more lucrative advertisers than any other syndicator, and even rivalling the networks in their sponsor clientele.[54]

Anticipating a boom in color television, Ziv added to its luster in 1954 by announcing that its series would henceforth be produced in "Zivcolor," a process that enabled them to shoot programs in both monochrome and color. In *Variety*, Ziv President John L. Sinn boasted of the firm's $4 million investment in Zivcolor and boldly proclaimed that

> those film producers who are willing to discard inexpensive production and go all out with high quality and lavish productions, those producers who are willing to shoot in color, to build up backlogs of color films which will result in secure residual income in the future, those television producers will chart the future of the television film industry.[55]

While Sinn's faith in residual value was certainly founded, Ziv's investment in color unfortunately came a decade too early. By the time all three networks had switched to an all-color schedule in 1966, United Artists had absorbed Ziv, and its color-produced series were well out of date.[56]

Though they continued to promote live broadcasting over their interconnected webs, the networks also participated in the telefilm market, as each of the emerging Big Three had a film division that syndicated series to local stations. As noted above, NBC had not moved completely over to film during Russ Johnston's tenure—and was in no position to go into even limited film production on its own—but it had acquired a few film series and packages for local distribution. Some of these were older theatrical fare, such as the Monogram *Hopalong Cassidy* westerns, originally produced in the 1930s and 1940s, which soon became the first mass "rerun" success on television, airing nationwide.[57] But the network also sought telefilms, and helped finance productions for which they would retain the television rights. These early deals would be the precursors to the program procurement policies that solidified network control of programming in the late 1950s.

In January 1948, NBC entered into a five-year contract with Jerry Fairbanks Productions—producers of theatrical short subjects and travelogues—which resulted in the first filmed series made for television: *Public Prosecutor*.[58] Although the Fairbanks contract was nullified only two years later, the precedent had been set, and from then on, the networks would be not only time brokers, but *program* brokers as well, selling telefilm to local stations and extending the identity of the "network" into "nonnetwork" time. Significantly, most of these early network-distributed film programs were intended all along for first-run syndication, and had not had network runs. Accordingly, programs were sold to advertisers and local stations, but not necessarily to affiliates.[59] While NBC was live television's loudest supporter throughout the 1950s, it was also the most prolific of the Big Three in first-run telefilm syndication, and met with great success distributing such nonnetwork programs as *Dangerous Assignment*, *Hopalong Cassidy*, *International Theatre*, and *The Lilli Palmer Show*, no doubt to the chagrin of its non-network competitors.[60]

Successfully exploiting the gaps in the networks' interconnections, first-run telefilm syndication continued to grow through the middle of the decade, generating more production, more investment, and more advertising revenue.[61] Nevertheless, this sector of the industry began a steep decline in 1956, and was virtually extinguished by 1960. What happened to cut off this nonnetwork alternative in only a few years? Several market factors combined to force first-run syndication into the television margins in the late 1950s, but they all can be summarized in one word: repetition. While Ziv, UTP, Flamingo, and other firms had successfully established the telefilm as a legitimate and lucrative form of programming, this success had eventually crowded the market, forcing them to cut the production of new series so that they could concentrate on selling and recouping the costs of already-existing series. In addition, the competition for time on local schedules intensified considerably in the second half of the 1950s, with the dominant and familiar, in the form of theatrical film and off-network telefilm, eventually winning out. The rerun had arrived.

Repetition Takes Hold

Rerun programs are probably the most under-rated programming on TV today.[62]

The sheer volume of new telefilm available in syndication throughout the early 1950s seemed to indicate that only the newest telefilm programs would be acceptable to broadcasters. With new episodes of so many series of various genres available, why would a station program the less-prestigious repeats? Even though there were many new packages of telefilm series, as well as an increasing amount of Hollywood cinematic material available by the mid-1950s, reruns of these same films began to gain acceptance as a legitimate programming form. This was a significant change in the conventional wisdom about broadcasting *per se*, which until that point had been governed by the near sacrosanct belief in live, quasi-theatrical programming. The presence of film chains—an arrangement of a film projector and a television camera that enabled the broadcasting of film—and the numerous cans of film at virtually every television station provided the physical ability to repeat programs; the fast-growing television audience and the necessity to expand the broadcast day furnished the economic logic. Still working from the premise that viewers were only interested in fresh material, programmers reasoned that since most of the burgeoning television audience had not seen a program on its first run, subsequent runs could attract new viewers. In addition, a second, third, or later run of a program in the same market was always considerably less expensive to acquire than a first run. Accordingly, although a few viewers complained, reruns provided an economical alternative to new programming. By 1955, however, the ratings evidence established that reruns were more than a cheap susbstitute for new programs. The "new audience" rationale had been only partially accurate; instead, repeat programs were also consistently drawing repeat viewers, to an extent that had not been foreseen, but would soon be relied upon. Consequently, the local syndication market shifted decisively away from new series and toward the exploitation of established, previously aired film and television properties: in short, reruns.

Even prior to the 1956–57 deluge of major studio titles, theatrical films were particularly prone to rebroadcasting. New York independent station WPIX virtually specialized in programming feature films, pioneering daytime and late night film blocks in the late 1940s, and obtaining multiple runs of packages whenever possible. In September 1952, they even programmed the *same* film five nights a week, from 7:30 to 9 p.m., directly replicating the cinema-going experience. As Carol Levine, the station's film supervisor noted, "re-issues are money in the bank for movie production companies. There is no sound reason why the same cannot be applied in television."[63] Echoing those sentiments, her General Manager, G. Bennett Larson, speaking at a BMI Television Seminar in early 1953, lamented the lost programs of live radio, and predicted that television had to reuse film to remain viable: "our expenses are much greater, advertising costs a lot more and if the advertiser can't get some replays or encore dates or residual value, I think we're all headed for a very expensive, wasteful business."[64] Similarly, the Program Manager of another independent station, Chicago's WGN, told the same audience that without a network affiliation, film buying was his "number one problem," and that you had to program third, fourth, and fifth runs of features or series in order to stay viable.[65]

Thus, while new series and film packages would always be acquired at local stations, the bulk of nonnetwork time would be given over to repeated programs from the mid-1950s onward. The higher up-front cost of a new series was a significant factor, but only part of the consideration. More influential was the fact that reruns were not losing audiences, as all available ratings evidence showed that their audiences were comparable to, or in some cases even greater than, the original airings.[66] This was partially attributed to the continued increase in television households cited above; most programs would not be experienced as reruns to many new TV families. However, the ratings data also indicated that viewers were content to watch the same program more than once. A 1953 Nielsen analysis of "repeat films" on the networks' schedules found that not only were the ratings of summer reruns higher than their first-run competition; 41% of the audience had watched the repeat despite having seen the episode in its initial broadcast.[67] Echoing these findings, Leslie Harris wrote in a 1954 *Broadcasting* article that "a film can be re-run as many as seven times, with a steady improvement in its ratings history," and that "almost without exception it has been proved that a re-run does not diminish the appeal of a program or a station's position."[68]

Reruns had arrived as a legitimate program form, and the economic effects were being borne out in the increased revenue of syndicators. At the end of the freeze in 1953, several syndicators offered new stations discount program packages, which generally enabled the acquisition of hundreds of hours of older telefilms at a much lower cost than comparable first-run series. In addition, these titles were often made available on a library basis, which granted stations the rights to unlimited usage of the films for the duration of the contract. For new stations short of cash and programming, these packages were a godsend, while for distributors they offered a legitimate means to continue to market their otherwise dated series. In 1954, Ziv established a separate division— the appropriately named Economee TV—to handle the sales of their older titles.[69] By 1956, Economee's 575-episode, 11-series library had been sold to 175 stations, mostly in smaller markets.[70] Similarly, Consolidated Television offered a Station-Starter Plan, an inexpensive package of nine shows with unlimited exhibition rights, while United Television Programs, MCA, Official Films, Du Mont, and others followed soon thereafter with similar plans.[71]

Despite their public stance in support of live television, the proven viability of filmed reruns was not lost on the networks, who had only recently started allowing film series on their prime-time schedules, let alone marketing them "off network" to local syndication. As noted above, the networks' film divisions had successfully sold telefilm series in first-run syndication throughout the early 1950s, but their business lagged behind syndication giants like Ziv, UTP, and MCA. Accordingly, realizing the long-term profits to be gained from syndication rights, the networks began to shift their prime-time schedules to formulaic, episodic filmed series, instead of selling large blocks of time to single sponsors, or producing expensive, one-off live spectaculars.[72] After its merger with United Paramount Theaters in early 1953, ABC took the lead in film programming; their unprecedented use of Hollywood studio-produced series in the mid to late 1950s—beginning in 1954 with *Disneyland*—has been much noted in television histories.[73] However, the shift to film also has roots in a few earlier network programs that became runaway hits as off-network reruns.

Under the leadership of Sylvester "Pat" Weaver, NBC still advocated live programs as a general philosophy throughout the 1950s. Nonetheless, they also programmed a few prominent telefilms on their prime-time schedules. As Vance Kepley notes, NBC's expensive decision to run the World War II film documentary series *Victory At Sea* as a sustaining program in 1952–53 had to be offset by profitable distribution to local stations. Released to local stations in May of 1953, *Victory* became a staggering success, consistently running in some markets for over a decade, and thus indicating that off-network syndication could be a lucrative long-term endeavor.[74] Consequently, NBC film division head Robert Sarnoff touted "the emphasis we have placed on rerunning successful film series" as the primary key to the success of the division.[75] NBC placed reruns of their co-owned telefilm police dramas *Dragnet* and *Gangbusters* in syndication in 1953—as *Badge 714* and *Captured*, respectively—and both garnered solid ratings for local stations well into the 1960s. At CBS, while live broadcasting was a dominant value, it was never dogma. Instead, according to William Boddy, their developing strategy in the 1950s had specifically called for formulaic, 30-minute filmed series—sitcoms in particular. No doubt the success of *I Love Lucy*, beginning in 1951, heralded this development.[76] CBS' reluctance to allow *Lucy* to be shot on film is legendary, and appeared to be shortsighted only two years later. In the wake of *Lucy*, several of their early live television sitcoms—some of which were already *de facto* "reruns," being TV versions of long-running radio shows—had switched to film by 1953, including *Our Miss Brooks*, *My Little Margie*, *My Friend Irma*, and *The George Burns and Gracie Allen Show*.[77] However, CBS Films' first real off-network success was not *I Love Lucy*—which would not become available locally until 1967—but rather *Amos 'n' Andy*, which left the network in June of 1953 after only a two-year run (its sponsor, Blatz Beer, had withdrawn support), and became a staple of local rerun programming into the 1960s.[78] Continuing their cultivation of the 30-minute sitcom form in off-network, CBS made other significant series available to syndication throughout the decade, including the 39 filmed episodes of *The Honeymooners*.[79]

An additional spur to the development of reruns was the expansion of "fringe time" in broadcast schedules. So-called because of its placement on both ends of the prime time viewing period, fringe time generally ran from 4 to 7:30 in the evening and 11 to signoff during the night.[80] By the end of 1956, the average commercial television station was on the air almost 102 hours a week, meaning many available daily hours outside of prime time.[81] As Boddy notes, the "discovery" of afternoon and late-night audiences solidified the film syndication market, and established the traditional home of off-network reruns.[82] September 5, 1955 marked a largely forgotten milestone in television history in this regard. On that date, Philadelphia station WPTZ began an unusual programming experiment. Off-network reruns were already becoming common by that time, but were run only once per week, generally in the evening. WPTZ decided to run Official Films' *My Little Margie*—an off-CBS sitcom distributed by Official Films—five afternoons a week, thereby initiating the practice of "stripping" a rerun on weekdays. Perhaps the most significant programming innovation since the weekly episodic series began on 1920s radio, stripping schedules a series "horizontally," i.e., at the same time across the weekly broadcast schedule. Stripping allows for daily viewing of a series originally produced in weekly installments, accelerating its consumption. Although the earlier anxiety about overexposure would seem to mitigate against this practice, the ratings data again indicated that viewers were content to watch the same program day after day. *Sponsor* called stripping "The Trend" of 1956, and identified NBC, CBS, and Official Films as the most active syndicators who advocated this programming strategy.[83] That fall, stripping became common practice across the country, with familiar network series such as *Dragnet, Life With Father,* and *Amos and Andy*, and syndicated series like *Highway Patrol, Foreign Intrigue,* and *The Cisco Kid* becoming daily, rather than weekly, fixtures on stations.[84] By early 1958, according to a study commissioned by California National Productions, a telefilm subsidiary of NBC, stripping amounted to 46% of all syndicated film hours in 60 major markets.[85] From this point forward, off-network series would generally run five days a week on local stations, exponentially increasing their repetition and familiarity.

In addition, the sheer number of first-rate Hollywood films sold in local television syndication in 1956 caused many to speculate whether there would be enough time on schedules for both feature films and telefilms. Proponents of the new film packages cited the superior "quality" of Hollywood features over episodic telefilms, and argued that this dose of quality could only improve the overall state of the medium. Robert Manby, Vice President of RKO Teleradio Pictures, was certain that these "quality features" would "[create] obsolescence in the pool of...half-hour films that have been run to death."[86] Conversely, Frederick Ziv shot back that the pre-1948 films would "easily set back the standards of the 'living room medium' five or ten years," and that only film made for television could serve as an effective advertising vehicle.[87] While most stations did buy into the flashy new packages of star-driven, 1940s Hollywood films—often adding additional feature film blocks to their broadcast schedules—syndicated telefilm did not take an immediate hit. Instead, according to *Sponsor*, the new features most often came at the expense of older, well-worn titles, rather than in time slots that would have gone to telefilms. In addition, the growing practice of stripping required a steady diet of 30-minute episodes rather than only longer feature films. Because they were now consumed so rapidly, programs with relatively long production runs (i.e., 50 or more episodes) were more successful than those with shorter runs.[88] Furthermore, advertisers and local stations alike generally preferred the half-hour episodic format; the former for its stability as an advertising vehicle, and the latter for its flexibility in filling out a program schedule.[89]

Thus, the rerun's reputation for being a cheap-yet-reliable program form had established itself. Stations could easily program their non-network hours, and syndicators could keep profiting from already-produced series. However, even with reruns being devoured at this accelerated pace, with new stations coming on-line, and with film becoming more and more prevalent despite the increase in overall broadcast hours, the market was still becoming oversaturated with programming. In July 1956, *Sponsor* estimated that there were already over 20,000 episodes of syndicated telefilms available.[90] While some in the industry, such as Norman Knight, the general manager of Boston station WNAC, regarded this glut as "an important plateau" in the industry, and believed that more film simply meant "a large supply of quality rerun product," others were concerned that the supply was growing too fast, and that the window was closing on new telefilm production.[91] Moreover, the 20 largest markets—vital to the success of any telefilm, regardless of how many other markets were sold—were becoming particularly difficult to break into.[92]

As early as 1954, some syndicators raised concerns that first-run telefilm syndication would fade away in deference to reruns and newly available theatrical film. *Variety* industry analyst Bob Chandler called telefilm syndication a "paradox": "a desert in the midst of plenty, a gold rush to a gravel pit." The paradox stemmed precisely from repetition, and the medium's new addiction to reruns. Successful telefilm producers had to balance the up-front costs of new production with the back-end profits gained through rerun sales. More episodes meant more costs, but potentially more profits, although having too *many* episodes was also problematic. Too few episodes meant that a series would not be as attractive as a rerun, particularly after stripping took hold, and series were consumed five times faster than they had been. A single season of 26, or even 39, episodes lasted only a few weeks at that pace. As Chandler summed up the dilemma:

(1) Don't go into it unless you're prepared to spend a lot of money; (2) Once you are in don't expect to get that money back for at least 18 months after time [sic] your series is produced.... The profit, if there is any—and there are only a couple of outfits in the business operating at a profit—will come with the replays, and at present the market is chock full of those too.[93]

A narrowing market was already forcing several firms to merge in the mid-1950s to consolidate their resources.[94] In addition, syndicators dealt themselves a double blow by engaging in a self-defeating pricing war in order to keep their properties moving to local stations, and simultaneously increasing their production budgets to aim for more "network-quality" productions.[95] At the November 1955 meeting of the National Television Film Council, Dwight Martin, Vice President of General Teleradio estimated that there were twice as many films in circulation than the market could bear, while John Mitchell, the Vice President of Sales at Screen Gems, claimed that desperate price-cutting was driving many firms out of business.[96] Echoing those concerns, Frederick W. Ziv cautioned that the artificially low prices paid for syndicated films were reducing the quality of the productions, making it difficult to finance a second or third year of a series.[97]

By the end of the decade, that concern was a reality. The "Golden Age" of first-run syndication of fictional programs was ending, and production plummeted from 29 series in production in 1956 to only one series by 1964.[98] By the early 1960s, first-run telefilms had been almost completely crowded out by the monster they had helped create: the rerun. This transition, which solidified the practices of televisual repetition, and assured that the future of syndication would be dominated by off-network programming, was largely the result of the factors detailed above, and, more directly, the growing hegemony of the networks and major studios over national television production, scheduling, and syndication.

The Rise of the Network-Studio Hegemony

The overall outlook for independent telefilm firms in the late 1950s was not promising. Local prime-time slots had all but vanished to the networks, and fringe time was increasingly filled with old theatrical films and telefilm reruns. In addition, as the networks moved away from in-house or single-sponsored live programs in favor of major studio-produced telefilm series, the entry requirements for telefilm syndication were raised. A successful network run was fast becoming an essential element for local syndication, as the legitimate market for first-run telefilm series was effectively reduced from hundreds of local stations to three national networks.[99] As Boddy details, because the networks enjoyed a virtual monopoly on prime-time hours, producers and advertisers alike generally had to give in to their demands, which usually entailed syndication rights and/or financial interest in the series they aired.[100] Frustrated by what they saw as an illegal network-level monopsony— i.e., a market with only one buyer—several major telefilm distributors, including Ziv, TPA, Official, Screen Gems, and RKO Teleradio, formed a coalition called the Association of Television Film Distributors (ATFD) and took their complaints to Washington in 1956, appealing to the FCC's Network Study Committee, the Senate Commerce Committee, and the House Anti-Trust Subcommittee. Their primary target, as stated specifically in a proposal made to the FCC Network Study Committee in May 1956, was the longstanding option time provision local stations had to grant in the network affiliation contract, which gave the networks exclusive accessibility to particular time slots in markets nationwide, severely limiting the amount of time available to nonnetwork programming.[101] Secondarily, the ATFD sought to curb network control and ownership of programming, noting that the networks' "financial interest may impel them to choose that program which they own or in whose profits they participate."[102] The networks, best represented by NBC's indignant and lengthy response to the charges, listed the expenses and public services of a national network, and defended option time and financial interest as "necessary and proper procedures in conducting a national network service."[103] The eventual committee reports, though critical of network practices, did not result in any immediate legal action against the network system.[104] With local schedules locked up, and the networks the only buyers of telefilm, fictional first-run syndication virtually disappeared within a few short years.

The 1950s had thus been a roller coaster for the independent film producers and their sponsors. The good news was that the networks were eliminating live programs and instead buying film from producers. The bad news was that they were also the only ones who could afford to buy new telefilms, tightening an already narrow market. The worst news was that the elusive network runs often came at the price of off-network syndication rights.[105] As Boddy writes, the net result of these developments "[gave] the networks unprecedented power in relation to affiliates, advertisers, and program suppliers."[106] Even though a network run meant less control and even financial interest, most firms had concentrated their efforts on that market by the end of the decade because first-run syndication was an almost assured loss. In a 1959 analysis of this issue in *Television Digest*, producer Phil Krasne of UTP explained how his firm had moved from producing entire series on speculation to investing more money in fewer pilots for network runs, with the hopes that one or two might be picked up as a network series. "Getting money out of reruns in syndication is a hard sell," claimed Krasne, as a buyer's market controlled a glut of old telefilm.[107] Through acquisitions and bankruptcies, the number of independent telefilm producers and packagers shrunk to a few giants by the early 1960s, almost all of which were subsidiaries of the major studios or the networks. Despite a few holdout programs, like Twenty Mule Team Borax's *Death Valley Days*, single sponsorship had similarly disappeared from the local syndication front, and accordingly local program directors had few first-run programs to choose from. Off-network programs—most of which were licensed by the networks' syndication divisions—poured into the syndication market, adding to the networks' *de facto* control over broadcast time.[108] Thus, by the end of the 1950s, the networks had tightened their control over television broadcasting by ironically abandoning the liveness principle that they had sanctimoniously defended as late as 1956. With few first-run properties available for local use, and a marketing route of network-to-syndication becoming routine, the stage was set for a decade of virtually complete dominance by the Big Three and their major studio cohorts.

Canned Goods

In a 1957 *Variety* article, TV industry analyst James Reeves advises that "[the] astute buying of film today is of the utmost importance to a station. . . . The necessity of high quality canned goods becomes more and more significant to the station operation each time a study of the ratings charts and sales figures is made."[109] By the 1957–58 season, the film vs. live debate on network television was effectively over, as Reeves' "canned goods" had decisively edged out live programs, claiming 53% of all prime-time hours. However, this debate had been resolved a few years earlier on local stations, as syndicated film had become the most economical and popular programming form during nonnetwork hours.

Most accounts of this first decade of television have focused on film's impact on network program schedules. While the networks' transition to film was undoubtedly the most significant shift in the history of American television, dictating the subsequent development of the medium and its programming, its foregrounding in historical studies has neglected the syndication of film to individual stations. Film's programming flexibility and, most significantly, capacity for repetition, were key in its ascendancy at the local level. In its ostensibly "pure," live form, a television broadcast is transmitted once and gone forever, existing only in that moment. Conversely, film is by its nature of the past; a permanent inscription, rather than a momentary expression, capable of being reviewed and reproduced. While the logic of the interconnected network as established by radio broadcasting was predicated on the central control of broadcast time and the simultaneous transmission of live events, film separated the event from the necessity of simultaneity, making the time of broadcast a local decision. More importantly, film allowed for the repetition and commercial reexploitation of existing programs. Once repetition became a standard practice of the U.S. television industry, the foundation was set for 20 years of industrial consolidation centered on the rerun, and the eventual cultural legitimation of past television.

Notes

1. William C. Eddy, *Television: The Eyes of Tomorrow* (New York: Prentice-Hall, 1945), 143–44.

2. Joseph H. Udelson, *The Great Television Race: A History of the American Television Industry, 1925–1941* (Tuscaloosa: University of Alabama Press, 1982), 24–27.

3. See Christopher Anderson, *Hollywood TV: The Studio System in the Fifties* (Austin: University of Texas Press, 1994); Tino Balio, ed., *Hollywood In The Age of Television* (Boston: Unwin Hyman, 1990); and Michele Hilmes, *Hollywood and Broadcasting: From Radio to Cable* (Urbana: University of Illinois Press, 1990), for accounts of how the major Hollywood film studios dealt with television.

4. "Non-commercial" in name only, as corporations with interests in advertising sales and equipment manufacture—particularly RCA—underwrote most of the research in this period.

5. National Broadcasting Company, *Television Programming Planning*, mss., NBC Collection, Wisconsin State Historical Society, Box 102, Folder 5.

6. "Movie Transmitted as Television Test," *New York Times*, 1 June 1938, p. 21; Jack Banner, "Feature Film is Televised by NBC-RCA for First Time," *Motion Picture Daily*, 2 June 1938.

7. National Broadcasting Company, *Summary Outline of Television Program Activities: Station WNBT, National Broadcasting Company, June 1942 to date*, mss., NBC Collection, Wisconsin State Historical Society, Box 113, Folder 29.

8. Despite the fact that 80% of its schedule during the 1939 World's Fair consisted of films, NBC Vice President Thomas H. Hutchinson claimed that they weren't to be "taken as examples of the kind of program service NBC is planning as a regular fare for its television audience." Qtd. in "Telecast Schedule Is Drawn by NBC," *Broadcasting*, 1 May 1939, p. 21.

9. Harry Gordon, "The 1940 Report on Television Reaction...Second and Concluding Study of a Survey of New York World's Fair Visitors," NBC Collection, Wisconsin State Historical Society, Box 103, Folder 21.

10. E. A. Hungerford, memo to Thomas H. Hutchinson, 24 May 1940, NBC Collection, Wisconsin State Historical Society, Box 103, Folder 9; E. A. Hungerford, letter to E. A. Alexander, 23 April 1941, NBC Collection, Wisconsin State Historical Society, Box 104, Folder 5.

11. Orrin E. Dunlap, *The Future of Television* (New York: Harper & Brothers, 1942), 76.

12. Many stations were also connected via line-of-sight microwave towers and receivers, which amplified broadcast signals in lieu of cable connections. In addition, because many of these early stations were the only ones in their markets, multiple network affiliations were relatively common, frustrating the networks' clearance goals but offering new stations more program possibilities. As a result, the period of the licensing freeze, from 1948–53, saw network prime time clearances hovering at an anemic 39%. See William Boddy, *Fifties Television: The Industry and its Critics* (Urbana: University of Illinois Press, 1990), 115.

13. Thomas H. Hutchinson, *Here Is Television, Your Window to the World* (New York: Hastings House, 1946), 230.

14. Sidney N. Strotz, letter to John F. Royal, 10 June 1947, ts., Wisconsin State Historical Society, NBC Collection, Wisconsin State Historical Society, Box 113c, Folder 32.

15. Russ Johnston, memo to Pat Weaver, 4 August 1949, ts., NBC Collection, Box 118, Folder 10.

16. Russ Johnston, *An Insurance Policy for NBC Television: Film Network and Programming*, ts., NBC Collection, Wisconsin State Historical Society, Box 118, Folder 10.

17. "Bicycling" is a term for shipping films (and later, tapes) around the country by ground or air transportation. Prior to the full interconnection of the networks, this was the only possible method of national distribution in many areas of the country.

18. Hilmes, *Hollywood and Broadcasting*, 149–150; Bob Stahl, "Tele-transcription service," *Variety*, 30 July 1947, pp. 33+.

19. Paramount's Los Angeles independent station KTLA pioneered the use of non-network kinescope distribution in 1949. "Paramount's kine recording...," *Television Digest*, 17 September 1949.

20. For example, the Sci-Fi Channel utilized kinescopes of the early live dramas *Lights Out!* and *Tales of Tomorrow* in its late-night lineup in the mid-1990s.

21. Leonard F. Kramer, "Canned video as solution," *Variety*, 9 July 1947, p. 32.

22. "Television Receiver Ownership and Use: 1946–1988," in Christopher H. Sterling and John M. Kittross, *Stay Tuned: A Concise History of American Broadcasting (2nd Edition)* (Belmont, CA: Wadsworth Publishing, 1990), 657.

23. See Dunlap and Eddy, as well as the ambivalence of the NBC executives on the issue of film.

24. See James L. Baughman, "The Weakest Chain and the Strongest Link: The American Broadcasting Company and the Motion Picture Industry, 1952–60," in Balio, *Hollywood in the Age of Television*, 91–114; William Lafferty, "Feature Films on Prime-Time Television," in Balio, *Hollywood in the Age of Television*, 235–256; David Pierce, "'Senile celluloid': Independent Exhibitors, the Major Studios and the Fight Over Feature Films on

Television, 1939–56," *Film History* 10 (1998): 141–164; Barbara Wilinsky, "First and Finest: British Films on U.S. Television in the Late 1940s," *Velvet Light Trap* 40 (Fall 1997): 18–31.

25. Lafferty, "Feature Films," 238. A.H. Cole, owner of several theaters in Texas, worried that the poor quality of films on television would ultimately affect film exhibition: "My only fear about TV is that it is going to kill the picture business because of those terrible films the stations are using. I'm afraid some audiences, after seeing them, will swear off ever seeing pictures anywhere." Qtd. in "'Kines' & 'oldies' find ready use," *Television Digest*, 4 February 1950.

26. Lafferty, "Feature Films," 238; Thomas N. Pryor, "Statistics Given In Anti-Trust Suit," *New York Times*, 19 October 1955, p. 40.

27. Hilmes, *Hollywood and Broadcasting*, 116–139.

28. Lafferty, "Feature Films," 239.

29. Lafferty, "Feature Films," 242.

30. "$24 Million Worth of Films Involved in Transactions," *Broadcasting*, 2 January 1956, p. 44; "Motion Picture 'Gold Rush' to Free Many Films for TV," *Broadcasting*, 9 January 1956, p. 31; "Warner Films Bought for $21 Million; Largest Library Yet for Television," *Broadcasting*, 5 March 1956, p. 42.

31. "NTA, 20th Century Fox Sign Gigantic Double Agreement," *Broadcasting*, 5 November 1956, pp. 48+.

32. Gordon Gray, "They got us into the black," *Sponsor*, 11 June 1956, p. 66.

33. "AAP Buys 'Popeye' Films for TV Station Release," *Broadcasting*, 11 June 1956, p. 52; "Prolific Profits From Popeye," *Broadcasting*, 12 August 1957, p. 64.

34. "Kids Crowd To Meet 'Rascals'," *Broadcasting*, 4 June 1956, p. 107.

35. "KTTV (TV) Los Angeles Takes Leaf From Earlier Generation's Book," *Broadcasting*, 15 July 1957, p. 116.

36. This is a point worth exploring in more detail than can be offered here. Perhaps two Sid Hix cartoons from *Broadcasting* can illustrate this popular cultural response to televised Hollywood cinema (or at least how it was perceived from the perspective of the industry's mouthpiece). In one, two elderly women are walking in front of a cinema marquee which reads "TODAY: CARY GRANT." One turns to the other and says "I'd rather see him on the late, late show...He's twenty years younger." In another, a middle-aged couple sits at home watching a monster movie on TV. The husband says "I've been looking forward to tonight's late, late show. Mom wouldn't let me see it when I was a kid!" Sid Hix, cartoons, *Broadcasting*, 3 July 1961, p. 122; 6 May 1963, p. 98.

37. "Is film good or bad for TV?" *Variety*, 15 October 1952, p. 21.

38. Interestingly, this contention elided the fact that recordings had always been prevalent in radio broadcasting via electrical transcriptions, indicating that the dominant view that radio was initially "live" still held. "Teleconomics," editorial, *Broadcasting*, 7 January 1952, p. 75.

39. "Levoy Poll; 700 executives prefer live TV," *Broadcasting*, 1 Dec. 1952, p. 68.

40. "Films Favored; Nat Wolff Cites Benefits," *Broadcasting*, 8 Dec. 1952, p. 84.

41. John L. Sinn, "The Case for Filmed Television," *Broadcasting*, 26 January 1953, p. 78.

42. "Network-affiliate relationship," editorial, *Broadcasting*, 4 May 1953, p. 134.

43. "'Go film, young stations'," *Variety*, 6 May 1953, p. 21.

44. "How Important Is Film?," *Broadcasting*, 13 July 1953, p. 87.

45. "Film Basics," *Sponsor*, 12 July 1954, p. 184. Moreover, *Variety* noted that by using film, stations avoided the union fees associated with live talent, thus fostering the medium's reliance on the "tried-and-true" in the name of cost cutting. "Vidpix dooms new live talent," *Variety*, 22 October 1952, p. 21.

46. Boddy, *Fifties Television*, 140. One of the more controversial telefilm firms at this time was Revue Productions, which was owned by talent agency Music Corporation of America (better known as MCA). Due to union agreements, talent agencies were forbidden from owning production companies, but MCA received a special dispensation from one of its most powerful clients— SAG president Ronald Reagan—and started Revue, as well as acquiring Universal Pictures and Decca Records. In 1959, however, the government forced them to choose between the management or production business, and MCA became a full-fledged Hollywood studio, MCA-Universal, which would go on to become one of the largest suppliers of network television series in the 1960s and 1970s. Hal Erickson, *Syndicated Television: The First Forty Years, 1947–1987* (Jefferson, NC: McFarland & Company, 1989), 9.

47. At this time, the usual sales process involved first selling the film to a regional or national advertiser, and then seeking time on local stations. Thus, a brewer, dairy, oil company, or supermarket chain would be the sole sponsor for a particular series over a particular array of stations. However, sales were also made directly to stations, particularly if a program was past its first run and could be offered at a discounted rate. In addition, the practice of "barter"—giving unsponsored films to stations in exchange for several national advertising spots—became a widely utilized, if controversial, practice by the late 1950s.

48. It should be noted that Midland-Odessa was a relatively wealthy area, due to oil production and distribution firms, and thus could more readily afford TV sets in comparison to other areas.

49. "In Midland, Texas—Films Build Sales and Set Count," *Broadcasting*, 10 May 1954, p. 84.

50. Marjorie Ann Thomas, "Film Builds Ratings: How Film Helped KTTV Get Into The Black," *Broadcasting*, 12 July 1954, pp. 94+.

51. "Ziv's zippy $25,000,000 biz," *Variety*, 22 April 1953, p. 25.

52. Morleen Getz Rouse, "A History of the F.W. Ziv Radio and Television Syndication Companies: 1930–1960" (Ph.D. diss., University of Michigan, 1976), 102.

53. Rouse, "A History of the F.W. Ziv Radio and Television Syndication Companies," 56–63, 77–88, 92–98.

54. "Ziv TV to double film production," *Broadcasting*, 4 October 1954, p. 32.

55. John L. Sinn, "Zivcolor: A Tint Mint," *Variety*, 5 January 1955, p. 108.

56. In the 1990s, producer J. Michael Straczynski similarly prepared for future TV technology, shooting his science fiction series *Babylon 5* in a widescreen format in anticipation of the upcoming 16:9, high-definition television standard. Unlike Ziv, Straczynski was able to market *Babylon 5* in widescreen, first on rerun syndication on the Sci-Fi Channel, and then in DVD box sets.

57. Hilmes, *Hollywood and Broadcasting*, 150–151.

58. Because it was the first film series for television, Fairbanks had no established models to work from. As a result, *Public Prosecutor* was an odd mix of radio and film conventions, with cramped sets, talk rather than action, and a minimalist visual style. The publicity materials boasted that

    > Every foot of this film was shot especially for television. You will notice an unusual number of close-ups, half shots, and the complete absence of long shots. Subjects are well centered to keep them away from the outer limits of the television receiving tube. Story treatment follows closely radio program technique as applied to television, with main characters addressing the television audience directly, providing an intimate link between film and home audience.

    In addition, Fairbanks intended the series to be repeated, planning for only seventeen new episodes, and allowing stations to run two repeats of each of them, making for a total of fifty-one weekly episodes. National Broadcasting Company, "Official Preview: First Dramatic Feature Film Made Especially for Television," 26 August 1947, ts., NBC Collection, Box 589, Folder 4; "Films especially lensed for tele to be ready for screenings by August," *Variety*, 2 July 1947, p. 34.

59. NBC reiterated this "first-come, first-serve" policy in 1953, after Denver affiliate KFEL had complained about the Film Division's sale of *Hopalong Cassidy* to rival station KBTV. By extending their market beyond their affiliates—by not even favoring their affiliates in the bidding process—NBC hoped to extend its control of local television. "NBC film division's Sarnoff says no station preference to be shown," *Broadcasting*, 5 October 1953, p. 31.

60. "NBC Film Div.; Sarnoff Announces Plans," *Broadcasting*, 22 September 1952, p. 84; "NBC notes step-up in film div. sales," *Broadcasting*, 18 May 1953, p. 34; "NBC film division plans expansion," *Broadcasting*, 13 July 1953,

p. 74; "NBC Film Status Report," *Broadcasting*, 12 July 1954, p. 31; "NBC Film Division Reports Record Year," *Broadcasting*, 16 January 1956, p. 49.

61. "Telepix's $25,000,000 gamble," *Variety*, 24 December 1952, pp. 1+; Dave Kaufman, "H'wood doubles telefilm production budget for '55 with $80,000,000 tab," *Variety*, 29 December 1954, pp. 1+.

62. Frederic W. Ziv, qtd. in "Why Ziv Is Gambling Millions In TV Film," *Broadcasting*, 4 June 1956, p. 48.

63. Carol Levine, "Film re-runs can pay off," *Broadcasting*, 10 August 1953, pp. 92–93.

64. G. Bennett Larson, "Film Buying—Film Costs and Problems of Film Operation," in Broadcast Music Inc., ed., *Twenty-Two Television Talks* (New York: BMI, 1953), 3.

65. Jay Faraghan, "Film Buying—Film Cost and Problems of Film Operation," in Broadcast Music Inc., *Twenty-Two Television Talks*, 125.

66. Levine, "Film re-runs," 92; "TV film panel studies economics," *Broadcasting*, 4 May 1953, p. 56; "Film Basics," *Sponsor*, 12 July 1954, p. 188; "Nielsen: Film Re-Runs Hold Audience," *Broadcasting*, 24 January 1955, p. 30; "Film: Can Reruns Still Draw Large Audiences?," *Sponsor*, 7 February 1955.

67. "Film Basics," *Sponsor*, 12 July 1954, p. 189.

68. Leslie Harris, "The Thorny Side of Syndicated Film," *Broadcasting*, 8 November 1954, p. 95.

69. Rouse, "A History of the F.W. Ziv Radio and Television Syndication Companies," 238–239.

70. Rouse, "A History of the F.W. Ziv Radio and Television Syndication Companies," 239.

71. "Consolidated sets 'starter' package," *Broadcasting*, 16 March 1953, p. 38; "UTP wraps up full-year package for new video market at 14G," *Variety*, 1 April 1953, p. 56; "13 Good Film Deals for New TV Stations," *Broadcasting*, 13 July 1953, p. 102.

72. Over the next several years, this shift also incorporated the "magazine"-style sale of advertising time, as detailed in standard broadcasting histories, which split up programs between several advertisers, and gave the networks more control over their schedules and the content of their programs. However, as Boddy details, this transference of program control also enabled the networks to become the primary brokers of *syndicated* television programs as well by the early 1960s. Boddy, *Fifties Television*, 175.

73. For analysis of ABC's network strategy at this time, see Anderson, *Hollywood TV*; Baughman, "The Weakest Chain," Hilmes, *Hollywood and Broadcasting*, 153–154.

74. Vance Kepley, Jr., "Documentary as Commodity: The Making and Marketing of *Victory At Sea*," *Film Reader* 6 (1985): 109; "Victory At Sea sales reach 44," *Broadcasting*, 20 July 1953, p. 32. In 1958, it still ran in

fifty-three markets, and was on its seventh run in New York and Los Angeles. More importantly, its revenues had already doubled NBC's initial investment. "'Victory' Still Going Strong," *Broadcasting*, 13 January 1958, p. 52.

75. Qtd. in "NBC Film Division triples its sales," *Broadcasting*, 21 Sept. 1953, p. 32.

76. William Boddy, "Building The World's Largest Advertising Medium: CBS and Television, 1940–60," in Balio, *Hollywood In The Age of Television*, 76; "Burns & Allen on film," *Broadcasting*, 7 July 1952, p. 79.

77. Eighty-six network and syndicated radio series were eventually made into television series by the 1960s.

78. "CBS expands television sales," *Broadcasting*, 4 May 1953, p. 70. Though popular, particularly in the south, *Amos 'n' Andy*'s profile began to wane during the early 1960s amidst the civil rights movement. Chicago station WCIU's plans to return the series to that city's airwaves in 1964 were cancelled after viewers protested, and sales to Kenya in 1963 were similarly cut off. CBS quietly removed the series from the air in 1966 in the light of increasing complaints about the program's representations of African Americans, and it has yet to resurface in syndication despite periodic calls for its return. See Boddy, "Building," 74; "CBS TV hypo in syndicated shows," *Variety*, 6 May 1953, p. 21; "'Amos 'n' Andy' show banned by Kenya TV," *New York Times*, 5 October 1963, p. 53; Val Adams, "Amos 'n' Andy: all tuned out," *New York Times*, 20 February 1966, sec. B, p. 23.

79. "'Honeymooners' in 50 Markets; Gross Sales Over $1 Million," *Broadcasting*, 29 July 1957, p. 58. Continuously run in local syndication since 1957, the series is the longest-running off-network rerun in television history, and one of the most prominent contributions to the television heritage that emerged in the 1970s in the wake of televisual repetition (see Chapter 5).

80. Earlier in the 1950s, late fringe time started at 10:30 or even 10 p.m., as network schedules didn't always run that late, and local stations were more prone to pre-empt a less popular network series to make room for a more popular syndicated show.

81. "TV Program Time Tops 100 Hours Per Week," *Broadcasting*, 17 December 1956, p. 28.

82. Boddy, *Fifties Television*, 141.

83. "Films $100 Million Year," *Sponsor*, 23 January 1956, p. 31.

84. To guard against perceived overexposure and confusion with their newer, first-run episodes, many programs were retitled for rerun syndication. For example, NBC Films' *Dragnet* became *Badge 714*; MCA's *Man Against Crime* (which had run on CBS, Du Mont and NBC) became *Follow That Man*; Ziv's *Highway Patrol* became *Ten 4*; and CBS' *Private Secretary* became Television Programs of America's (TPA) *Susie*. Regardless of the change in title, however, these reruns were desirable programming for local stations

and sponsors in that they represented established network or first-run successes, and were considerably inexpensive compared to first-run programming.

85. "Syndicators off and running toward new highs," *Broadcasting*, 24 February 1958, p. 162.

86. "*Sponsor* Asks . . . How do you view the effect on television of the greatly increased availability of feature film?," *Sponsor*, 11 June 1956, p. 67.

87. "Ziv Says Hollywood Movies May Set Back TV Standards," *Broadcasting*, 2 April 1956, p. 40.

88. This stark fact quickly led to the "magic number" of one hundred episodes as the goal for a network run which would assure enough material for stripping.

89. "Flood of Features Isn't Hurting Syndicated Film," *Sponsor*, 1 December 1956, p. 35.

90. "Film Basics," *Sponsor*, July 1956, p. 142. The same article cited a June 1955 NARTB study which estimated that network programs took up an average of 53% of total broadcast time on the typical station, while syndicated film claimed nearly 32%; local live programming was well behind at roughly 16% of all weekly time.

91. Norman Knight, "Film and the TV Station," in Broadcast Music, Inc., ed., *Television Talks 1957* (New York: BMI, 1957), 71.

92. Harris, "The Thorny Side of Syndicated Film," 94; "Anybody got a time slot?," *Variety*, 15 December 1954, p. 45.

93. Bob Chandler, "Syndication: paradox of '55," *Variety*, 5 January 1955, p. 101.

94. Gross-Krasne Productions and Studio Films merged with the larger United Telefilm Productions (UTP) in late 1952, while UTP itself merged with MCA in 1955. Ziv held out until a 1960 merger with United Artists, by which point it had ceased producing new series and was concentrating on acquisition and distribution. "'55-vidpix year of decision," *Variety*, 22 December 1954, p. 39.

95. Art Woodstone, "Vidpix economics vs. webs," *Variety*, 11 July 1956, pp. 35+.

96. "Surplus of Films Portends Era of Intense Competition," *Broadcasting*, 21 November 1955, p. 27–28.

97. "Ziv Urges Caution in Buying 'Bargain' Film Packages," *Broadcasting*, 23 January 1956, p. 42.

98. Boddy, *Fifties Television*, 180.

99. Boddy, *Fifties Television*, 169–172.

100. Boddy, *Fifties Television*, 173–174.

101. Boddy, *Fifties Television*, 119–120.

102. "ATFD's Secret Proposals For Curbing Networks," *Broadcasting*, 17 September 1956, p. 39.

103. "NBC Charges Film Interests Are Behind Network Attacks," *Broadcasting*, 28 May 1956, p. 36.

104. The Minow FCC ultimately banned option time in May 1963.

105. Boddy, *Fifties Television*, 169–181.

106. Boddy, *Fifties Television*, 181.

107. "Shying away from syndication," *Television Digest*, 12 October 1959, p. 14.

108. Boddy, *Fifties Television*, 181.

109. James Reeves, "Criteria for film buying," *Variety*, 31 July 1957, p. 29.

4
Familiarity Breeds Content: Reconfiguring Television in the 1960s and 1970s

A hunk of film is as tangible an asset as a piece of real estate.[1]

Regular, televised film had not only become viable by the end of the 1950s; it had proven dominant. Network prime-time programming was almost completely produced on film in Hollywood, while local stations relied upon several varieties of syndicated film, including older features, animated shorts, and reruns of network-originated series. Like the stereotype plate, theatrical film, phonograph record, and electrical transcription before it, television film had solidified its status as a tangible cultural property that could be repeatedly exploited over time. Accordingly, the syndication of film to local stations was an increasingly lucrative sector of the television industry. The Big Three networks, their initial resistance to film now all but forgotten, embraced film as a means of extending their control of programming, while minimizing its production, promotion, and development costs. Having conquered Hollywood, vanquished first-run telefilm syndicators, and (increasingly) wrested the programming reins from sponsors, they were the only viable buyers of new fictional television series remaining in the national market, and often acquired proprietary and distribution rights to new series in exchange for a network run. Accordingly, network film divisions greatly expanded during the 1960s, bolstering their firms' domestic and foreign syndication market shares with these new acquisitions. By the end of the decade, and at the height of their power, the networks even made some tentative forays into feature film financing.

Off-network syndication had only just begun to impact the U.S. television industry in the late 1950s. Over the next two decades, the rerun would move from the periphery of the industry to its very center, becoming no less than the ideal product of U.S. commercial television: the perfect incarnation of stability in an often unpredictable programming game. Because of its increasing significance, rerun syndication helped usher in new practices, priorities, and powers throughout the industry in

69

the 1960s and 1970s. Organizations like NATPE (the National Association of Television Programming Executives) and INTV (the Independent Television Association) formed to promote the syndication trade, and the rerun functioned as the dominant nexus of national and local broadcast distribution. The rerun also marked the rise and fall of network power during the same period, as unprecedented network control over broadcasting was met in the 1970s by extensive federal broadcasting regulations and a growing number of independent stations. Although the FCC ostensibly intended the new broadcasting rules—the Financial Interest and Syndication rules (i.e., Fin-Syn), which forced the networks to divest their ownership stakes in programming, and the Prime Time Access Rule (i.e., PTAR), which scaled back the evening hours of network prime time—to foster diversity in programming, the rules ultimately only assisted the growth of new program buyers and sellers, in the form of independent producers and stations. The resultant nonnetwork television was not a striking alternative to the networks, but instead largely relied upon safe, familiar genres (e.g., game shows and talk shows) and, increasingly, safe, familiar programs (off-network reruns). Rerun syndication was such a staple of the industry by the mid-1970s that a futures market was developed which attempted to cash in on today's network hits with projections of tomorrow's off-network profits. By the end of the 1970s—the peak of the over-the-air broadcast era—off-network syndication had profoundly affected network and local station schedules, FCC regulations, production guild and union contracts, studio and distributor profitability, the formation of trade organizations and events, and, with Paramount's Christmas 1979 release of *Star Trek: The Motion Picture*, had even generated a successful feature film franchise.

The off-network rerun became the key form of television in the United States at this time because of its market flexibility and durability. As previous chapters explored, the primary motive of the U.S. broadcasting industry has always been the sale of potential audiences (in the form of scheduled time) to advertisers. However, the sale of programs to broadcasters represents the beginning of that cycle; generally speaking, the more appealing a program is to an audience, the more appealing that same program is to an advertiser. Accordingly, in a conservative industry that, as Thomas Streeter describes, is predicated much more on stability and "systems maintenance" than on innovation or even true competition, a known quantity, a safe bet, is always sought.[2] A successful rerun, an *I Love Lucy*, *Star Trek*, *M*A*S*H*, or *Friends*, has been as safe a bet as they come: programs that can be efficiently exploited time and time again. This chapter traces how off-network syndication (i.e., "off-net") fostered significant changes in the industry in the 1960s and 1970s. The syndication market both expanded and reorganized in the 1960s, resulting in the development of new industrial practices, and the long-delayed blossoming of UHF and independent stations. In the 1970s, the networks, bowing to new FCC regulations, ceded sectors of the industry and local broadcast schedules to independent interests. However, these rules were not the reorientation of television broadcasting toward localism and alternative voices that they were ostensibly intended to be. Instead, the regime of repetition was further solidified, as off-network reruns were not only ensconced but also virtually codified into particular parts of the schedules on local stations nationwide, sanctioning the development of the television heritage in the 1970s, which redefined television's role in American culture.

The Syndication Market in the 1960s

By the end of the 1950s, repetition was already well established on television at every level. Local stations, particularly independents, were already gaining a reputation for constantly rerunning the same feature films, and aging syndicated telefilm series like *Highway Patrol* and *I Led Three Lives* were well into multiple runs in most major markets. While they were not the most prestigious programs on the air, the ratings evidence consistently validated their economic benefits. Theatrical film series like *Our Gang* (rechristened *The Little Rascals* for television), *Popeye*, and *Looney Tunes*, had already become all-time television staples, drawing increasing ratings and continuous renewals over multiple runs. United Artists Associates' (UAA) package of Warner Brothers' *Looney Tunes* cartoon shorts was particularly successful at this stage, drawing first-run rates even after several renewals. Robert Rich, the General Manager of UAA, reported to *Broadcasting* in 1959 that not one station had failed to renew their initial contract, as "the cartoons seem to be ageless." As a caption under the article's illustration of Bugs Bunny put it: "They never grow old, never depreciate."[3]

This pie-eyed faith in the endless viability of past film and television was enough to change American television. If an old program could draw an audience almost as well as a new one, why not continue to utilize it? Better yet, if *particular* old programs could become television standards, consistently popular with audiences, why not exploit them to their fullest potential? This recycling principle grew to become conventional wisdom in 1960s television, and was practiced at the networks, where reruns were increasingly utilized all over the schedule, and even more dramatically at local stations, where a key rerun acquisition could mean the difference between net profit and loss. A 1958 *Printer's Ink* article noted that the term "rerun" had been a "dirty word" a few years earlier, but it was now respected: "a syndicated series that has proven its staying power through a half-dozen re-runs [sic] is the nearest thing to a sure thing that any advertiser will ever find in television."[4] The same article also reported that WGN in Chicago had gone through 10 runs of Ziv's *Boston Blackie* since 1951—and had just signed a contract for four more.

Print advertisements from syndicators began to tout their series' strong local ratings as reruns, and made sure to mention their particular viability to stripping (i.e., running daily episodes of the same series in the same time slot), which had already become a standard programming tool.

Even though the medium itself was barely more than a decade old, a few long-term successes had already emerged in rerun syndication. Series like Official Films' *The Trouble With Father* and *My Little Margie*, and Ziv's *I Led Three Lives*, *The Cisco Kid*, and *Highway Patrol* continued to be renewed in well over 100 markets even after several runs.[5] Similarly, NBC's acclaimed World War II documentary series *Victory At Sea* continually ran on local television schedules for over a decade after its debut in syndication in 1952, despite having only 26 episodes. Meanwhile, Ziv had even gone as far as forming an entire *Cisco Kid* division to continue the distribution and merchandising of that program even after it had ceased production, while Roy Rogers Enterprises continued to exploit the licensing of over 400 products via its *Roy Rogers* reruns.[6]

As these examples indicate, it was now clear that the acquisition and control of existing films and/or telefilm series was an essential component of the television industry, a logical companion to the control of the means of distribution and exhibition (i.e., the networks and broadcast channels). New production was expensive, and the initial returns were not lucrative; barring a radical restructuring of the entire broadcasting system, reruns were the producers' best bet for profitability. Accordingly, many firms scrambled to buy out promising extant properties or merge with other distributors. United Artists was particularly aggressive in this regard, as it acquired Associated Artists Productions (Warner Bros. animated shorts, *Popeye*, some features) in 1958, merged with Ziv in 1960, and ceased producing their own series in 1962.[7] Similarly, the networks' expanding film distribution arms had all ceased first-run production in 1958 to focus on acquiring and distributing independently-produced series and specials.[8] National Telefilm Associates (NTA) had even built up enough capital to attempt a new, film-based network via the shrewd acquisition of existing films. Though this venture was ultimately unsuccessful for various reasons, *Forbes* remarked that film distribution *per se* was "probably a good deal more profitable" than new production.[9]

Thus, the rerun had simply become the standard form of syndicated television by default, almost completely squeezing out first-run production, which was already reeling from the disappearance of local prime-time time slots. As the last chapter indicated, the networks had gained control of telefilm series in the late 1950s; by the early 1960s, the first of these series became available in off-net. Accordingly, the networks' and major studios' syndication arms came to dominate.

After the shakeout of first-run, prime-time syndication, the market adapted to this new regime of off-net dominance. First-run syndication was still a viable program form, but it now referred to a wide variety of less expensive, shorter, and more demographically focused nonfiction programs, rather than the once-standard, 60-minute action-adventure series of the 1950s. This was essentially a shift to *narrowcasting* (although the term itself is anachronistic): programs with particular interests (e.g., sports, music, talk shows, game shows, etc.) packaged for smaller audiences and fringe time slots.[10] *Broadcasting* editorialized in 1962 that this new first-run syndication trend was "promising," and that it offered "more diversified programming," an ostensible antidote to the saturation of off-network material that was already dominating the local schedules at the time.[11] By the end of the decade, buoyed by the greater viability and number of independent stations, a drop-off in the number of off-network series released to syndication, and the wide-scale replacement of film with videotape as a production and distribution medium, the number of first-run syndicated series would exceed its mid-1950s peak.[12]

While many new, nonfiction first-run series were certainly successful, the mass audience was ceded almost entirely to off-network reruns, which dominated all other forms of syndicated programming throughout the 1960s. This was particularly the case early in the decade, when the first tsunami of studio-produced network telefilm series hit the syndication market, pushing aside well-worn 1950s programs like *Mr. District Attorney* and *Highway Patrol*. In 1960, only seven former network series were released into local syndication. In each year from 1961 to 1963, 35 off-network series became available; by 1964 this had added up to over *one hundred* off-net series in syndication. Under such conditions, *Broadcasting* wondered how long the networks and major studios could continue to syndicate so many series, claiming that "simple mathematics is working against the off-network concept for the future."[13] Making programming variety even more limited for local stations, the networks also began to usurp the feature film supply. Feature films had long been the flagship program form on local station schedules, but prior to the 1960s, network feature film presentations were rare. Beginning with NBC's regularly scheduled *NBC Saturday Night Movie* in September 1961, however, all three networks began claiming the cream of the post-1948 Hollywood crop in a rapid series of lucrative deals with the major studios.[14] While plenty of films were still available for local syndication, stations could no longer afford the more desirable recent films.

With so many off-net programs in circulation, syndication marketing also became more elaborate in the 1960s, indicating reruns' increased stature in the television industry. As noted above, trade advertisements in the late 1950s were already using programs' network and local ratings histories in their promotion efforts, noting in particular their success in stripping. However there was no central organization or annual event centered specifically around syndication until the formation of the

Television Film Exhibit (TFE) in 1963. The TFE began as a film-sales-only convention scheduled simultaneously with the annual NAB convention. Syndicators and station programmers had always felt too dispersed or crowded out amongst the advertisers, broadcasting executives, engineers, and policy wonks that dominated NAB, and the TFE quickly became a major event for the syndication market during the mid-1960s. Just as the NAB convention was an important space for industry recapitulation and formation (particularly in regards to technology and FCC policy), the TFE served to galvanize buyers and sellers alike, helping to further solidify a growing market.

However, it was still an ad hoc arrangement dominated by major distributors, and never quite gelled into a permanent industry fixture. After five years of consistent problems with venues and participation, the TFE was held for the last time in 1968. In its place arose an organization dedicated to television programming issues, rather than simply an annual event. The National Association of Television Program Executives (NATPE) was founded in 1964 to focus the economic and policy energies of programming concerns. Its greatest contribution to the industry as a whole, however, has arguably been its annual convention, which has expanded well past the TFE's initial footprint to become a major industry event separate from the NAB. Scheduled early in the winter to facilitate deal-making for the subsequent fall's programming slate, NATPE became the primary place for syndicators and programmers to spin hype, make deals, and debate programming issues away from the NAB's more policy and technology oriented atmosphere.

The expanded marketing of syndicated television in the United States at this time indicates how TV's industrial culture has had a significant impact in its development. By industrial culture I refer not only to abstract issues of capital, profit, loss, supply, and demand; I also mean the formation and reproduction of real economic and discursive practices through the actions of particular human agents within these organizations. Like the earlier forms of cooperation among publishers and film studios, the refinements of television program marketing indicate how the everyday decisions of television industry institutions and workers shaped the overall organization and dominant practices of the medium as it matured. Thus the TFE, NATPE, and all the other forms of syndication market-ing are best understood as significant industrial apparatuses, like ratings tables, genres, or stars: means of producing knowledge about television programming that is enacted upon by the appropriate agents. Everyone involved in the programming trade—producers, distributors, advertisers, trade journalists, station managers, etc.—helped solidify the rerun in the 1960s, preparing the industrial and conceptual ground for its cultural "discovery" in the 1970s as the television heritage. Syndication in general—and reruns in particular—had been in the ascendancy before the arrival of these new organizations; however the TFE and especially

NATPE concretized the trend with institutional backing and concomitant individual actions.

"New" Technologies: Color and UHF

Just as the elaboration of the programming trade helped solidify the stature of off-network syndication during this period, changes in television technology also affected programming and policy decisions at every level of the industry. This is not to say that technology "naturally" emerged to change the medium. As Raymond Williams observed, technologies are generally produced out of changing social and economic relationships and hegemonic priorities, rather than the other way around.[15] In this case, the new priorities were the expansion of broadcasting outlets (i.e., local stations) and the bolstering of the television receiver market, and the resultant technologies were the promotion of color television and the long-delayed development of the Ultra-High Frequency (UHF) band of the electromagnetic spectrum for television broadcasting.

Color television had been a working technology since 1953, after the FCC controversially approved RCA's system as the national technical standard. However, color programming only became standard at the network level over a decade later, due largely to the shift to telefilm production and the increased programming of feature films.[16] The transformation to prime-time color programming on the networks took place over the 1965–66 and 1966–67 seasons. Despite the additional costs of equipment, most local stations also began switching completely to color during this period to keep up with the networks. The number of color sets in use, however, would not reach a majority of viewers until the early 1970s. Still, the rapid transition to color TV concerned film syndicators, as almost all of their available features and telefilm series were in black and white.[17] Would these black and white programs—which represented well over 90% of all available syndicated film in early 1966—still be viable on color television?[18]

Initially, most color programs available for syndication were low-budget first-run series produced on videotape.[19] However, these series did not address the demand for off-network reruns. Fearing that the future returns of black-and-white reruns were uncertain, off-net distributors rushed many monochrome series to the market, including network stalwarts like *Perry Mason, Dr. Kildare, Rawhide, The Patty Duke Show*, and *McHale's Navy*, which had all ended their network runs in 1966.[20] Some distributors were more prescient, however. Certainly, color programs would be in demand, but there was little indication that it would necessarily mean the end of monochrome television. Indeed, several monochrome off-net series had already become steady hits in local syndication by the mid-1960s, and their distributors were not concerned about realistic competition from upcoming color shows. Some argued that color was primarily a marketing gimmick to sell new television sets, as the sales of monochrome sets had leveled off.[21] Accordingly, syndicators with color properties were marketing the same hype to station managers as manufacturers were to home consumers. As one unnamed distributor philosophically pointed out, "color cannot help a bad show."[22] While the supply of color programs lagged behind their rise on the networks for the remainder of the decade, several "quality" monochrome series still commanded large sums in the market.[23]

The other, more significant, technological shift was the similarly postponed expansion of the Ultra High Frequency, or UHF band of the broadcast spectrum. The FCC's Sixth Report and Order had officially prepared the UHF band for broadcasting in 1953. However, UHF had met with little success due to the entrenched economic power of the networks and their more powerful Very High Frequency (VHF) stations and affiliates in major markets, and the reluctance of major manufacturers (most notably RCA, the parent company of NBC) to produce sets that could receive both VHF and UHF signals. As a result, applying for a UHF license in the 1950s was financial suicide in established markets, and only somewhat less so elsewhere.[24] The crux of the problem was that viewers needed a separate set to receive UHF stations. The lack of stations in most markets, and the band's notoriously weak signal strength, were hardly major selling points. The FCC was justifiably frustrated at this lack of development, but showed little ingenuity in dealing with it.[25]

Under the Newton Minow-led FCC, however, UHF's prospects began to improve. After several "deintermixture" plans—which would have rearranged U.S. television broadcasting into all-VHF and all-UHF markets—were all soundly opposed, the new FCC wanted to make UHF more attractive for potential broadcasters.[26] Again, as Streeter argues, there is nothing "natural" about broadcasting. The government originally "created" UHF with the intent to foster more programming outlets, and maintained that principle throughout the 1960s and 1970s.[27] When the existing interests were ultimately not all that interested in that prospect, the government simply changed the rules of the game. In 1961–62, with deintermixture off the table, the FCC and 87th Congress sought to make UHF more viable on the reception end, by requiring all new television sets manufactured and/or sold in the United States to receive both VHF and UHF bands. The All-Channel Receiver Act, as this new law came to be known, was passed in 1962 and went into effect in May of 1964. One of its results was to dramatically increase the number of viewers with access to UHF signals. During the first year of the All-Channel Receiver Act, the number of UHF-equipped sets jumped from 10 to 16% of the total, and climbed to 73% by the end of the 1960s.[28] Regardless of the actual ratings results, this at least meant that UHF stations were now accessible to most viewers, giving them a fighting chance to succeed, particularly in the larger, VHF-dominated markets. With this new potential for development, more

UHF applications were filed and more stations began broadcasting. Larger firms with deeper pockets also became involved to a greater extent, as they had during the earlier VHF license freeze, helping to keep stations on the air until they could finally turn a profit. Even after the All-Channel Act went into effect, the development of UHF remained a priority of the FCC throughout the rest of the 1960s, with the Commission even suggesting a "program sharing" plan in which network affiliates in 18 small-to-medium markets would relinquish several hours of its network programs to independent, "have-not" UHF stations.[29]

The spurring of UHF directly enhanced the viability of nonnetwork television stations, thus creating more nonnetwork time, and enhancing the syndication market. Calling the expansion of UHF "the single brightest development in the syndication industry in 1966," *Broadcasting* reported that that year alone saw a four-to-five fold increase in syndication sales to UHF stations.[30] Two years later, despite a lack of popular network series debuting in off-net syndication, distributors were still experiencing increased sales due to the new clout of UHF; some UHF stations even outbid their more established VHF rivals in several markets.[31] Throughout the rest of the decade, the number and viability of UHF stations would continue to grow; by 1972, a slim majority of UHF stations had even begun showing profits.[32]

Independent Stations

The development of color and UHF, the reconstruction of programming around off-net and "specialty" first-run series, and the establishment of TFE and NATPE combined to produce a larger, more elaborated syndication market in the space of a few years. At the same time, the prospects for greater program diversity and truly nonnetwork television seemed to be increasing as well, as independent stations, long considered the unclean stepchildren of broadcasting, became more viable. However, as with the other developments in television technology and industrial practices, these new stations did not diversify television programming near as much as repeat it. Indeed, rather than provide an alternative vision to network-originated programming, independent stations were instead the single most significant factor in the expansion of off-network rerun syndication in the 1960s and 1970s.

Despite the inevitable conflicts which arose in the national–local relationship, network affiliation still carried great prestige for local stations. Affiliates were able to sell themselves to sponsors and audiences on this national identification. They consistently had more desirable channel allocations (almost exclusively on VHF), larger audiences, higher rate cards, and thus more advertising revenue. Independents, by contrast, had no network affiliation, and had to distinguish themselves from the network stations to prove viable broadcasters. Significantly, however, their reputation—and survival—was largely based on the use of reruns. In a 1963 *Television* article, Morris J. Gelman noted that independent stations were seen within the broadcasting and advertising industries as "film grinders," "glutted with ancient feature film packages and mediocre film series in one of their countless reruns."[33] Network programs and stations still carried more stature with advertisers and audiences.

However, independent stations made significant audience gains against affiliates in the 1960s primarily via off-network syndication. In the same article, Gelman called off-net series "adrenalin shots for lackluster independent programming schedules," and most indie station managers would have agreed.[34] Independent stations made off-net programs— in most cases the very network series they were competing against a few years earlier—their flagship programming form, increasing their stature in their markets with advertisers and viewers. While these gains were most pronounced in large markets like New York and Los Angeles, where several independents operated on the more established VHF band, it also occurred throughout the country, where both VHF and UHF independents at least established a permanent presence.[35]

The key weapon in the independents' arsenal was the off-net strip: a rerun series run at the same time five days a week against network programming during evening prime time, or, more successfully, in the three previous hours (5–8 p.m.), which some indies began touting as "independent prime time." As early as 1960, New York independent WPIX proclaimed itself, perhaps too eagerly, to be "the prestige *independent* with *network* programming!" in a trade advertisement which listed such their lineup of former network series including *M Squad, San Francisco Beat, You Are There,* and *The Honeymooners.*[36] This trend of stockpiling various off-network reruns had developed into standard procedure for independents by the end of the decade. Chicago independent WGN touted the familiarity of its fall 1968 prime-time lineup of *The Flintstones, Mike Douglas, I Love Lucy, Steve Allen,* and *Perry Mason* as "broadcasting's Who's Who."[37] By the fall of 1969, all three of New York's VHF independents had made inroads into network prime-time audience share via the stripping of off-net series such as *I Love Lucy, The Dick Van Dyke Show,* and *Star Trek. Broadcasting* noted that "that hoary warhorse" *I Love Lucy* was a particularly key off-net series in early evening nationwide, while series like *Gilligan's Island* and *McHale's Navy* were enjoying higher shares than their network runs.[38] Ironically the gains in independents' prime-time ratings were a result of reversing the programming base established in the 1950s; in the 1960s, the networks ran several nights of feature films in prime time, while the independents countered with old network series.[39] However, both strategies reveal a significant investment in familiarity and repetition, even beyond the formulaic appeal of established series or genres. Despite the substantial changes occurring in society and culture in the 1960s, television audiences readily accepted the old and familiar throughout the decade.

By 1970, the syndication market was decidedly larger, and decidedly different than it had been a decade earlier. Though the number of stations had expanded by roughly half due largely to the viability of UHF and independents, and new organizations and events facilitated the broadcast trade to local stations, the result was not a resurgent fictional first-run syndication. First-run syndication did come back from the precipice, but it was now a relatively diverse mix of lower-budget game, talk, variety, and other "specialty" series, rather than the mass-audience, fictional entertainment series that had been the rule in the 1950s.[40] As far as fictional programming went, the predominant influence on syndication was, and would remain, the off-network rerun. Its presence on local schedules throughout the 1960s was continually validated by ratings growth, if rarely acknowledged by the mainstream press, and kept many old series in circulation long past their network demise, covertly ensconcing them in American cultural memory. However, the sheer volume of rerun programming, and its new centrality in the industry as a whole, would come to the forefront in policy debates over the regulation of broadcast time and property in the 1970s.

"On-Network" Reruns

Although the growth of the local off-net syndication market was the most important contribution to the solidification of televisual repetition in the 1960s, there was also a significant increase in the use of reruns *on* network schedules. The decisive late 1950s shift to film programming on the networks did not only result in original material; indeed, as the previous chapter examined, the reusability of film was regarded as one of its major advantages over live television. Reruns of popular series became more and more essential to network schedules throughout the 1960s and 1970s, in every part of the broadcast day. Reruns drew comparable ratings to first-run programming, but for a fraction of the cost. These stable ratings assured the networks and their advertisers that reruns were a legitimate form of network programming.

The highest-profile use of reruns was in prime time. Although the practice of reairing previous episodes had been used sparingly in both network radio and earlier television, it was not until film became dominant that the use of reruns became standardized at the network level. Up until the 1957–58 season, the usual yearly broadcasting schedule consisted of 39 new installments of a series; the remaining 13 weeks (almost all in the summer) consisted of a mix of specials and short-lived replacement series. Once the studio-produced film series became standard, however, most of those 13 weeks were given over to reruns. There were two, interrelated reasons for this shift. While series production costs were escalating, this rise was partially offset by standardized genre and program production, similar to the "B-movie" production techniques utilized by the major Hollywood studios prior to the Paramount Decision in 1948. The formulaic nature of most series lent more consistency and predictability to the network schedule; just as it was economical to continue with the same sets, cast, crew, and even scripts in producing a series, it was even more so if the episodes themselves were reused.[41] For producers this was especially significant, as they generally could not recoup their costs in the initial network sales and needed reruns to attain profitability. In addition, a change in the federal tax laws in 1959 contributed to the spread of reruns from summer to winter; it became more profitable for producers to spread out their income from film series across the year.[42] The growing residual payments mandated in newer union contracts added some additional costs to reruns, but they were minimal when compared to the cost of entirely new productions. More importantly, as examined in the last chapter, the much-feared audience revolt against reruns never materialized. While there was still a general drop-off in overall HUT (Homes Using Television) levels during the summer, the audience shares of rerun programs were mostly consistent with those of new, in-season episodes, and were nearly always much higher than the ratings for a one-off special or replacement series. Accordingly, reruns were more profitable than first-run episodes, for networks and advertisers alike. A rerun episode cost the network a fraction of the cost of a new production, while the advertising time itself (at least in the summer) could be sold on a discount basis to sponsors. On the bases of the ratings evidence and resultant economics, summer reruns quietly, but quickly, became a standard network practice in the early 1960s.

As the presence of reruns increased, however, the practice became more controversial. In 1962, prominent *New York Times* television critic Jack Gould lamented the lack of new programming, commenting that "the summer replacement, once the means of introducing new faces or experimental ideas, has gone the way of the 10-inch picture tube. Save for baseball players, live performers are even more extinct." He cited the lack of quality of most filmed reruns, the network and advertiser penny-pinching at work, and the concomitant loss of employment for creative personnel in broadcasting. For Gould, for whom "liveness" was still perhaps the prime virtue of television, reruns indicated a continuing downward spiral into tired convention and mediocrity.[43] The 39 episode standard, however, was short-lived. The relationship between production costs and network revenues made it more feasible to decrease the number of original episodes per season; why produce 39 episodes if only a third of them could be used as reruns on network schedules? By the early 1970s, the typical prime-time fictional series had only 22 to 26 episodes per season, a drop of one-third or greater from 10 years earlier.[44]

At this time, however, the prevalence of prime-time network reruns came under increased political fire, fueled no doubt by the proactive regulatory climate at the FCC (see below). In 1972, a freelance Hollywood film editor, Bernard A. Balmuth, compiled his own research on the amount of network reruns, and determined that they represented almost 50% of total prime-time hours. He then compelled major Hollywood production guilds and unions—who were suffering employment losses due to the increase of reruns—to take action. They formed the Film and Television Coordinating Committee, with the aim of increasing prime-time production and limiting the use of reruns. In late August of that year, the AFL-CIO came out against network reruns, and urged that the FCC enact rules limiting the use of reruns to no more than 25% of the prime-time schedule. Several prominent California politicians sided with the unions, including then-Governor Ronald Reagan, and President Richard Nixon, who was, by that point, no friend of the networks anyway, and transparently courting voters in his imminent reelection bid. Nixon authorized his Telecommunications Policy director Clay Whitehead to look into curtailing "the spreading blight of reruns."[45] Producers and syndicators chimed in favorably to these proposals, noting that fewer episodes per season diminished the long-range off-network potential of their series, which needed a stockpile of roughly 100 episodes to satisfy the appetites of local stations. In their defense, the networks, publicly represented by CBS President Robert Wood, predictably claimed that reruns were a "public service" to viewers and a financial necessity for network operation.

However, the networks were all alone in defending the practice. Buoyed by the positive political and cultural response to the complaint, the Screen Actors Guild (SAG) submitted a study to the President's Office of Telecommunications Policy (OTP) in December 1972 which documented that a rise in residual payments from 1966–71 was offset by a loss in employment and real wages over the same period. They conceded that reruns were a necessity, but demanded that they still be cut back in favor of more original productions, and that residuals be raised to 100% of the original salary. The OTP's official study on the issue was published in February 1973 and argued that intense network competition was to blame, resulting in cost-cutting and quick cancellations rather than new productions. While the FCC was already going after the networks for similar concerns at this time, this specific furor made reruns an actual "problem" that needed to be solved. In the summer 1974 contract negotiations with television producers, SAG was able to win an extension of residuals into "indefinite" runs, and increase their royalty percentages in the first several runs. In early 1975, formal positions on the issue were finally filed with the FCC, with both sides sticking to their guns.

The networks restated their dubious "public service" argument, and pointed out that the FCC had no jurisdiction over network programming.[46] CBS claimed that a loss of reruns would negatively impact new productions: "In no event could the networks regularly invest the amounts of money now spent on new program production and acquisition, were such programs intended for only one prime time broadcast."[47]

In the end, the topic fizzled at the federal level, perhaps because most of the prominent Hollywood unions and guilds had eventually won better residual packages from television producers, and thus ceased their demands. Nevertheless, the uproar that surrounded prime-time reruns indicates how repetition had affected industrial relations and had garnered the attention of the federal government. The networks' reliance on reruns did not end at prime time, however. From the end of the 1950s through the late 1980s, long-running prime-time series were stripped daily in other parts of the schedule. This represented a particularly shrewd strategy on the networks' part, as popular series could be successfully "milked" yet again—for the network and national sponsor—before being released to local syndication.

In the 1960s and 1970s, these reruns were primarily scheduled in the mid-morning, where they ran adjacent to soap operas and game shows. CBS was the dominant practitioner of this strategy, utilizing a 2-hour sitcom block featuring such series as *I Love Lucy*, *The Andy Griffith Show*, *The Dick Van Dyke Show*, and *The Beverly Hillbillies* throughout the 1960s.[48] Similarly, ABC also relied on series like *Bewitched* and *Make Room For Daddy* to fill out its daytime schedule. NBC, conversely, chose to program mostly game shows and soap operas in its post-*Today* time slots, although it did occasionally run sitcoms as well. Regardless of the network, though, in almost every case these were series in which the network had vested interests. While license fees for additional network runs were still negotiated with the producers for these runs, as part of the initial financing arrangement, the series were kept off the local syndication market. This enabled the networks to exploit a popular series' familiarity before a local station could schedule it. Though this was not local syndication *per se*, it helped foster the overall standardization of the rerun strip, adding another level of viability to televisual repetition. Indeed, the networks' daytime schedules—particularly CBS'—were the most prominent use of stripping in the 1960s. As early as 1963, syndicators and stations were worried that this network use was "siphoning" off too many popular series from local syndication, potentially wearing away their appeal after years of network exposure, and leaving local stations with relatively unmarketable product.[49] However, this fear was soon found to be unjustified, as many of the most-repeated series—*I Love Lucy* in particular—were still solid hits for local stations when they finally entered local syndication late in the decade.[50]

Similarly, in the 1970s and 1980s, both ABC and CBS utilized reruns of 30-minute sitcoms and 60-minute drama series at the other end of the broadcast schedule, in late fringe time (i.e., after 11:30 p.m.). NBC did not need this strategy, as its *Tonight Show* was the benchmark for late-night programming, and its subsequent late-night series (*The Tomorrow Show* and *Late Night with David Letterman*) extended the network's schedule into the early morning. ABC and CBS attempted to compete with NBC during this time slot in the 1960s and early 1970s with new talk and variety series, but to no avail. By 1973, both networks had resorted to rerun blocks. CBS utilized a variety of reruns in its *CBS Late Movie*, aired on weeknights from 1972 to 1989.[51] Most of the programs during this block were current or recent CBS crime series (as well as a few sitcoms like *M*A*S*H*, *Archie Bunker's Place*, and *WKRP In Cincinnati*), although series that originally aired on other networks also wound up there, including NBC's *The Rockford Files*, *Columbo*, and *Remington Steele*, and ABC's *Hart To Hart* and *TJ Hooker*. Not to be outdone, ABC also featured a late-night rerun lineup that ran from 1973–82, and featured almost exclusively former or current ABC series, including *The Rookies*, *S.W.A.T.*, *Police Woman*, and *Soap*.[52] Crime series were the usual fare in this period in part because of the NAB's "family hour" mandate—an attempt to head-off federal program regulation first adopted in the mid-1970s—which effectively banned several popular action-oriented 60-minute series from local syndication in late afternoon or early evening timeslots just as they were coming on the market. Under the voluntary provision, stations pledged to avoid violence in the afternoon and early evening (until 9 p.m.), but could actively exploit it during late-night broadcasting, where the bumper crop of crime-related network series of the 1970s found its rerun niche.

By the mid-1980s, however, a variety of factors combined to eliminate both the daytime and late-night rerun periods. The morning block was eroded on both ends. A dearth of successful sitcoms in the early 1980s (see Chapter 6) and the promise of increasingly greater fees available in both local and cable syndication prompted most producers to opt for the local money, while the networks drastically reworked their daytime schedules, dropping the afternoon completely by the end of the 1980s—thus ceding more time to local stations—and focusing their energies on news and soap operas. At the other end of the schedule, ABC's and CBS's efforts to develop late night finally paid off with ABC's *Nightline* in 1980, and CBS's arguably network-saving hiring of David Letterman to go against *The Tonight Show* in 1993.

Whatever the specific use of reruns by the network, the key principle remained the same: reruns were uniquely lucrative. Networks controlled the vast majority of the series they aired in the 1960s, and continued to exploit this control via network-aired reruns. These reruns furthered the repetition by keeping old series on American network television day after day, making them familiar, *expected* aspects of the television experience. By the early 1970s, however, this network domination, which had long been under skeptical federal scrutiny, prompted significant new FCC regulations that drastically altered the face of U.S. television.

PTAR, Fin-Syn, and the Restructured Television of the 1970s

The changes engendered in the television industry in the 1960s were largely the result of active development: of stations, of broadcast time, of new audiences, and of extant programming through off-network syndication. However, despite the arrival of nonnetwork stations as a legitimate market for programming and advertisers, the networks were never more powerful. They had editorial control over virtually every program they aired, held domestic and foreign syndication rights to most of them, and—despite the ban on option time clauses enacted in 1962—dominated affiliates' schedules in the morning, afternoon, and evening.[53] This fact was not lost on local stations, series producers, syndicators, or the FCC, as the networks' dominance over television time became a target of focused investigation and criticism beginning in the late 1950s, setting off a chain of proposals and policies in the 1960s and 1970s ostensibly aimed at curtailing this power.

Thomas Streeter describes U.S. commercial broadcasting as a "simulated market" in that the fundamental unit of the industry—the broadcasting station/license—is nothing but an arbitrary designation of signal frequency in the electromagnetic spectrum: a "simulated property."[54] Similarly, as both Streeter and Eileen Meehan describe, the ultimate product of commercial broadcasting—the consumer audience—is another convenient simulation, measured through statistically dubious but economically significant ratings.[55] The government, through the FCC, coordinates these exchanges, historically favoring regulations that foster overall system stability rather than real gains of any of the participants, including the viewing public. However, the 1970s policies that resulted from proposals and investigations commenced more than a decade before were largely seen at their inception as something different, far-reaching in their potential transformation of U.S. commercial broadcasting away from network domination and toward greater diversity. Although they did remove a degree of industrial control from the networks, the ultimate effect of the Prime-Time Access Rule (PTAR) and the Financial Interest and Syndication Rules (fin-syn) on the overall shape of U.S. television was fairly negligible. Rather, the rules ultimately resulted in a system which heavily favored safety, formula and repetition in programming: the very definition of the "system stability" this simulated market required.

These rules have become some of the most cited in FCC lore and broadcasting history. The significance of these regulations and their accompanying debates for off-network syndication lies in a conjunction of noble rhetoric, self-deceptions, and industrial politics. Reruns were not the stated focus of these regulations, but viewed retrospectively, from a time in which none of them are still on the books, they help form a nexus of discourse and policy that codified a particular structure of broadcast television for nearly 20 years. The regulations affected virtually every local station schedule and had a profound effect across the entire industry. However, they were not a radical departure from the 1960s industrial status quo that commentators of the time alternately sought and feared. Instead, while they restructured industrial relationships, shifting some power away from the networks, they fell well short of taking down the network system in principle, ultimately sanctioning the growing reliance on repetition, and standardizing the continual reuse of past television as part of the American television experience.

In the aftermath of the Barrow Report of the late 1950s, which detailed the networks' monopolistic practices, and the quiz show scandals, which shattered the industry's perceived integrity, the FCC's Office of Network Study, headed by Ashbrook Bryant, finally released their recommendations in January 1965. Presenting evidence of network domination in program procurement and syndication, the report outlined several policies for the oft-stated goal of increasing competition in the programming market. This explicit goal would become the mantra of the entire regulatory cycle of the 1960s and 1970s, and the evidence in its favor was difficult to dispute. The Bryant Report stated that, as of 1964, the networks controlled over 90% of the "independently produced" programming they aired, and that they constituted a monopsony in the programming market, forcing producers to trade control and large percentages of syndication revenues for production financing and network exposure. While independent first-run syndication had withered in the late 1950s and early 1960s, the networks' domestic and foreign syndication arms had increased their net profits by 126%. Accordingly, the report recommended banning the networks from syndicating any program they did not actually produce, setting a 50% limit on the amount of nonnews programming a network could have financial interests in, and splitting network profits 50–50 with their affiliates.[56] The networks responded with the usual outrage and allegations of their own. At the 1965 NBC Affiliates Meeting, president Robert Sarnoff claimed that the new rules could "shatter the structure of network television," while CBS's Frank Stanton told the American Association of Advertising Agencies (AAAA) that the proposed rules "are bad all around—for networks, for producers, for you in advertising and for the public."[57] While most in the industry, such as the AAAA, were initially opposed to the proposals— perhaps cowed by the networks' political weight—these sentiments were not unanimous. The networks' staunchest institutional allies at this time—the National Association of Broadcasters and *Broadcasting* magazine—unsurprisingly came out opposed to the changes, but stations themselves were divided, and program distributors generally supported limiting network participation in syndication.

Variations on these recommendations were debated and proposed throughout the rest of the 1960s. A bill introduced in early 1968 in the House Commerce Committee would have banned the networks from virtually any enterprise outside of a narrow definition of "network operation": no syndication of any kind, no network ownership of programs, no ownership of sports teams or sports promotion firms, and no controlling interest in any outside business. Though the bill fell well short of becoming law, it indicated the heightening climate for broadcast regulation, and continued the general debate on network power. A major proponent of the Bryant Report's recommendations emerged later that year with its own proposals. This was Group W, the broadcasting arm of the Westinghouse Corporation, which owned five television stations in major markets, and produced several prominent first-run syndicated series, including talk-show hits *The Merv Griffin Show* and *The Mike Douglas Show*. Officially, they argued that the networks had too much determination in what local stations could air, and one way to correct this was to carve out a space in prime time for nonnetwork programming. However, they also sought to advance their own syndication prospects. They felt they had the resources to produce and syndicate network-quality programming; they just had to get the networks out of the way to gain more access in local markets. The networks contracted the Arthur D. Little firm to provide some defensive research, but the FCC was skeptical of the findings. The networks' 1969 Little Report argued that there was no need to limit network programming, since "nonnetwork" program outlets and sources were on the rise. It noted that 61 of the 84 new commercial broadcasting stations over the previous four years were independents, and that nonnetwork prime-time hours had doubled over the previous decade. However, the report failed to highlight the significant fact that the bulk of so-called "nonnetwork" programming and time was in fact dedicated to off-network reruns; the Commission felt this could hardly be referred to as "nonnetwork."[58]

After years of these skirmishes, the proposals became official policy in March 1970, as the FCC formally approved several regulations designed to scale back network control and foster local programming. The primary mechanisms were the Financial Interest and Syndication Rules, collectively known as "fin-syn," which would bar the networks from domestic syndication and program acquisition, and force them to divest all their existing syndication rights. The networks balked at these policies, and maintained that they hardly "controlled" domestic syndication, as they represented only 18% of the market. However, according to *Broadcasting*'s own calculations, the networks' syndication divisions were the three leading domestic syndicators, with CBS Enterprises clearly dominating through its popular sitcoms such as *I Love Lucy, The Honeymooners,* and *The Beverly Hillbillies.*[59] The other major rule, the Prime-Time Access Rule (PTAR) was ostensibly created to open up the most lucrative evening viewing hours for "independent," that is, local, nonnetwork programming. Technically, it limited network affiliates in the top 50 markets to 3 hours of programming between 7 and 11 p.m. In practice, however, this meant that all markets would fall under these rules, as over 70% of viewers were located in the top 50 markets; it was not feasible to produce a separate network schedule for the remaining markets.

Though the rules were due to become effective on September 1 of the next three years, implementation was delayed several times due to court battles; the networks were not going to cave in without a fight.[60] Significantly, the networks were split on the rules, due largely to competition and political jockeying. CBS stunned the industry in July of 1970 when it announced plans to "spin-off" its lucrative syndication and cable television holdings into a new, separate company, Viacom, thus beating the FCC to the fin-syn punch. While their attempts to get Viacom off the ground were held up over the next 18 months due to dubious FCC scrutiny and disgruntled shareholders, CBS eventually succeeded in "coming clean" with the Commission, and scaled back virtually all CBS voting interests from the new company.[61] The formation of Viacom was a major development in television history, as it indicated the growing capital of popular reruns such as *I Love Lucy, The Andy Griffith Show, Hogan's Heroes,* and other 1950s and 1960s CBS sitcoms, and some not-insignificant cable television holdings.[62] After the formation of Viacom, CBS dropped their opposition to the fin-syn rules, leaving NBC and ABC—who were much less prepared to start their own Viacoms—to fight that battle. NBC was particularly upset about the divestment aspect of the rules that set a strict deadline which they maintained would make it difficult for to get a fair price for its series.[63] NBC and ABC did get the FCC to delay the implementation of the rules, but eventually acquiesced to the FCC, and divested their remaining syndication holdings—which were nowhere near as lucrative as CBS'—by 1973.

Conversely, CBS was most strident in its opposition to the Prime-Time Access Rule (PTAR). It filed petitions against the rule in the summer of 1970, claiming that it violated the First Amendment, the Communications Act, and the Federal Administrative Procedure Act.[64] Station groups Metromedia and Group W, the major industry proponents of PTAR, filed counter-briefs several months later, citing the precedents of the 1943 Chain Broadcasting and 1969 Red Lion Supreme Court decisions in supporting the FCC's "protection" of local station rights over network broadcasters.[65] In May 1971, the U.S. Second Circuit Court of Appeals ruled unanimously in favor of the FCC, upholding both PTAR and fin-syn. Dismissing CBS' arguments, the court stated that the FCC "has acted in discharge of its statutory duty" in fostering more competition in the programming field, and that it is not "dictating" programs but rather "ordering licensees to give others the opportunity to broadcast."[66]

Thus, the rules eventually went into effect at various times throughout the early to mid-1970s. Even after the court battles had subsided, however, controversy still raged. Fin-syn had met with greater approval from the industry at large, with only two of the three networks dead-set against it; its acceptance had been surprisingly smooth. PTAR was another matter entirely; its implementation, opposition, and revision cut to the heart of televisual repetition, and the new stature of syndication. As the reconfigured television of the 1970s developed in the wake of the new policy, every aspect of PTAR generated debate.

PTAR and Fin-Syn in Practice

The networks resolved the dilemma of exactly which portion of prime time would be ceded fairly quickly, as they uncharacteristically agreed to an 8 to 11 p.m. Monday through Friday schedule effective fall 1971.[67] Thus, the FCC considered 7 to 8 p.m. to be the "access period" of prime time, where nonnetwork programming would be able to find the largest audiences of the broadcast day. However, debate centered on what kind of programming would be granted this "access." Since this was to be ostensibly local time, would truly "local" programs be required? Similarly, would any national syndication be viable in that slot, and if so, what forms could it take?

A major provision of the initial rule forbade network-owned-and-operated stations (O & O's) and affiliates from scheduling off-net series in the newly freed hour. This was anathema to the affiliates, but an unexpected coup for independents, who would now have a codified advantage over affiliates in the acquisition of off-net series. Indeed, until PTAR was repealed in 1995, the strongest independent stations in every market almost always obtained the top off-net programs. However, the Commission delayed the implementation of this part of the rule for one year to give stations more time to comply. Accordingly, during the 1971–72 season, most network affiliates programmed off-net sitcoms during the second half of the access hour, using as much of that resource as they could before they had to surrender it the following season. Major market affiliates stayed close to home in a similar manner, and programmed first-run syndicated continuations of popular family-oriented series that had all ended their network runs in 1971, such as *Wild Kingdom* (NBC), *Lassie* (CBS), and *The Lawrence Welk Show* (ABC).

However, once that grace period was up, affiliates were forbidden from programming any off-net series during the access period. Accordingly, independents—who were already reportedly "ecstatic" about PTAR even before its effective start—seized on this advantage, outbidding affiliates for key off-net series, and scheduling their most popular programs during the access period, thus accelerating their already impressive growth over the previous decade.[68] The 1972 formation of INTV (a national coalition of independent television stations) coalesced these energies, lobbying to insure that PTAR would never be revoked. One year later, Ward L. Quaal, the president of prominent Chicago independent station WGN, became the first nonnetwork-affiliated figure to win the NAB's Distinguished Service Award, validating the independents' new stature within the industry. Again, repetition in general—and series stripping in particular—were cited as the primary programming forms that sparked the independents' ascendancy. As *Broadcasting* wrote, "in the ecology of television, the independents discovered endless recycling."[69] However, stripping was not necessarily "endless," as there were definite winners and losers in the programming stakes heightened by the implementation of PTAR and fin-syn.

The shift of time from networks to local stations was also of significant concern to series producers. Those with network series or experience were generally opposed to PTAR, fearing a further narrowing of their already-narrow market. In mid-1973, a group of these producers, including Norman Lear, Gene Roddenberry, Jack Webb, and Bud Yorkin formally petitioned to repeal PTAR. They claimed that they were all in initial support of the rule, but were now against it, maintaining that the innovation it was designed to promote was not going to materialize in the present environment, and that a return of time to the networks was the only way to improve prime-time programming. Only the networks, they reasoned before the Commission, had the resources and "courage" to support real innovation on television.[70] On the other side, producers already providing successful first-run syndication— mostly affiliated with the National Association of Independent Television Producers and Distributors (NAITPD)—supported PTAR. When the FCC attempted to modify the Rule in late 1973 by allowing network affiliates to air off-net series in the 7–7:30 portion of the hour, the NAITPD vehemently opposed the decision, arguing that it would discourage new syndicated programming, and revoke the intent of the original rule.[71]

The Commission would ultimately return to something closer to the original Rule with "PTAR 3" in 1975, due to a court revocation of the second version. The Commission's strategy this time was to attempt to strengthen the language regarding which types of programs were acceptable during the access period. This impacted the syndication market immediately, as the interpretation of the "children's programming" requirement come license renewal time was not firmly established. Most stations had claimed their afternoon off-net sitcom blocks as "children's programming," but were uncertain if this would continue to suffice under PTAR 3. Conversely, independent producer Sandy Frank did not think the new version went far enough to protect new development, and targeted off-net series specifically, lobbying the FCC to add a ban of "multiple exposures"—i.e., stripping—of a program during access time.[72]

Despite the attempts at fine-tuning, and the almost annual chaos it would cause in the syndication market, the overall effect of every version of PTAR was, ironically, but predictably, given the already-established tendency towards repetition, to foster conservatism and formula in programming. In what should have been seen as an omen, two separate studies published in early 1972 found that the new rule was having virtually the opposite effect that it was ostensibly intended for. Industry analysts Telecom Associates of New York, and advertising agency Foote, Cone, and Belding, compared the fall 1970 and fall 1971 ARB ratings in major markets in separate studies, and found that "known quantities" such as off-net reruns, remakes of older series, or first-run continuations of network series, easily outdrew both new first-run series and local-originated programming. Herb Jacobs, president of Telecom, reported that the new programming finished "third or worse" during PTAR's first few months, while Foote, Cone, and Belding claimed that the average independent station—stocking its schedules with off-net reruns—had increased its share 149% between October 1970 and October 1971, mostly at the expense of NBC and CBS affiliates.[73] Another analysis firm, Ogilvy and Mather, echoed these findings, and baldly stated to its clients that "programs should be familiar in subject matter, have family appeal and be uncomplicated in content."[74] As Karla Salmon Robinson documented in her 1996 dissertation, several government, industry, and academic studies corroborated these findings for the next decade and a half, further delegitimating PTAR's aims to increase programming diversity.[75]

Of course, these ratings analyses do not necessarily give the full picture of the marketing environment in which new programming ideas were consistently tried out against series that were heavily promoted to stations as "old favorites." Advertisements in trade journals during this period bear this out. NBC Films trotted out the local syndication of *Ponderosa* (aka *Bonanza*) by trumpeting it as "the most popular program in television history," Screen Gems claimed that "*Bewitched* works like magic," and UA-TV simply declared "because... *Gilligan's Island* rates 92.7% renew."[76] The promotion activities and conservative fiscal practices of the industry seems at this point to have doomed new ideas—which PTAR was ostensibly intended to promote—to failure. The saying "nothing succeeds like success" has always been a mantra in the media business, and its endemic preference for formula and familiarity over innovation and challenge has consistently been, as I have argued throughout, a standard operating procedure in almost every commercial media form, from publishing all the way through to home video. As a cordoned-off part of the television schedule, the evening access period provided a laboratory to prove the aphorism correct.

PTAR had not only failed to promote innovative and/or local television; it had fostered the very entrenchment of recycled formats (e.g., evening versions of daytime game shows), fluffy "news" programs (e.g., Group W's *PM Magazine*), and, most dramatically, off-network reruns. Indeed, as Robinson wrote, "industry structure, program economics and profit maximization could not be eliminated by administrative fiat."[77] The resulting economic imperatives shifted even more attention and energies in the 1970s into developing successful off-network reruns, programs that would become the key products of an industry increasingly built upon repetition, and the key texts of a culture increasingly awash in the recent past.

Today's Hits Tomorrow: The Off-Net Futures Market

It would be an understatement to say that popular off-net series were "hot commodities" in the late 1970s. The Prime-Time Access Rule, the increased competition of independents, and the burgeoning sense of the television heritage in 1970s popular culture (see the next chapter) had greatly expanded the market and stature of past television. Even series which were never considered to be serious off-net contenders, such as *The Brady Bunch* and *Star Trek*, were generating high audiences for local stations, and, in the case of *Star Trek* in particular, developing into whole multimedia entertainment franchises. Accordingly, network series producers now hastened the jump to local syndication by selling syndication "futures": the rights to locally broadcast a series several years later (usually, though not necessarily, after the end of its network run). Before the 1970s, series had been offered for syndication during the winter prior to their debuts in local markets, a gap of six to nine months. The futures, or "presell" approach to syndication moved the date of this sale back a year or more; thus a station would have to purchase their fall 1978 schedule in spring 1976. While proving quite lucrative for major distributors with access to hit network series—most notably Paramount and Viacom—this practice generated far more hype than results for local stations, who often put out large amounts of cash up front for less-than-spectacular ratings several years later. This change in program marketing indicates how local stations' insatiable appetites for repetition and having "proven hits" were easily exploited by program distributors, and continued to be for years afterwards.

While a few programs were sold as "futures" in the late 1960s, the practice ascended in earnest in 1972, when MCA-Universal, the producers of many long-running NBC crime dramas, announced the sale of their popular detective series *Ironside* to local syndication. Spurred by the off-network success of Viacom's *Perry Mason*, which also starred Raymond Burr, MCA attempted to sell *Ironside* two years ahead of its network cancellation (reached in an agreement with NBC), for local broadcasting beginning fall 1974. Within a month, MCA had sold all 175 projected 60-minute episodes of *Ironside* to 125 markets, and the series became the all-time grosser in off-net syndication, before a single episode had even aired on local stations.[78] MCA continued this strategy the following year, recording heavy sales for its *Marcus Welby, MD*, and *Adam-12*. Sparked by the success of this plan, which had generated much higher fees for these series than were otherwise projected, other prominent distributors, including Viacom, Screen Gems, Warner Brothers, and MGM, began preselling their programs as well.[79] Despite a lull in recent programs actually coming to the local market at this time, presells of "hot" network shows such as *The Six Million Dollar Man* (MCA), *The Odd Couple* (Paramount), *The Bob Newhart Show* (Viacom), and *M*A*S*H* (20th Century Fox) continued at a rapid clip.[80]

The largest sales in off-net futures were had by sitcoms, which had already established their place in the local television schedule as the consummate repetitive program form. This bias was exacerbated even further by the NAB's family-time provisions, which had a chilling effect on the afternoon scheduling of off-network 60-minute crime series, and sent stations scurrying after suitable "family" sitcoms. Accordingly the popular, long-running sitcoms of the early to mid-1970s, such as *The Mary Tyler Moore Show, Sanford and Son*, and *M*A*S*H*, were rushed to off-net syndication. While some of these series, most notably *All In The Family* and *Maude*, were held out of local syndication out of concern that their style was becoming dated or their material too controversial for daily stripping, others were heavily promoted in the presale market.[81] When Viacom announced the preselling of *The Mary Tyler Moore Show* in 1975 (for local airing in fall 1978 at the latest), NBC quickly recorded a record deal for a seven-year, unlimited run of *Mary* on its O & O's, paying over $50,000 an episode, despite the fact that they would be unable to run it at the most lucrative early-evening time slots due to PTAR.[82] Though the O & O's and major station groups were the largest buyers of these properties, Paramount opted to go market-to-market—even staying out of the 1977 NATPE—when it sold *Happy Days*, successfully raising its price further than projected; New York station WPIX even accepted Paramount's opening price of $35,000-per-episode right off the bat.[83] For the rest of the decade, popular sitcoms such as *Happy Days, The Bob Newhart Show, Laverne & Shirley*, and *Three's Company* would set new records in local sales, entirely on the basis of their current status on the networks. Distributors leapt upon any advantage they could find in an increasingly crowded market. For example, after *Laverne & Shirley* recorded the highest-ever rating for a prime-time network sitcom episode (on January 10, 1978), Paramount quickly presold the series later that winter, over three years before its fall 1981 debut in local syndication.

While these futures sales drove the prices of particular series through the roof in the late 1970s and early 1980s, only a few of these programs would become long-term syndication staples. Neither *Laverne & Shirley* nor *Happy Days* would match their network heights of popularity, and did not last long in local syndication. Conversely, slightly less popular but more consistent series like *M*A*S*H*, or, to a lesser extent, *The Bob Newhart Show*, became solid off-network hits throughout the 1980s. Although the futures market cooled down temporarily by that point, due in large part to an almost total dearth of newer hit sitcoms (see Chapter 6), it remained a lucrative method of selling series to local markets, generating quicker profits for producers and distributors. While the programming marketplace of today is much more complex than it was in the 1970s, a well-chosen off-network series is still a "hot commodity," by any measure, as stations and cable networks alike still hope to cash in on televisual repetition.

Do It Again

Over the course of the 1960s and 1970s, U.S. commercial television had significantly transformed. By the early 1980s, the networks still dominated prime-time programming, but, in the wake of PTAR and fin-syn, other players in the television industry had become much more viable. Independent stations in particular had made significant inroads into network affiliate shares nationwide, and were now serious competitors for local and national advertisers. The key factor throughout this period was the off-network rerun, which fostered the growth of UHF and independent stations, affected the development of syndication marketing and programming methods, and spurred federal regulations. Off-network syndication had established itself firmly at the center of the television industry by the end of the 1970s, validating industrial and cultural principles of cultural repetition, and helping set the stage for the further exploitation of past television. Flying in the face of calls for diversity and local origination, distributors and stations instead placed their bets with known quantities, ensconcing repetition as the *lingua franca* of the U.S. television industry.

As a result of these economic practices, which consistently favored repetition over innovation, the daytime off-network series strip—whether on networks or local stations—became a fixture on virtually every commercial station nationwide during this period, and its effect on the experience and memories of American television is difficult to deny. It was one thing to have caught a few episodes of *I Love Lucy*, *Batman*, or *Star Trek* on their original prime-time network runs, but quite another to watch the same series daily, catching many episodes several times, and building up a bank of American cultural memories. Together, producers, networks, distributors, unions, advertisers, local stations, and the federal government had generated this regime of repetition. After a generation had grown up with television, viewers and critics—all virtually incidental to the industrial and regulatory development of the medium—now generated their own understandings and experiences of all this "old TV," and began to consciously shape a *television heritage*: a common postwar history of the new rerun nation. Their discourses will be explored in the next chapter.

Notes

1. Ely Landau, President of National Telefilm Associates (NTA), 1958. Qtd. in "The 'used movie' czars," *Forbes*, 15 May 1958, p. 22.

2. Thomas Streeter, *Selling The Air: A Critique of American Commercial Broadcasting* (Chicago: University of Chicago Press, 1996), 268–274.

3. "Cartoons Endure For UAA," *Broadcasting*, 10 August 1959, pp. 74–75.

4. "TV re-runs: how they bring advertisers big audiences at low cost-per-thousand," *Printer's Ink*, 15 August 1958, pp. 41–42.

5. Advertisement, *Trouble With Father*, Official Films, Inc., *Broadcasting*, 25 August 1958, pp. 26–27; Advertisement, *My Little Margie*, Official Films, Inc., *Broadcasting*, 18 August 1958, pp. 28–29; Advertisement, *The Burns and Allen Show*, Screen Gems, *Broadcasting*, 23 June 1958, pp. 12–13.

6. "How The Cisco Kid Stays Ageless," *Broadcasting*, 24 August 1959, pp. 52+; "He Just Keeps Ridin' Along On TV," *Broadcasting*, 18 July 1960, pp. 78–79.

7. United Artists merged with Ziv in early 1960, continuing distribution of some series while eventually selling the rights to others. "UA Finally Gets Its Hands On Ziv," *Broadcasting*, 14 March 1960, p. 84; "First-run film series: its heyday is past," *Broadcasting*, 8 May 1961, pp. 84+.

8. Hal Erickson, *Syndicated Television: The First Forty Years, 1947–1987* (Jefferson, NC: McFarland, 1989), 105.

9. "The 'used movie' czars," *Forbes*, 15 May 1958, pp. 21–22. NTA ultimately failed to live up to its own logic. Its New York-based flagship station, WNTA, offered an innovative array of new live and film programming, but was unable to draw either viewers or advertisers, and was sold to a non-profit group in 1962. Ironically, WNTA lost out to the other New York independent stations, which relied on film and television reruns rather than new series.

10. "Syndicators woo select audience," *Broadcasting*, 27 August 1962, pp. 27–29; "Market brisk for diversified programs," *Broadcasting*, 15 March 1965, pp. 73+.

11. "New style in syndication," editorial, *Broadcasting*, 27 August 1962, p. 94.

12. This form would become particularly lucrative for independent syndicators in the 1970s, as the Prime Time Access Rule cleared valuable

early-evening time on network affiliates for first-run syndication. "All systems go for record TV syndication," *Broadcasting*, 17 March 1969, pp. 74+.

13. "Off-network program scarcity ahead?," *Broadcasting*, 30 September 1963, pp. 52–55.

14. William Lafferty, "Feature Films on Prime-Time Television," in Tino Balio, ed., *Hollywood In The Age of Television* (Boston: Unwin Hyman, 1990), 245–246.

15. Raymond Williams, *Television: Technology and Cultural Form* (New York: Shocken Books, 1974), 14.

16. Tino Balio, "Introduction to Part I," in Tino Balio, ed., *Hollywood In The Age of Television* (Boston: Unwin Hyman, 1990), 38–39.

17. Only Ziv had shown the foresight to produce some of their series in both monochrome and color in the 1950s, though their faith in the market for color programs turned out to be premature.

18. "Color only small part of total film backlog," *Broadcasting*, 3 January 1966, pp. 88+.

19. "Color tones up syndication sales picture," *Broadcasting*, 21 March 1966, pp. 69+.

20. This surge in off-net supply—the largest crop of new offerings in the mid-1960s—also resulted from the growing development of late afternoon as the primary daypart for off-net series. "Off-network bonanza for buyers," *Broadcasting*, 2 May 1966, pp. 25–27.

21. RCA had been marketing its color sets since the standard was first agreed upon, via the heavily-promoted use of color programs on NBC, the network with far and away the most color programming prior to 1966. CBS, the top-rated network, had no set manufacturing arm, and was thus the most reluctant to switch over to color, though it saw no choice in the face of competition by the mid 1960s.

22. Qtd. in "Boom times for color backlog," *Broadcasting*, 20 September 1965, pp. 27+.

23. "Syndication color still short of demand," *Broadcasting*, 2 January 1967, pp. 74+.

24. "TV permits dropped," *New York Times*, 23 November 1960, p. 59.

25. At the end of the Eisenhower FCC, 234 UHF licenses had been either revoked or denied by the Commission due to the inability of potential broadcasters to meet regulatory service deadlines.

26. "FCC announces channel shifts," *New York Times*, 29 July 1961, p. 39. At the 1963 NAB convention, Minow also made the intriguing suggestion that the networks be allowed one VHF and one UHF affiliate in each market; the latter would be used exclusively for off-network reruns. This suggestion was never developed further, but it demonstrates the acceptance of the rerun as

a standard form of programming. "Minow proposes second run UHF network," *Broadcasting*, 8 April 1963, p. 60.

27. Streeter, *Selling The Air*, 248.

28. It was perhaps fortuitous for UHF proponents that the All-Channel Act went into effect coincident with the networks' transformation to color television. There were millions of new color sets sold in the late 1960s, and every one of them had both VHF and UHF reception. "Ownership of Television Receivers: 1946–1988," table, in Christopher H. Sterling and John M. Kittross, *Stay Tuned: A Concise History of American Broadcasting* (Second Edition) (Belmont, CA: Wadsworth Publishing Company, 1990), 658.

29. "New moves to force-feed UHF," *Broadcasting*, 16 March 1964, pp. 58+; Jack Gould, "Government asks TV show sharing," *New York Times*, 17 March 1964, p. 71.

30. "U's newest syndicator prospect," *Broadcasting*, 14 November 1966, pp. 31–34.

31. "Syndicators see bullish market," *Broadcasting*, 25 March 1968, pp. 75+.

32. "A first for UHF: 'typical' station in the black in '72," *Broadcasting*, 9 July 1973, p. 30.

33. Morris J. Gelman, "Life without networks," *Television*, pp. 61+.

34. Gelman, "Life without networks," 86.

35. Metromedia stations WNEW (New York), WTTG (Washington), and KTTV (Los Angeles) showed the biggest gains, doubling their prime-time shares between 1966 and 1968. "The Independents' Bigger Bite," *Broadcasting*, 14 October 1968, pp. 42+.

36. Italics in the original. Advertisement, WPIX-TV New York, *Broadcasting*, 26 September 1960.

37. Advertisement, WGN-TV Chicago, *Broadcasting*, 30 September 1968, p. 6.

38. "The new tricks of counterprogramming," *Broadcasting*, 10 November 1969, pp. 36–38.

39. "Counterprogramming," *Broadcasting*, 17 June 1968, p. 5; "The Independents' Bigger Bite," *Broadcasting*, 14 October 1968, pp. 42+.

40. There were some 1960s first-run contenders that hewed to the old action-adventure formula, however these were relatively rare in comparison to the dominant form. These first-run dramas include series such as *The Blue Angels*, *Ripcord*, and *Shannon*. According to Hal Erickson, American series in this mold had disappeared by 1963, to be replaced by Australian, Canadian, and British productions. ITC, the predominantly British producer-distributor, was particularly successful in placing its entertainment series in U.S. first-run during the Anglophilic sixties, including *The Saint*, *Thunderbirds*, *Captain Scarlet and the Mysterons*, and *Stingray*. Hal Erickson, *Syndicated Television: The First Forty Years, 1947–1987* (Jefferson, NC: McFarland, 1989), 106.

41. Christopher Anderson notes that the Warner Bros telefilm series of the late 1950s and early 1960s, which aired primarily on ABC, were notorious for exploiting these principles in production, and that even scripts were routinely reworked for use on other Warner Bros westerns or private eye series. Christopher Anderson, *Hollywood TV: The Studio System in the Fifties* (Austin: University of Texas Press, 1994), 248–252.

42. Jack Gould, "TV reruns to run on," *New York Times*, 17 March 1960, p. 67.

43. Jack Gould, "Summer reruns," *New York Times*, 5 August 1962, sec. B, p. 13.

44. This is still, give or take a few episodes on particular series, the usual season order today. However, the recent successes of shorter-running reality series (e.g., *The Bachelor, Survivor*), premium-cable-based fictional series (e.g., *Sex and the City, The Sopranos*), and DVD releases of television series has caused some speculation about the continued feasibility of the twenty-plus episode season; see Chapters 7 and 8.

45. Albin Krebs, "President backs coast unions in fight to limit reruns on TV," *New York Times*, 15 September 1972, p. 1.

46. As Les Brown noted in a contemporaneous *New York Times* article, the networks could always point to the fact that the majority of viewers did not see the episode the first time, meaning that a rerun was, broadly speaking, in the "public interest." However, the networks' own research, not as widely publicized, also indicated that the majority of rerun viewers *did* in fact see the episode the first time as well, still leaving a majority of viewers not exercising their "public interest." Les Brown, "Broadcast Notes: How Come So Many Reruns?," *New York Times*, 23 March 1975, sec. II, p. 29.

47. Qtd. in "A rerun on reruns," *Broadcasting*, 3 February 1975, pp. 54–55.

48. CBS only ended this strategy when they prepared to spin off their syndication rights to these and other series into the newly-formed Viacom in 1970; see below.

49. "Off-network program scarcity ahead?," *Broadcasting*, 30 September 1963, pp. 52–55.

50. Indeed, there seemed to be no audience satiety with many of these series, leading to their establishment as "evergreens" in the television heritage and, thus, on the American cultural terrain. The next chapter will explore this phenomenon more fully.

51. From 1972–77, *The CBS Late Movie* was literally that: reruns of previously broadcast feature films and made-for-television movies. During the program's last dozen years, however, films were only broadcast sporadically, as old episodes of current or recent network series were primarily utilized.

52. The only non-ABC show utilized in *ABC Late Night* was CBS' *Mannix*.

53. Option time clauses were provisions in network-affiliate contracts which granted networks exclusive rights to particular broadcast hours on affiliates.

54. Streeter, *Selling The Air*, 212.

55. Eileen Meehan, "Why We Don't Count: The Commodity Audience," in Mellencamp, ed., *Logics of Television* (Bloomington: Indiana University Press, 1990), 117–137; Streeter, *Selling The Air*, 212–213.

56. "Upheaval in TV program control?," *Broadcasting*, 25 January 1965, pp. 27–28.

57. Qtd. in "It's war on FCC program control," *Broadcasting*, 22 March 1965, pp. 74–76; qtd. in "Not an FCC Friend in Sight," *Broadcasting*, 26 April 1965, pp. 58–60.

58. The same report also determined that local advertising revenues represented a growing percentage of total affiliate profits, while the importance of network compensation in this total was shrinking. "Resurgence seen in non-network product," *Broadcasting*, 28 April 1969, pp. 66–67.

59. "Major moves to rip up broadcasting," *Broadcasting*, 30 March 1970, pp. 27–30.

60. The three primary aspects of the fin-syn rules were originally due to go in effect on September 1, 1970 (ban on program acquisition), 1971 (ban on domestic syndication), and 1972 (divestment of subsidiary syndication rights), while PTAR was due to commence on September 1, 1971.

61. Though CBS had made clear from the beginning that Viacom was to be a completely distinct company with no CBS control, the network repeatedly had to revamp its divestment plans to curtail the participation of CBS executives and major stockholders in the new company. At the same time, they had to stave off a lawsuit from minority shareholders in a San Francisco Bay area cable company, who felt their rights were being trampled in the new arrangement. By November 1971, the path was clear, and Viacom was on its way toward eventually becoming one of the largest media corporations in the world. "Spin-off: one way to beat the system?," *Broadcasting*, 6 July 1970, pp. 19–21; "Double trouble for CBS spin-off," *Broadcasting*, 21 December 1970, p. 34; "Sudden halt to Viacom spin-off," *Broadcasting*, 11 January 1971, pp. 32–33; "CBS reassures FCC on Viacom," *Broadcasting*, 25 January 1971, pp. 29–30; "Viacom receives CBS' cable TV," *New York Times*, 5 June 1971, p. 40; "A belated natal blessing for Viacom," *Broadcasting*, 7 June 1971, pp. 32–33; "FCC upheld on Viacom," *Broadcasting*, 22 November 1971, p. 44.

62. Viacom would continue the domination of former CBS series in off-net syndication into the 1970s and beyond, as many of their series were afternoon and evening staples in virtually every market in the country. These series' consistent renewals and status as "evergreens" fueled the growth of the corporation, aiding their acquisition of cable networks such as MTV and Nickelodeon in the 1980s, their buyout of Paramount Communications in 1994, and their eventual acquisition of their corporate parent, CBS, in 2000. Clearly, were it not for televisual repetition, and the

cultural embrace of reruns promulgated in the 1970s, Viacom would not have become one of the planet's half-dozen largest media firms by the end of the twentieth century.

63. "Access becomes a free speech issue," *Broadcasting*, 30 November 1970, pp. 37+.

64. "Networks hit prime-time rule," *Broadcasting*, 15 June 1970, p. 9.

65. "WBC, Metromedia defend prime-time rule," *Broadcasting*, 21 December 1970, pp. 42–43.

66. "Appeals court upholds prime-time access," *Broadcasting*, 10 May 1971, p. 36.

67. There was a brief exception to this on Tuesday nights for one season, as the networks, in deference to ABC, retained 7:30–8 p.m. and instead relinquished 10:30–11 p.m.

68. "New breed, new battle in program sales," *Broadcasting*, 5 April 1971, pp. 26+.

69. Qtd. in "The hard way to make money in television," *Broadcasting*, 5 March 1973, pp. 39+.

70. "The biggest access show to date: oral arguments at the FCC," *Broadcasting*, 6 August 1973, pp. 13+.

71. "Top of the Week," *Broadcasting*, 3 December 1973, p. 6; "NAITPD denounces prime-time-access changes by FCC," *Broadcasting*, 10 December 1973, p. 35.

72. "PTAR III may have touched off a fuse," *Broadcasting*, 27 January 1975, p. 19; "What troubled program chiefs on NATPE eve," *Broadcasting*, 10 February 1975, pp. 38+.

73. "Not exactly off to a roaring start," *Broadcasting*, 17 January 1972, p. 25.

74. Qtd. in "Blur in the prime-time vision," *Broadcasting*, 7 February 1972, pp. 52+.

75. Karla Salmon Robinson, "The Performance of First-Run and Off-Network Syndicated Television Programs, 1964–1993" (Ph.D. diss., Northwestern University, 1996), 17–22.

76. Advertisement, *Ponderosa*, NBC Films, *Broadcasting*, 27 March 1972, p. 3; Advertisement, *Bewitched*, Screen Gems, *Broadcasting*, 18 February 1974, p. 35; Advertisement, *Gilligan's Island*, United Artists Television, *Broadcasting*, 29 October 1973, p. 1.

77. Robinson, "The Performance of First-Run," 22.

78. "Programer's consensus: better times," *Broadcasting*, 17 April 1972, p. 46; "Heavy sales for 'Ironside'," *Broadcasting*, 15 May 1972, p. 67.

79. "Closed circuit," *Broadcasting*, 31 December 1973, p. 3.

80. "Prime-time access to get different types of programs," *Broadcasting*, 1 March 1976, pp. 26+.

81. Tandem's experience with *Maude* was telling in this regard. They removed the series from syndication after only three months on the market in 1977 due to a "chilly reception" from local stations. The following year, however, they embarked on a unique "discount plan," designed by McCann-Erickson, under which they would offer *Maude* at a discount rate with an option to cancel the run after one year. While this plan did place *Maude* in local stations, the series was predictably deemed too "strident" and "controversial" by conservative station managers, and soon faded from off-net syndication. *Maude* eventually returned to television under the cover of nostalgia on the cable network TV Land at the turn of the century; see Chapter 7. "'Sanford,' 'Good Times' off-network sales said to be at record prices," *Broadcasting*, 25 July 1977, p. 84; "Tandem joins forces with McCann-Erickson to market 'Maude'," *Broadcasting*, 18 December 1978, p. 68.

82. "'Mary Tyler Moore': biggest yet for TV syndication?," *Broadcasting*, 7 July 1975, pp. 34–35.

83. "Happy days for syndicators of network comedies," *Broadcasting*, 10 January 1977, pp. 34+.

5
Our Television Heritage: Reconceiving Past Television

> [T]here are very few moments from the TV past that our children will not
> witness, over and over again.[1]

One morning in November 1976, longtime CBS chairman William S.
Paley stood in front of a building in midtown Manhattan and announced
the opening of a new cultural institution. The Museum of Broadcasting
would join the ranks of familiar New York monuments to the Great
Achievements of History, such as the American Museum of Natural
History, the Metropolitan Museum of Art, and the Guggenheim Museum.
"Now in 1976," said Paley, "on the fiftieth anniversary of network
broadcasting, [radio and television] have become a mature, responsible
and important force in our national life... it is time that we take stock
of our past, so that we can know and understand the heritage of the
broadcast media in building our future."[2] The Museum was an instant
success as soon as it doors opened, drawing much more attention than its
eight audio-visual consoles could handle. Its thousands of hours of past
radio and television were made available to academic researchers and
lay visitors alike, legitimating past broadcast media as it had never been
before. Still, despite this success, some questioned the validity of a
museum devoted primarily to television programs. Noting the popularity
of the museum, and the growing enshrinement of television among the
arts, *New York Times* TV critic John J. O'Connor wondered in 1978 if
such veneration was appropriate:

> ... [H]as the time arrived for serious television retrospectives? As sure as
> the Paley family once made little brown cigars, television is bound to
> follow the cultish pop-entertainment path discovered by the movies.
> Art of various persuasions will suddenly be detected in products that
> were largely churned out for the sole purpose of entertaining a mass
> audience. Charlie Chaplin became a subject for serious discourse. So too,
> no doubt, will Lucille Ball. The movies are now enshrined in museums,
> and television is already beginning to hear the first rumblings of the
> same fate.[3]

The opening of the Museum of Broadcasting was a signal event in media history, as it crystallized a growing legitimation of television in American culture. Once broadcasting's past was enshrined in monolithic form, it would never be the same.

The Museum of Broadcasting is part of a broad cultural shift in the perception of television that began in the early 1960s and coalesced by the early 1980s. New critical perceptions of what was now as likely to be called "popular" as "mass" culture offered a greater acknowledgement of the everyday culture of modernity. This new validation of the popular was also reflected through an unprecedented and highly mediated nostalgia that defined much of the cultural landscape at this time. During the seventies,[4] these discourses, and others, would construct a new narrative of American television. Consider these two statements, from roughly a decade apart. The typical response to television reruns in the mid-1960s was one of disdain or sarcasm, as indicated by Charles Morton's comment on the sitcom in *Atlantic Monthly*: "Laughter, however improbable as a reaction to situation comedy, simply does not deteriorate once it is canned and put in storage." By 1975, *Chicago Tribune* television critic Gary Deeb could eulogize the oft-ridiculed Ozzie Nelson:

> He was perfectly matched to the 1950s . . . a benign guy for a benign era. Ike was President. Times were tranquil. Life was painless. And even later, when the world got noisy and frightening, Ozzie and Harriet provided a popular service. They were a dependable respite for those who were terrified by the pace of the world.[5]

In contrast to Morton's highbrow *bon mot* at nameless sitcoms, Deeb's tribute exemplifies the particular combination of cultural legitimation and generational nostalgia circulating around television by the mid-1970s. Ozzie Nelson meant something different in 1975 than he had in 1965.

The seventies marked the beginning of television's *historicity*, that is, its articulation into discourses of history and memory. This is not solely because, as a rather literal-minded view of historiography would have it, that "enough" time had simply passed in order to form something resembling a "history." Rather, television's history was already being activated in the multiple contexts produced by the shifts in cultural and industrial production described in the previous chapters. My concern in this chapter is with the primary result of these shifts by the seventies: the formation of the *television heritage*. The television heritage serves as a base of legitimacy for television, a mechanism for locating television—series, genres, stars, policies, stations, logos, advertisements, or viewing experiences—in American history and memory; i.e., as something worthy of attention, preservation, and tribute.

"Heritage" is precisely the right term for this altered perception. Its etymology lies in the word "heir," as in "property that descends to an heir," as my Merriam-Webster Dictionary puts it.[6] It conveys a sense of a natural inheritance to this property, a birthright. Past television clearly functions in this manner today, as a cultural and historical resource for all generations. It is widely used as a cultural touchstone, instantly signifying particular times. Moreover, like particular natural and historic sites considered as "heritage," past television is now protected and exploited as both private and public property, through copyright and continued cultural recirculation. This transformation of past television into the television heritage was not inevitable. Many other societies have decades of past television to draw from, but none do so near as extensively as the United States. Like all forms of media before it, television had to be placed into history and memory, rendered culturally significant at particular times and for particular reasons.

The seventies were that time for television, and the primary spark was a growing interest in the recent past. In an era marked by political struggle, stagnant economies, and the proverbial "malaise," the past several decades became a major source of cultural identity and reflection for Americans. Memories of the twenties through sixties were activated through an unprecedented nostalgia that affected virtually every aspect of popular culture during this period. Television—that most uncanny of all the tools of modernity—provided a vivid connection to the recent past, helping cement the dominant narratives of the post-World War II era in popular memory, and fostering the subsequent development of the cultures of retro and nostalgia that pervaded the last quarter of the century. Television had always served, in part, as a kind of time machine, constantly presenting and representing sounds and images of the past. Paradoxically, however, the medium was rarely considered in this light during its first two decades. The idea of seriously studying television as a cultural form of discrete programs and a distinct history—let alone attributing any long-term cultural value to it at all—is a relatively recent development, dating back no further than the mid-1960s. Prior to that time, television was perceived to be any of a disparate array of categories; it was innocuous, therapeutic, apocalyptic, debasing, educational, worthless, and transcendental. Its programs and discourses were perceived as part of a contemporary condition, as symptoms of modern life. Television simply did not, could not, have a past. As detailed in the previous chapter, however, the regime of repetition had already established itself on broadcasting. By the end of the 1960s, recirculated programming, in the form of off-network syndication, filled commercial television, both locally and nationally. The past had become as much a part of television as the present, if not more so, as the sheer volume of reruns on the typical television station of this time indicates.[7] As the ubiquitous semiotic capsules of the recent past, off-network reruns played a key role in the new nostalgia of the seventies, and would eventually become legitimated as part of the American cultural heritage.

The changing status of past television in the seventies was expressed via several different forms. Many of the actual programs and accompanying documentation of television's early years—now known as the "Golden Age of Television"—were physically archived for scholarly research, and presented to the public in new broadcasting museums. As stated above, the Museum of Broadcasting opened in New York in 1976, providing a sanctioned, highly public organization of past television series and events. Mainstream articles and books focusing on particular 1950s and 1960s television series, stars, genres, and general trivia were regularly published. The majority of this work was created through the lens of baby boomer nostalgia, extending the cultural lifespan of many ostensibly defunct former network series by linking them to a generational television heritage. Meanwhile, amidst the ivory towers—which had only barely begun to acknowledge the academic legitimacy of the study of film— television's practices and, more significantly, texts, began to be analyzed by a new generation of scholars who were born into the world of television. Horace Newcomb's landmark *TV: The Most Popular Art* (1974) is arguably the ur-text of this American brand of television studies, which was based in the humanities rather than the social sciences. Finally, during the same period, television fans began to emerge as a significant subculture, producing their own histories, mythologies, and critiques of their favorite series, performers, and auteurs.

This new acknowledgement of the past had not gone unnoticed or unexploited by the television industry. While television and radio broadcasting at every level were already saturated with the past, the difference, starting in the mid-1970s, was that old programs could be promoted with more than simple familiarity; they could now be touted as "classics." Accordingly, all three networks aired several splashy retrospectives of their own television heritages in the seventies, including massive, multi-hour specials commemorating their anniversaries, tributes to various Golden Age performers, and TV-movie "reunions" of the casts of familiar rerun series such as *Father Knows Best, Gilligan's Island*, and *Maverick*. At the same time, the coupling of the regime of repetition with the new television heritage assured that particular past series would, in principle, always be repeated. Accordingly, *I Love Lucy*—two decades removed from its original CBS run—was still one of the most popular series on television, by any measure, airing in off-network syndication in virtually every market in the country, and ultimately becoming hailed as the consummate American television program.[8]

Simply put, the television heritage became the dominant cultural embodiment of the recent past in the United States, an active memory bank of images and sounds, easily communicated across the culture. Over the course of the seventies, television became the subject of active nostalgia, historical exploration, and cultural preservation. It was seen to be a medium at least capable of cultural significance, and even artistic achievement. Most importantly, however, it was now perceived as a cultural form with a rich history, a past worthy of not only examination, but also valorization.

This chapter traces how past television became the television heritage in the seventies. The television heritage—made up of the retrospective classifications of television museums and archives, journalistic commentary, academic inquiry, and nascent fan cultures—validated the medium in ways that it had never been before, giving it an acknowledged role in the recent life and memory of the nation, and thus an assured place in American cultural history. Televisual repetition may have been initiated by broadcasting industry economics, but it became part of the expected experience of television only once reruns had entered the cultural domain in their own right. In short, while a rerun of *I Love Lucy* might have been greeted in 1967 with derision ("*look* at that old show!"), by 1977 an opposite, appreciative reaction ("look at that *old show!*") was much more viable.

The Television Heritage

The cultural climate in the early 1970s was primed for the reevaluation of past television. Americans were beginning to reflect upon the tumultuous experiences of the past few decades, and television was seen as a source and symptom of those times. Despite earlier critical and creative forays, television had not entered into the traditional artistic canon. It had left an incomplete, contentious discursive field of criticism; accordingly, its overall meaning was still up for grabs. While the mass communications and mass culture critiques of television remained dominant throughout this period, some critics and scholars grew skeptical of their dire perceptions. These scholars began acknowledging the variety, vitality, and social significance of what was now increasingly called *popular* culture. In addition, as the smoke cleared from the upheavals of the sixties, baby boomers—who were indelibly linked with TV—began to reflect upon their own life experiences. As the dominant mass medium, and primary source and mediator of mass and popular cultures since mid-century, television was in a critical position to convey—and produce—historical and cultural legitimacy.

The new legitimation of television was based not on the canon, as it had been with film, nor with the scientific principles of mass communication, but on the idea of *heritage*. A heritage suggests a rootedness in social experience and history that neither of the previous terms could possess. While the canon tends to be separated from everyday life and located in a refined, timeless sanctuary, a heritage, while also protected to a certain degree, is part of the lived, historical experience of a culture. It becomes a critical social resource, blurring the concepts of history and memory and forging national and cultural identities. It represents where we are from, and who we are, linking past and present through tangible relics and practices. Television, in its unparalleled accessibility, its endless flow of processed sounds and images, its connections to economic and state institutions, and its constant repetition, is thus the most prolific heritage generator in our culture. While the parade of past television had been a staple form of the medium since the mid 1950s, it was not until the mid-1970s when it became singled out and noticed as a significant contribution to the culture in general. It began to be seen to possess a *real* (that is, culturally and socially effective) past, a trajectory of series, stars, and events that culminated in the oft-cited "new television" of the 1970s, but also described, defined, and "reflected" the nation. The television heritage was more than a history of a particular industry or technology; it was the effectual Rosetta Stone of post-World War II America.

The concept of a television heritage has generally been referred to with a wink and a nudge, as in Nick At Nite's mid-nineties slogan, "preserving our precious television heritage." The idea that entertainment television is "precious," has a "heritage," and is anything more than innocuous is still dealt with through barely disguised irony.[9] However, even within this usage there is a core of sincerity: television, in fact, *is* our cultural heritage as postwar Americans; we are just loath to admit it. Television has long been the United States' top leisure activity, while *TV Guide* has been the most widely-circulated periodical. In short, television viewing is what Americans *do*. Accordingly, some of this country's most prominent collective memories of the last 50 years have centered on television. During the seventies, these memories were activated through museums and archives, popular literature, humanities-based academic television studies, and collective viewerships (i.e., fandoms). In return, the development of these endeavors prompted an ersatz historicism in the medium itself. As the later chapters will argue, in the eighties and afterwards, as television's metamorphosis toward narrowcast forms and technologies accelerated, the television heritage was firmly ensconced as one of the dominant generators of programming. This was well beyond the mechanical logic of repetition established in the 1950s and 1960s; this was a holistic, thoroughly cultural reconception of television, which enshrined the rerun as its key form. Considered together, these discourses validated Americans' experiences of television and transformed TV from simply the massest of mass cultures to an important cultural institution with all the trimmings: serious rumination, academic study, zealous celebration, and even physical preservation. Of course, while TV would still always constitute a sociological "problem" or a hopeless wasteland of philistinism for some factions, it was now also increasingly plausible to perceive it in a legitimate cultural and historical light.

A Sense of History: Creating the "Golden Age of Television"

The classification of past television actually started in earnest in the early 1960s. While in retrospect the sense of a break with the past was not as acute as it would be several years later, there were significant reasons to posit differences between "then"—the 1950s—and "now"— the Minow era—on television, even though the medium was just over a decade old. Foremost among these rationales were the quiz show scandals of 1958–60, which had punctured the veneer of innocence that surrounded early television, and had made viewers, critics, regulators, and television professionals feel not only duped but also complicit in the use of the medium to perpetrate contrived American myths of genius and instant celebrity. As historian Kent Anderson described, these were "scandals without precedence," which set off many significant changes in the industry, its regulation, and its perception in American culture.[10] In their aftermath, the federal investigations of network television practices were accelerated, including the Barrow Report, the establishment of the FCC's Office of Network Study, and Senator Dodd's hearings on television violence. Similarly, just as the election of John F. Kennedy had ostensibly produced a new optimism and momentum in the federal government and the nation, the appointment of Newton Minow to head the FCC signaled a major shift in the relationship between government and broadcasting, after the disgrace of the scandal-ridden Doerfer years. However, Anderson notes that the perception of significant change between the late 1950s and the New Frontier exaggerated the reality of those changes, particularly in regards to industry policy.[11] "Perception" may be a largely discursive phenomenon, but that's precisely the point. Changing perceptions, more than anything else, have had the most significant effects on the cultural status of television. The past itself cannot change, but its meanings and uses for the present can.

Thus, even before the social and cultural turbulence of the mid to late 1960s, past television was already perceived as somehow "different." Accordingly, the recent past of only a few years before became mythologized as the "Golden Age" of television. The objective quality of any period of any creative medium is always a contentious discursive struggle, as lines are drawn, arguments are made, and reputations vacillate. With the power of hindsight, certain periods are singled out and held up as peaks of achievement, models for excellence, which subsequent eras somehow fail to measure up to. For American television, this period is roughly the medium's first decade, from 1948–58, when (or so the myth goes) program forms and norms were not yet entrenched, and the level of ingenuity and sheer talent on display was unparalleled. The oft-cited energy and creativity of live television dramatic production are at the heart of this myth, contrasting with the safety and formula of the telefilm series that replaced the live dramas. This Golden Age is a myth not because its premises are objectively false (although they are certainly arguable), but rather because the term has generated a particular hold and signifying power over television. It is the formative myth of the medium, signifying a lost, "magical" time, which can never be recaptured again, and a diffuse body of work retrospectively designated as "classic." Over the intervening years, this myth has solidified, as all effective myths do, and has become a fixture of television histories. Attempts to tell an alternative TV history, such as William Boddy's *Fifties Television*, must inevitably engage with the myth of the Golden Age.[12] Thus, as the most prominent era in television history, the Golden Age has played a key role in the development of the television heritage.

As Boddy notes, the Golden Age myth had long been impervious due to the widely accepted and unchallenged assumption of television's seemingly perpetual downward trajectory toward banality generated by 1950s and 1960s critics and consistently repeated in most subsequent histories.[13] Horace Newcomb locates the origins of the myth with these critics:

> [N]otions of the 'Golden Age of Television' rely on a very limited set of examples and a particular evaluative scheme that honors particular aesthetic choices. The focus on psychological realism of so-called 'ordinary' characters, on contemporary settings, on nonformulaic narrative structures, and, for most early television critics, on probing particular types of social problems, elevated some of the early live dramas on television into exemplary texts.[14]

While Erik Barnouw, television's first significant historian, makes no explicit reference to the Golden Age in his three-volume study *The Golden Web* nor its condensation, *Tube of Plenty*, the implication is clear in his championing of live anthology drama and scathing treatment of telefilms: in his assessment, television had once been a more open forum for innovative and artistically significant work, and has since been supplanted by formula and conservatism.[15] In addition, as Boddy notes, for many years there were no reference books on past TV programming, so that much of the information about past television remained in the past, out of the reach of present-day scholars. In lieu of direct access to programs, the critical assessments of Barnouw, *New York Times* television critic Jack Gould, and others were handed down as common knowledge.[16]

The myth began almost as soon as the era it encompassed had ended. But it blossomed in the seventies, as biographies, insider accounts, and retrospectives of 1950s programs such as *Your Show of Shows*, *The Honeymooners*, and *The Garry Moore Show*, as well as the aforementioned live dramas, were published, painting a picture of a new, innocent medium, and implying a narrative of innovation and achievement, followed by a grand fall into mediocrity and vulgarity.[17] Accordingly, all of these books approach their subjects through nostalgia, wistfully describing legendary figures and lost times. The fact that many of the most highly regarded programs of the Golden Age were broadcast live, and not recorded on kinescope, added to this nostalgic construction, giving them an almost unimpeachable air of "lost classics." Many programs only existed in memory, through the anecdotes and embellishments of viewers, artists, journalists, and critics. In fact, for some critics, these programs' very ephemerality testified to the romantic appeal of live television (i.e., "you had to be there"). A 1982 *New York Times* op-ed by longtime television writer–director Fielder Cook indicates the appeal of the Golden Age myth along these lines:

> The era was golden, in my estimation, because the productions were essentially in the hands of their creators—and the situation has never been quite the same since. ... The excitement of presenting original thoughts and feelings, of concentrated creative endeavor, plus youth's fierce energies flavored by ever-possible crisis—a heady brew. ... Thus, when the subject of the Golden Era of live drama comes up, it can be fiercely remembered—and justifiably so.[18]

Similarly, the film *My Favorite Year*, released a few months after Cook's reminisces, paints a glossy, romantic picture of this period (1954, to be exact), championing this "fierce energy" of youth through its protagonist, a young TV assistant on a live comedy show similar to *Your Show of Shows*. Cook's account was typical of most Golden Age participants, and was bolstered through other discursive means, not least of which through television itself.[19] Iconic Golden Age performers, including Desi Arnaz, Lucille Ball, Sid Caesar, Milton Berle, Imogene Coca, Jackie Gleason, and Rod Steiger were frequent guests on 1970s TV talk shows like *Dinah, Merv Griffin, Mike Douglas*, and *The Tonight Show*, where they invoked the Golden Age through the ritual anecdotes and lamentations of a bygone era.[20]

However, the primary spark to the Golden Age myth in the seventies (as opposed to earlier) was not so much the programs' "liveness" but rather their "*fifties*-ness." In an increasingly nostalgic era, past television's visual and narrative styles were increasingly perceived as a quick audiovisual reference to "how it was." Accordingly, the Golden Age tag was broadened to incorporate series and genres otherwise far removed from the live dramas with which it was originally associated. It eventually blurred enough to take in virtually any series first produced and aired in the "fifties," a diffuse cultural category that, since the seventies, has stretched from the end of the 1940s to the early Kennedy Administration. The Golden Age began to refer to the time itself (i.e., of American economic and cultural stability) rather than a particular mode of television production. Some key fifties series had long been rerun staples—most notably *I Love Lucy* and *The Honeymooners*—but now found new legitimacy in the seventies under the Golden Age banner. Viacom, the distributor of both of these series, could now market them as classics, as indicated in the text from one trade ad: "Now more than ever, Lucy's madcap antics with Desi Arnaz, Vivian Vance, and William Frawley are praised as priceless performances with timeless appeal."[21] In addition to the most prominent series, eager distributors exhumed several other fifties programs that had not been syndicated in years (if at all), in order to take advantage of the Golden Age mystique. The sketch comedy series *Your Show of Shows* returned to television via the legitimating mechanism of theatrical film; several surviving sketches were blown up from the original kinescopes for 35 mm projection and compiled in a 90-minute feature called *Ten From Your Show of Shows* which had a successful, critically-praised run in revival houses and on college campuses in 1973. The film was later aired on television, and a subsequent package of episodes was moderately successful in syndication.

The Golden Age myth also functioned at a more pragmatic level for many stations. The National Association of Broadcasters' Family Hour mandate, which prevented many more recent off-net series from running in the early evening fringe period, due to their ostensible sex and violence, paved the way for the retrieval of several relatively squeaky-clean series of yesteryear, which were now touted as "family viewing." For example, in 1973, Groucho Marx and his original television producer John Guedel obtained the syndication rights to 235 segments of their *You Bet Your Life* game show, and the series became one of the surprise syndication hits of the 1974–75 season.[22] Similarly, Disney resyndicated the original *Mickey Mouse Club* in 1975, and it quickly became one of the top-rated programs in afternoon syndication, prompting the production of an updated version, which began airing in 1977.[23] The fifties nostalgia binge clearly benefited these syndication efforts, but distributors hoping to create long-term properties also emphasized their programs' timeless appeal. As George Faber of Viacom commented in 1976, "I think there's a certain amount of nostalgia involved but there's a certain amount of professionalism, too. If a show is good, it doesn't matter if it was made in 1950, 1960, or 1970—it's still good."[24] This comment reveals how the discourses of the television heritage enabled different standards of evaluation. Faber's contention that all that matters is if "it's still good" tries to separate a more objective idea of aesthetic value ("good") from the more subjective, emotional discourse of lived time ("nostalgia"). Thus, a Golden Age "classic" may come from the fifties, and may function as a vehicle of nostalgia, but it may also function in the realm of timeless aesthetic quality, i.e., the canon.

Along these lines, some of the most prominent Golden Age texts were broadcast instead on public television, indicating how far TV had come in its quest for cultural legitimation. Public television, after all, was ostensibly meant as the alternative to the commercial networks. In fact, many of the critics who had excoriated commercial television in the 1950s and 1960s had also fought to establish the Public Broadcasting System.

It was thus slightly ironic that past commercial television programs aired at various points on most PBS stations in the seventies. However, the television heritage could only be enhanced by the broadcasting of these programs on the more highbrow venue of public television. In the television industry, PBS may have been dismissed as an economics or ratings threat, but it could also grant a cultural legitimacy that the other networks could not.[25] A retrospective of Edward R. Murrow's news segments aired on PBS in early 1972, a ten-part compilation of Ernie Kovacs sketches ran in 1977, and several famous live dramas, including "Marty," and "Requiem for a Heavyweight," were broadcast in the early 1980s, complete with new interviews with all the principals. In turn, many of these PBS broadcasts were accompanied by critical praise in the press, which echoed the Golden Age myth, even while acknowledging its "mythical" status.[26] These broadcasts and their accompanying coverage linked past television with such conventional high and middlebrow PBS fare as nature documentaries, literary adaptations, and legitimate theater.

The commercial networks also jumped onto the Golden Age band-wagon, seeing it as an opportunity to produce large, ratings-grabbing specials, and promote their own roles in creating the television heritage. NBC was the first network to do this, airing a 4-hour retrospective called *NBC: The First Fifty Years* in November 1976, complete with stentorian narration by Orson Welles.[27] The following season, CBS more than doubled the ante, airing the nine-and-a-half hour, seven-night *CBS: On The Air* to commemorate its own 50-year history in April 1978. ABC had to content itself with a mere 3-hour compilation of its first 25 years of television broadcasting in February 1978. Meanwhile, beginning in the seventies and continuing through to the present, many old series—most of them long-running hits in off-network syndication—were revived as new series, or, as was usually the case, as made-for-TV movies. While the new series often utilized a new cast, thus differentiating them from the original, the movies often focused explicitly on the "reunion" of the series' principals, underlining the production of the television heritage as a form of personal and national memory.[28]

Regardless of how it was conveyed on TV and in popular and main-stream accounts, the Golden Age myth provided television with its first legitimate historical discourse. However, heritages do not consist of only discourses; they are also activated by two critical legitimating mechanisms helped provide a *material* foundation to this history of television.

The Museum and the Archive

While the Golden Age was most heavily promoted by television itself, it could only achieve long-term legitimation through more venerated cultural forms. Enter the Museum and the Archive: arguably, the most vaunted sites of cultural legitimation imaginable in modern societies.

As the ritualized space where society displays its capital-T "Truth"—largely through Art, History, and Science—the Museum legitimates its objects and their relationships to society. The Archive functions in a similar, if less public, manner, consecrating its documents into the raw materials of historical knowledge. While the television heritage was produced through the nostalgia of the Golden Age (in print and on television itself) in the seventies, it was also entering the realm of capital-H "History" in the Museum and the Archive.

As with the formative Golden Age myth, television's first forays into museums lay in the early 1960s. In 1963, the Museum of Modern Art, in conjunction with all three networks, put on a retrospective of television that drew considerable attendance and press notice. The primary draws were the same artifacts of 1950s television that remain on top-ten lists, televised retrospectives, and university screenings to this day: the 1954 *See It Now* series exposing Senator McCarthy, the highly-acclaimed live dramas "Marty" and "Requiem for a Heavyweight," and the comedy of Milton Berle, Sid Caesar, and Jackie Gleason. Thus, the key texts of the Golden Age were already constructed as "history," only a scant few years after their ostensible heyday. Again, this indicates how particular historicizing discourses were already active before explicitly coming together in the seventies. Indeed, the very act of producing a retrospective indicates a perception of change. Despite this sense of legitimated history, however, a sense of nostalgia for the Golden Age is also indicated by the show's curation and echoed in its reception. Lewis Freedman, a MOMA board member who helped select the screened material lamented that the live dramas of only a few years before "would be too strong or too gentle to be acceptable now." Reviewing the exhibition, John P. Shanley of the *New York Times* presciently noted that, "despite its relatively short history, television has already generated a certain nostalgia among its more ardent fans."[29] This indicates already how the television heritage conflates discourses of history and nostalgia, as the emotional contexts of memory are invariably entwined with the ostensibly more objective pursuits of history.

Over a decade later, the Museum of Broadcasting in New York was founded with similar concerns of historical legacy. In this case, however, the primary legacy at stake was that of longtime CBS chairman William S. Paley. As Paley's biographer Sally Bedell Smith commented, "a museum would assure that the man who symbolized television would be linked in the public mind only with the best of a medium that pandered far more than it enriched."[30] Paley was already involved in the Museum of Modern Art, and had a long history of ingratiating himself with the patronage community in New York. He felt that a broadcasting museum would monumentalize television and radio on a more prestigious level than would be possible in other venues, and was closely involved in the museum's organization, location, and architecture (though false modesty ultimately kept his name off the building). Significantly, while other museum planners advocated placing librarians, historians, and similar academics on the museum's board, Paley instead assembled the board from network executives and industry colleagues. Thus, despite the rhetoric of general historical and cultural heritage, Paley and his business cronies largely shaped the Museum of Broadcasting, with the man himself placed conspicuously at its center.[31] Still, the museum, now known as the Museum of Television and Radio, has expanded since its founding, moving to a new location in 1991, and opening a second branch in Los Angeles in 1996. Its primary goal remains cultural legitimation: educating the public about television.

As the Museum began to acknowledge television, so did another repository of legitimate history: the Archive. Archives are arguably even more legitimated cultural sites than museums. The clichéd binary of American academia is a useful analogy in this regard: museums are for "teaching," while archives are for "research." Archives are separated from the general public, so that the raw materials of historical knowledge are carefully preserved, their secrets waiting to be discovered by legitimate scholars. It is no coincidence that the most prestigious archival collections, unlike the most vaunted museums, are located at universities. In 1965, the Academy of Television Arts and Sciences (ATAS) sought to establish "historically representative" television libraries at NYU, American University, and UCLA. A board comprised of a mixture of academic, creative, and business figures initially screened the material selected to represent television history.[32] Other collections were soon started in the 1960s and 1970s at other universities, preserving the materials of television for historical research. During the mid-1970s, amidst the wider formation of the television heritage, these preservation efforts were considerably stepped up, as a coalition of historians and librarians sought to prioritize the material preservation of television texts. Speaking at the 1975 conference of the Popular Culture Association, American Film Institute director George Stevens, Jr. declared that past television was a "visual transcript of our culture." Noting that only 5% of programs produced since 1948 had been "consciously saved," and that the television industry had thus far shown little interest in preservation *per se*, he advocated more federal leadership in preservation.[33] The following year he obtained his wish, as a provision of the massive Copyright Revision Act of 1976 mandated that:

> The Librarian of Congress is directed to establish and maintain in the Library a library to be known as the "American Television and Radio Archives," the purpose of which is to preserve a permanent record of television and radio programs and to provide access to the programs to historians and scholars without encouraging or causing copyright infringement.[34]

These archives have facilitated the historical construction of television, relocating it from American living rooms to the hallowed, academically legitimated halls of written documentation.

Significantly, most of these historically legitimated materials, whether in museums and archives, have related to the creative rather than either the industrial or reception aspects of television, and have generally consisted of individual programs or entire series available on film and video, and the final drafts of scripts. While other areas of the production and reception of television—e.g., legal contracts, memoranda, viewer letters, etc.—are preserved in some collections, it is clear that artifacts conforming most to the traditional concept of the text are the primary mode of preservation. Moreover, the collection of props and sets from particular television series at the Smithsonian (including Archie Bunker's chair, and the Fonz' leather jacket), bolsters this construction of the heritage, locating its power in the familiar, mythical artifacts of television itself, rather than the more complex practices that brought these objects to the air to begin with. Thus, the heritage is largely constructed, even at the level of "legitimate" history, out of textual artifacts. Television is effectively remembered through its creative and cultural practices, rather than through its industrial practices or social effects.

Television in the Nation–Family

While the discursive function of the Museum and Archive is to represent and reproduce the nation, most popular writing on the television heritage in the seventies placed the medium firmly in the family, foregrounding personal memories of television, and even anthropomorphizing the set itself as a member of the family. However, the family, as constructed in this writing, is also emblematic of "America," encapsulating a nation–family centered largely on a representation of an archetypal fifties nuclear family. Accordingly, the television heritage is located in the home *and* the nation; the two concepts are elided.

As befitting a seventies (or rather, postsixties) representation of the nation–family, a perception of change permeates this era's writing about television, conveying a sense that the current times were different, and that the development of television was not only indicative of the changes of the recent past, but had helped produce them. In his 1974 study *Yearning For Yesterday*, sociologist Fred Davis speculated about the seventies' turn toward nostalgia. Drawing from Henri Bergson's concept of the *durée*, or "lived time," Davis argued "the ability to feel nostalgia for events in our past has less (although clearly something) to do with how recent or distant these events are than with the way they contrast— or, more accurately, the way we *make* them contrast—with the events, moods, and dispositions of our present circumstances."[35] By the early 1970s, the "lived time" of most Americans had gone through considerable changes; the Eisenhower era, only 15 years removed, seemed like another century. The perception of change was great, and thus the recent past was reexamined via nostalgia throughout the culture.

First and second person address was almost standard in this writing, suggesting a generalized experience of television that both reader and author shared as baby boomers. The baby boom generation had emerged into the shiny new post-World War II world as the children of the American Century, had enjoyed greatly expanded social spaces for youth culture, had shocked their parents with revolutionary styles of dress, behavior, music, chemical stimulation, and sexuality as teens in the sixties, and had taken center stage during one of the most tumultuous periods in the nation's history. Emerging into adulthood in the seventies, they viewed the changes of the recent past through their own life experiences. They looked back through their lives—to their fifties childhoods in particular—sharing their experiences with others of their generational cohort, thus creating a more stable sense of identity. This corresponds to what Davis called "nostalgic sharing." Davis writes that this is typical behavior of young adults *per se*, in any period: "nostalgic sharing enhances the sense of our own normalcy, something which adolescents and young adults stand in special need of, given the social dislocations and identity strains to which they are subject."[36] By addressing themselves and their audience as a common "we" the authors blurred concepts of nation, family, and generation fostered through television viewing in recent American history, placing the medium at the center of personal and social experience: television has "grown" and "we" have watched. Since the general tenor of these works is nostalgic, rather than historical, however, both television's past and present are described with ambivalence. Fifties television is idealized through the authors' memories as innocence lost, often comparing favorably to seventies television, but also lacking the latter's perceived sophistication. It wasn't so much that television—or the nation, generation, or family—had objectively degraded *or* improved; rather, as with growing from childhood to adulthood, there had been perceived trade-offs along the way.

Jeff Greenfield's July 1971 *New York Times Magazine* cover story on past television marked the first nostalgic paean to the medium in the "paper of record." He opened with a series of poetic vignettes of 1950s television, mentioning Milton Berle, Ozzie Nelson, Hopalong Cassidy, and Gorgeous George; all figures conjured from the mists of memory. He went on to link the experiences of television with the maturing of his generation, the Baby Boom, and was ambivalent about how television should ultimately be remembered:

> Yes, there were moments. Mary Martin and Ethel Merman singing on two stools for an hour; Sid Caesar, only 26 when he began on network TV with a brilliant stable of writers under 30...Ernie Kovacs and his electronic

wizardry and cheerful misanthropy; "See It Now" and the determined presence of Edward R. Murrow. . . . Yet what remains, the images that force their way back to the surface, are the collected remnants of incredible witlessness and outright stupidity: a self-portrait of a country coming out of a war for self-preservation and into a time that did not turn out the way it was supposed to. . . . We are still in a sense trying to come to grips with the things we learned about America at the knee of the 7-inch DuMont. [37]

Past television is an unsettling specter throughout the article and its presentation. TV screen-shaped images of past stars and vintage 1950s *Times* cartoons about television conveyed a typically nostalgic "Do You Remember?" tone to the article's illustration, but Greenfield was not quite as wistful. In his account, television's clear successes were relatively few, adhering closely to the Golden Age myth, while the medium's overall effect on its first generation was not quite as positive.

This ambivalent treatment of past television particularly surfaced when the subject of reruns was broached. Reruns were convenient subjects for analysis for seventies journalistic critics writing about television nostalgia; after all, they were readily available *on* television. The fact that reruns— via the regime of repetition—had helped produce this nostalgia was never remarked upon; indeed, the effect seemed to go the other way around in many critics' minds. In Chicago, UHF station WSNS (channel 44) was particularly bullish about its fifties rerun slate, prompting several features from *Chicago Tribune* television critic Gary Deeb. Noting the station's fall 1974 schedule, Deeb wrote that WSNS "continues to revive the Eisenhower era with a vengeance." A few months later, he reported that WSNS' airings of *Superman* were phenomenally successful, giving the station its highest-ever daytime ratings, and inspiring adult baby boomers to petition the station to air the series in the evening. Deeb wrote that this series' revival was particularly nostalgic, and could even be "labeled 'camp,' if it weren't for the fact that the show was 'camp' even during its initial run in the early '50s." [38] However, when covering WSNS' acquisition of *I Love Lucy* in 1977, Deeb was finding the whole endeavor to be getting a bit tiresome: "Our nation . . . seems to be trapped in such a militant adoration of the 1950s that virtually anything belonging to the sleepy Eisenhower era is the automatic recipient of coast-to-coast hosannas." [39] In each of his features on WSNS, Deeb describes reruns as embarassing, yet endearing, artifacts from the past. They virtually haunt the present (or at least Chicago's airwaves) in his analysis, representing a particularly visible incarnation of the fifties.

John Leonard of the *New York Times* found the mix of past TV to be particularly salient to the issue of children's television viewing. By the mid-1970s, weekday afternoons on local stations usually featured programs from the 1950s and 1960s, as well as cartoons and live action comedy shorts dating back as far as the 1930s (e.g., *The Little Rascals*). Observing his own children watching this unprecedented mix of past and present, Leonard reflected, "there are very few moments from the TV past that our children will not witness, over and over again. ... By and large, our children not only watch the same *new* programs that we watch, but they are scholars of everything that went before, everything we have forgotten or never knew."[40] Television is here cited as an historical source, but an historical source out of the range and control Leonard is familiar with. TV presented "everything that went before," in his estimation, but this is the pre-cable, pre-video, pre-Internet, pre-TiVo television of the 1970s; the regime of repetition has expanded exponentially since 1976, and Leonard's children, contemporaries, and *their* children have always known this experience of television.[41]

Feature articles about television nostalgia were significant, but sporadic. Many books on past television were published throughout the seventies that crystallized the ambivalent nostalgic discourse, lamenting the past gone by, but pointing out the continuities to the television of today. In these more comprehensive productions, the television heritage is not entirely distinct from the present, but continues to exist in activated memories and the legacies of contemporary programming.

Irving Settel and William Laas' *Pictorial History of Television* was published in 1969, but it already indicated how some of these nostalgic tropes were beginning to factor into writing about the medium. Their television history is ambivalent, indicating a voguish allusion to McLuhan, but skeptical of his optimism:

> In scarcely twenty years, a new kind of communication has wrought a cultural revolution, but it has done so in the guise of fun. All but the youngest readers will recall with nostalgia the great moments pictured here, whether 'great' in the memorable sense or the notorious. We were there, with our eyes glued to the flickering tube. We saw it grow in size and in competence; we felt its influence, though hardly realizing what it was doing to us. Now we know. Let us see how it came about.[42]

In this passage, television has "happened," and the book is situated as an attempt to make sense of its transformation of the national family. Television is a "fun cultural revolution" in Settel and Laas' estimation, a striking metaphor suggesting a transformation as quick and encompassing as Mao Tse-Tung's contemporary remaking of China, yet more enjoyable, thanks to the pleasures of postwar capitalism as presented on TV.

Arthur Shulman and Roger Youman's *The Television Years* is a 1973 collection of photographs and pithy "remember when"-type statements listed in chronological order from 1948 to 1972. Each of their "years" is christened with a title that encapsulates its "essence:" e.g., 1948 is The Year of Uncle Miltie, 1952 is The Year of the Polite Cop, and 1966 is The Year of the Bat. Past television thus becomes organized into convenient categories and short commentaries ideally suited as a trivia reference. Shulman and Youman also take the generational identity position, but to a new height of anthropomorphism:

> We witnessed the arrival of this miraculous gadget. It seemed childlike and innocent, eager for our attention and affection. We played with it, laughed at it, marveled as it learned new tricks, and watched expectantly to see what it would do next. We have seen it grow into a powerful giant. Confident that it has us in its thrall, it is too big and strong to wonder whether we still love it, yet always worried that we may not respect it.[43]

Television is a growing, sentient being in this conception, a somewhat sentimental rhetorical figure, but a telling one as well. This relationship is intimate and reciprocal, as that between siblings, or parents and children. Significantly, "we" relate to television in this book; it is part of "our" daily lives.

While the television set is constructed as a child in Shulman and Youman's book, past television programming is also described as the avatar of childhood comfort in much of this writing. In *The Great Television Heroes*, Donald F. Glut and Jim Harmon review dozens of children's and adventure series from the 1950s and 1960s. Like others who wrote about television nostalgia during this era, they admit that while some of earlier television was "bad," many series "have remained fondly in our memories." Here, past television is a safe zone of cozy childhood memories, devoid of the "difficult" issues of contemporary television. The television heritage is used here as an escape into a simpler past. Again, the nation and family are elided. Glut and Harmon invite the reader to return to a seemingly less cynical time, before the "hostilities of the Bunker family," or "the insipid formula plots and abysmal animation" of current Saturday morning cartoons, or "someone [trying] to teach you the number 3 or the letter R": "yes, those were more innocent days in which we, also more innocent, lived and found entertainment in this phenomenal new instrument of information."[44]

While these publications were completely and unabashedly awash in nostalgia and trivia, even the more systematic, researched, and respected reference works published later (in the late 1970s and early 1980s) were not averse to nostalgic citation. In the introduction to his 1977 *The Complete Encyclopedia of Television Programs, 1947–1976*, Vincent Terrace entices his readers with cherished television memories: "contained within these pages are nostalgic excursions into a time past...."[45] Tim Brooks and Earle Marsh's *The Complete Directory of Prime Time Network TV Shows*, the American Book Award-winning, standard reference work on the subject over six editions and 25 years, vacillates between rendering its subject as nostalgia or as historical knowledge. In the introduction to the first edition, published in 1979, the authors list 30 years of TV memories available in the book—ranging from Milton Berle to the Fonz—and then claim that "this is not simply a book of nostalgia": "This volume has been carefully researched for the scholar who wants to know what happened and when. But it is also—like TV itself—for your enjoyment."[46] In a similar vein, the introduction to Alex McNeil's equally respected *Total Television* notes that "more than half of the population alive today has never known life without television," and lists a panoply of the usual figures and events of past television—Dave Garroway, Captain Kangaroo, Lucy, Johnny Carson, the moon landing—that "we" have all watched.[47]

It is significant that the academic study of past television—which has always relied extensively upon these works—is placed conspicuously besides nostalgic browsing in the general understanding of the medium. While this approach no doubt made for an easier sell to large publishers, it also indicates the concept of the television heritage at its most powerful. As Lynn Spigel has argued, our experience of television is inextricably bound with the postwar expansion of the domestic sphere.[48] When the regime of repetition is factored in to television's domesticity, it seems inevitable that television's "history" would become as familiar as our family memories. Accordingly, the television heritage is shared by "all," or at least all who recognize its authority over American cultural memory. As a consequence, even in the era of legitimation opened up in the seventies, television scholars and historians have had to struggle to discursively locate past television not only as a gauzy array of vivid images and warm memories, but as a culturally and socially significant force worthy of serious, academically-sanctioned study.

Television Studies

While the academic study of television was still dominated by the psychological methods of the mass communications school, during the seventies television began to be understood as not only a set of psychic triggers, but also as a bearer of myth, history, and social representation. A new generation of intellectuals who had grown up in the era of television sought to complicate the either-or pronouncements that had largely comprised television criticism to that point. They were interested more in what television actually *was* than in what it ostensibly *did*. Drawing from new cultural theories and methods that valued culture on its own terms, these scholars began to put forward models of studying television in the seventies that fully blossomed into humanities-based Television Studies in the eighties and nineties. Their scholarly work should be seen as part of the television heritage, helping foster ways in which television was productively linked to questions of culture, memory, and history.

To be sure, there were then, and continue to be, many viable approaches to television in the academy. The mass communications methods dominant prior to and during the seventies have certainly not disappeared, and other schools of thought (e.g., "media ecology," political economy, policy studies, uses and gratifications, etc.) have also been influential. The difference with the humanities-based approach is its focus on particular television institutions, texts, and practices. It rarely describes the medium as an unbroken whole, or undifferentiated force. Rather, it focuses on how specific components of the medium, such as programs, stars, producers, networks, or audiences function to produce "television" as a major form of popular culture. The growing legitimation of past television helped enable an approach that assessed the medium's specific contributions to American culture.

Television's first, and most influential historian was Eric Barnouw, a veteran radio and television journalist. Barnouw completed his three-volume history of American broadcasting—still the standard compre-hensive overview of radio and television in the United States—in 1968, fostering new scholarly interest in the television and radio past. However, history was not the only new approach available to seventies television scholars. The Aspen Institute Program on Communications and Society, led by Richard Adler and Douglass Cater, held several conferences in the mid-1970s which sought to establish television as a subject within the humanities. While the ostensible goal was to generate the kind of text-focused critical standards that were already applied to other media, the essays in the two anthologies that resulted from the conferences— *Television as a Social Force* (1975) and *Television as a Cultural Force* (1976)—indicate the shifting nature of the perception of television. In Richard Adler's introduction to the second volume, he repeated many of the complaints offered by the authors of the critical anthology *The Eighth Art* 14 years earlier, claiming that "[t]elevision has become the primary source of news and entertainment for most Americans, yet it is ignored as a subject of serious criticism. By serious criticism, I mean the informed response and analysis that exists in abundance for literature, film, drama, and the other performing arts."[49] Adler wrote that the medium's centrality to American culture—even more pronounced in 1976 than in 1962—was not being acknowledged in criticism, and that "we"— i.e., intellectuals, scholars, and critics—were conditioned to disregard television. "While we are taught from an early age to be critical readers," he notes, "we learn at an even earlier age that television is watched without reflection."[50] At the end of the essay, Adler made a significant yet subtle claim for television not as an artistic form, but as a cultural form. He wrote that television is best thought of as a mediator "between fact and fantasy, between our desire to escape and our need to deal with real problems; between our old values and new ideas; between our individual lives and life of the nation and the world."[51] In this passage, as in the use of the word "force" in the titles of both anthologies, the editors attempt to locate television within the everyday life of the nation, rather than as just another creative medium. Their interest in its culture was meant to foster a humanistic, historical understanding of the medium as a significant part of American culture.

On a more critical and influential level, however, Horace Newcomb's 1974 *TV: The Most Popular Art* should be regarded as the founding text of U.S. television studies.[52] Writing explicitly against the dismissive tone of the mass culture thesis and the scientific methods of the mass communications school, Newcomb carefully separated television into discrete genres, describing it first-and-foremost as a textual medium. In doing so, however, he was cognizant of the limits of the aesthetic model, and connected television's aesthetics to its cultural role. He was the first to closely examine how television is an essentially formulaic medium. But rather than use the term as mere pejorative, Newcomb argued that TV's unique formulae reveal how the medium dramatizes social and cultural issues in an easily digestible form.[53]

For example, Newcomb makes a particularly strong case for the sitcom—and its subsidiary, the domestic comedy—as narrative forms completely unique to television. Rather than start from the perspective of earlier critics who railed at television's perceived "lacks" in comparison to other media, Newcomb suggests that sitcoms are the medium's quintessential narrative form, and should be understood within those parameters. Significantly, the example he chooses to illustrate this is the star persona of Lucille Ball, a model that could only have come from attention to the regime of repetition and the new television heritage. Newcomb regards Lucy as an historical icon of television performance:

> [The sitcom] form allows Lucy to excel and in it we find many of the elements essential to any understanding of television as popular art. It is a paradigm for what occurs in more complex program types, and its perennial popularity is probably due to the relatively simple outline it follows. There is something here that allows us to do more than enjoy and laugh. Something makes us 'love' Lucy.[54]

Again, "we" are inscribed in the national family, as with the nostalgic writers above. But Newcomb locates our enjoyment of Lucy, and of sitcoms in general, in distinct narrative forms. These forms, experienced over time, reinforce television's cultural significance. This significant thesis—that individual television texts matter to the culture—would become a fundamental principle of critical television study.

In the wake of Newcomb's landmark foray into television studies, the critical and scholarly methods and perspectives that now define the field began to emerge more clearly. The first edition of *Television: The Critical View*, edited by Newcomb, was published in 1976, and posited a new field of television research distinct from both aesthetic criticism and social science. Noting that those forms of analysis did not allow for a television heritage, or anything less than a general condemnation of the medium,

Newcomb called for more "careful descriptions" and "histories" of television programming.[55]

As essays in the Adler and Cater, and Newcomb anthologies indicate, the "relevant" sitcoms of the early 1970s, including *The Mary Tyler Moore Show*, *M*A*S*H*, and *All In The Family*, were popular subjects of early television studies, and were the first comedies—as opposed to news and live drama—to be legitimated as historically significant to both television *per se* and American culture. The reasons for this designation perhaps lie at the critical perception of the sitcom as television's quintessential genre, and further indicate how televisual repetition had structured the perception of the medium. These series succeeded in the general critical view not so much because they were thoroughly "new"—even if often referred to at the time as "the new television"—but because they engaged with and altered familiar sitcom conventions and narrative forms. Here, Newcomb comments on *All In The Family*:

> Patterned after the domestic comedy, it challenges every stereotype of that formula, and at times pushes to the edges of the most complex artistic productions. It is another mark of the deep cultural base of television that the innovations of "All In The Family" may be seen again as directly related to the family patterns established in more conventional forms of comedy.[56]

This perception could only have been possible by the continual presence of off-network reruns on local television. The "established family patterns" Newcomb refers to were constructed largely out of the reruns of popular family sitcoms of the fifties.

If *All In The Family* represented the state of the art of seventies television—it was mentioned in virtually every comparative account of U.S. television, and Archie Bunker even graced the cover of the first edition of *TV: The Most Popular Art*—then its antithesis was any of several late 1950s family sitcoms, such as *Leave It To Beaver*, *Father Knows Best*, or *Ozzie and Harriet*. Because the realism of *All In The Family* was considered its greatest virtue, the Cleaver, Anderson, and Nelson families of the earlier sitcoms functioned as cultural and sociological ciphers, markers of what "we" *had been*, while the Bunkers represented the family of the present:

> Physically the show [*All In The Family*] is an example of a way of life common to much of the audience. It stands in direct contradiction to the dreamlike world of most situation-domestic comedy. Rather than being a sample of the fantasy world of the American middle-class life, it is the representation of an actual world.[57]

While this conflation of the Bunker household with reality would be critiqued in the eighties, it is significant that the concern with social and cultural "relevance" would become the first critical benchmark in seventies Television Studies. Through such designation, the lines of an academic television heritage were drawn.[58]

While the work of these scholars laid the groundwork for television studies in the United States, by the early 1980s the insights of European theory and (in particular) British cultural studies began to be incorporated. During the 1970s, British scholars such as John Fiske, Stuart Hall, John Hartley, Raymond Williams, and the Birmingham Group had advanced a more critical approach to popular culture than was possible in the U.S. context. Their work combined a broadly Marxist conception of a class-based society with British sociological method, including content analysis and ethnography. The 1983 anthology *Regarding Television* is a key collection in the history of American television studies in this regard, as it indicates how these new British approaches were beginning to make their way across the Atlantic. It gathered essays that exemplified "new critical and theoretical approaches to commercial television," many of which remain classic studies to this day.[59] E. Ann Kaplan's introduction to the volume explicitly seeks a separation from the mass communications school: "This book aims to correct the one-sided disciplinary approach to television by offering articles written largely by people trained in film and in the humanities."[60] In one of the essays, William Boddy reviewed the available television literature, and found fault with not only the mass communications approach, but with the crusading aesthetic critics of the fifties and sixties who overvalued "quality" television. Echoing the loosely deconstructive ethos of the collection and its essayists, Boddy called for a questioning of the established terms of television study, and a new focus on long-neglected historical, economic, and theoretical concerns: "[The] new cultural critics recognize the social contradictions within the prevailing uses of media, and with them the grounds for cultural intervention. Their recent contributions from social theory, historiography, and textual analysis offer hope for a *theory* of television worthy of the name."[61]

By the eighties, television studies was situated as a significant component of academic cultural criticism distinct from prevailing aesthetic, mass culture and mass communication methods, and premised instead on an historical and theoretical sensibility. The nascent television heritage of the seventies provided a background of mainstream historical and cultural awareness from which this academic attention could function.

Television Fandom

While the academic study of television was expanding beyond its quantitative shell, many regular, nonacademic viewers were developing their own methods of understanding the medium and constructing the television heritage. Self-identified as fans, these viewers produced a wide variety of intensive and organized texts and practices centered around particular television series. While there had been a long history of industrially-promoted, "official fan clubs" of particular figures, many late 1960s television viewers began to formally organize themselves around their favorite series, often in an antagonistic stance to the "powers that be," i.e., the network or station broadcasting (or *not* broadcasting) their series. However, televisual repetition furnished daily reruns of favorite series, fostering, to a large degree, the entire idea of television fandom. Rerun syndication enabled viewers to see the same episodes multiple times, on a regular basis, thus encouraging the development of discourses and knowledge centered on particular series.

The most prominent example of this active viewing practice is the fandom centered on science fiction series *Star Trek*, which originated in the 1967–69 letter writing campaigns to get NBC to renew the series. Although these efforts were only partially successful—the series was eventually cancelled after three seasons—they laid the foundation for the fandom which fully flowered in the seventies, when the cancelled series became a surprise hit in off-network syndication, prompting the formation of local clubs nationwide, and the first phenomenally successful conventions based around the series.[62] As described by Henry Jenkins in *Textual Poachers*, fan communities take a proactive stance towards television, producing extensive creative works inspired by their favorite texts, and fostering a sense of community and identity based around the appreciation and understanding of particular series.[63] While the fans of *Star Trek* and other science fiction series have gained far and away the most notoriety of any fandom, many other series have generated comparable viewer communities. For example, fans of *The Andy Griffith Show*, *I Love Lucy*, and *The Honeymooners* have long produced a similarly extensive culture of events, publications, and groups based around their favorite programs. Similarly, more recent programs such as *The X-Files*, *Xena: Warrior Princess*, *Buffy The Vampire Slayer*, and *Farscape* have also engendered active fan followings through first-run episodes and the inevitable reruns.

Jenkins writes, "participating within fandom fundamentally alters the ways one relates to television and the meanings one derives from its contents."[64] While he warns that these exceptional fan formations are by no means indicative of television viewers in general, and that there are important and innumerable differences in production and ideology between and within various fandoms, I believe it is at least plausible to suggest that these groups and their practices have added to the overall historical construction of the television heritage since the seventies, helping legitimate television (and particularly *past* television) in myriad ways as a culturally significant medium. Truly popular culture, even television, always transcends its commodified roots; it means something other than just economics or just entertainment. Fans' multivocal and increasingly public appropriations of their series are another indication of how television had entered a new cultural stature in the seventies, and had acquired its own sense of heritage.

Rerun Nation 1976

The reconsideration of television that coalesced into the television heritage in the seventies affected how the medium was subsequently programmed, promoted, viewed, critiqued, celebrated, studied, and most importantly, remembered. The regime of repetition, which had already proven economically successful, was now applied across a broader cultural terrain. Discrete aspects of television—series, stars, slogans, and styles—became recognized as part of America's cultural heritage. From this period onward, past television would be a valid terrain of national memory, critical analysis, and fan activity, an array of texts and figures which could engage with contemporary social and cultural concerns: a *television heritage*.

The television industry was clearly cognizant of these developments. Even as the heritage was forming, it began to convert the increased cultural value of the heritage into the economic capital of televisual repetition. At the same time, as the previous chapter indicated, the most sweeping FCC broadcasting regulations in a generation attempted to reshape the industry. The next chapter explores how rerun syndication was reconceived in light of these changes, helping create a media industry more tied to cultural repetition than ever before.

Notes

1. John Leonard, "Old Sitcoms and Young Minds," *New York Times*, 28 March 1976, sec. B, p. 27.

2. Qtd. in "Paley opens broadcasting's own museum," *Broadcasting*, 15 November 1976, pp. 54–55.

3. John J. O'Connor, "'Prisoner' on TV tonight," *New York Times*, 16 January 1978, sec. III, p. 29.

4. I use words (e.g., "seventies") to describe a cultural period that centers on, but does not necessarily fall within, particular years. I use the actual years (e.g., "1975") to identify a more specific date.

5. Gary Deeb, "Ozzie Nelson: a nice guy who finished first," *Chicago Tribune*, 5 June 1975, sec. C, p. 11.

6. "Heritage," *Merriam-Webster's Collegiate Dictionary* (10th Ed.) (Springfield, MA: Merriam-Webster, 1996), 543.

7. Most commercial stations ran a few hours of off-network reruns during the daytime, in addition to the requisite old feature films in the afternoon and late night.

8. Bart Andrews, *Lucy & Ricky & Fred & Ethel: The Story of 'I Love Lucy'* (New York: E.P. Dutton, 1976), 7; Les Margulies, "Reruns: oldies for you, goodies for TV coffers," *Chicago Tribune*, 27 January 1976, sec. C, p. 8.

9. This irony is amplified by the cable network's programming, which has consisted almost exclusively of formulaic sitcoms, prompting an appropriately "jokey" tone. See Chapter 7 for more extensive analysis of Nick At Nite and TV Land.

10. Kent Anderson, *Television Fraud: The History and Implications of the Quiz Show Scandals* (Westport, CT: Greenwood Press, 1978), xi–xii.

11. Anderson, *Television Fraud*, 181.

12. William Boddy, *Fifties Television: The Industry and its Critics* (Champaign-Urbana, IL: University of Illinois Press, 1990).

13. Boddy, *Fifties Television*, 4–5.

14. Horace Newcomb, "The Opening of America: Meaningful Difference in 1950s Television," in Joel Foreman, ed., *The Other Fifties: Interrogating Midcentury American Icons* (Urbana, IL: University of Illinois Press, 1997), 108.

15. Erik Barnouw, *Tube of Plenty: The Evolution of American Television (2nd Revised Edition)* (New York: Oxford University Press, 1990), 154–167, 193–198, 213–218.

16. Boddy, *Fifties Television*, 5.

17. These include Bart Andrews, *Lucy & Ricky & Fred & Ethel: The Story of 'I Love Lucy'* (New York: E.P. Dutton, 1976); Donna McCrohan, *The Honeymooners' Companion: The Kramdens and The Nortons Revisited* (New York: Workman, 1978); and Ted Sennett, *Your Show of Shows* (New York: Collier, 1977).

18. Fielder Cook, "Why early TV was a golden era for drama," *New York Times*, 14 February 1982, sec. B, p. 31.

19. There were some dissenting views, however. In the 1973 autobiography *How the Golden Age of Television Turned My Hair to Silver*, director Kenneth Whelan remarked that the Golden Age "was not as Golden as you might remember." While there were considerable talents, they were few and far between, according to Whelan: "Yes there were several pure nuggets that created the myth of the Golden Age, but most of live television was just plain brass. ... The age of live television has been dead for 14 years. It is over and done with, and it will never return. ... Thank God!" Kenneth Whelan, *How the Golden Age of Television Turned My Hair to Silver* (New York: Walker and Company, 1973), 209–212.

20. In a telling mix of nostalgia, irony, and the "romance" of live television, Arnaz, Berle, Rick Nelson and even *Highway Patrol* star Broderick Crawford appeared as guest hosts of NBC's *Saturday Night Live* during the 1970s, sending up their 1950s TV personas and tacitly acknowledging the contributions of this new generation of television performers.

Their appearances could only have been possible under the regime of repetition, which had kept their star personas in circulation for decades. Thanks to Daniel Marcus for pointing this out.

21. Qtd. in Andrews, *Lucy & Ricky & Fred & Ethel*, 5.

22. Lee Dembart, "Groucho's 1950s Quiz Show is a Hit All Over Again," *New York Times*, 9 March 1975, sec. B, pp. 1+.

23. Though the burgeoning television heritage had certainly included references to *The Howdy Doody Show*, an updated version of this program was attempted in first-run syndication in 1976, and while it featured original host Buffalo Bob Smith, it was not successful. See Hal Erickson, *Syndicated Television: The First Forty Years, 1947–1987* (Jefferson, NC: McFarland, 1989), 200–201.

24. Qtd. in Les Margulies, "Reruns: oldies for you, goodies for TV coffers," *Chicago Tribune*, 27 January 1976, sec. C, p. 8.

25. This cultural legitimacy did not end with the Golden Age, as subsequent programs and series were rebroadcast on public television. In 1979, CBS News granted PBS stations unlimited rights to its 1960s and 1970s documentaries. Other commercial series were aired on local PBS stations as well during this time, lending them a similar air of credibility and legitimation. *The Prisoner*, a British commercial series that had originally run in the United States on CBS in 1968, was a particularly prevalent staple of PBS stations in the 1970s and 1980s, while some stations even ran *Star Trek*. The cultural battles over television were far from over, however. When Phoenix PBS station KAET began airing *The Twilight Zone* in 1981, Nick Salerno, the host of its *Cinema Classics* series of classical Hollywood films, resigned in protest.

26. The 1980 rebroadcast of "Requiem For A Heavyweight" inspired Richard Shepard to wax nostalgic about live television drama: "There is still challenge and tension in television, but the feeling of now or never that was once pervasive is somewhat harder to be found. . . . If nostalgia clouds actuality, this showing of 'Requiem' indicates that above the clouds there is a true gold quality worth remembering." Richard F. Shepard, "First rerun of a 24-year-old hit drama," *New York Times*, 22 August 1980, sec. C, p. 23.

27. Ironically, Welles' radio voice had actually become famous over on CBS in the 1930s.

28. Sasha Torres examines how particular series, and reruns in particular, function to perform national memory in "War and Remembrance: Televisual Narrative, National Memory, and *China Beach*," *Camera Obscura* 33–34 (Spring 1994–Winter 1995): 147–165.

29. Qtd. in John P. Shanley, "Fans relive infancy of TV at museum's kinescope series," *New York Times*, 6 April 1963, p. 47.

30. Sally Bedell Smith, *In All His Glory: The Life of William S. Paley, the Legendary Tycoon and His Brilliant Circle* (New York: Simon and Schuster, 1990), 514–515.

31. As Arthur Taylor, a Paley aide fired just before the museum's grand opening in 1976, commented, "what he did was to create a monument to broadcasting, knowing he was Broadcasting. He pushed ahead and took an aggressive approach to cementing his position in history." Qtd. in Smith, *In All His Glory*, 515.

32. Val Adams, "Libraries to house films of TV shows back to 1948," *New York Times*, 12 May 1965, p. 95.

33. Qtd. in Les Brown, "Program Archive for TV Proposed," *New York Times*, 22 March 1975, p. 63. Stevens' comments on the television industry were telling, indicating a general misunderstanding of the role of reruns and syndication in the health of the industry. On the contrary, syndicators and producers were quite interested in "preservation," in a general sense, as long as it maintained their programs' long-term viability as syndication properties. As the controversy surrounding the 1998 "AFI 100" list of films slated for perpetual preservation indicated, if there is no profit in preservation—in this case, from the reissues of restored films in theaters and on home video formats—there is little incentive for firms to preserve their properties.

34. U.S. Congress, Copyright Revision Act of 1976, P.L. 94–553 (S. 22), 19 October 1976, 533. Erik Barnouw, the most prominent US broadcasting historian at the time, was selected as the archive's first director, a position he served from 1978 to 1981.

35. Fred Davis, *Yearning For Yesterday: A Sociology of Nostalgia* (New York: Free Press, 1974), 11–12.

36. Davis, *Yearning For Yesterday*, 43–44.

37. Jeff Greenfield, "A Member of the First TV Generation Looks Back," *New York Times Magazine*, 4 July 1971, p. 11.

38. Gary Deeb, "Superman rescues ch. 44," *Chicago Tribune*, 5 December 1974, sec. C, p. 16.

39. Gary Deeb, "Channel 44 'loves Lucy' but is it merely for the love of the '50s?," *Chicago Tribune*, 6 January 1977, sec. B, p. 10.

40. Leonard, "Old Sitcoms," sec. B, p. 27.

41. Those contemporaries include this author (born 1969), who spent all too many weekday afternoons in the 1970s watching 40 years of cartoons, sitcoms and action series.

42. Irving Settel and William Laas, *A Pictorial History of Television* (New York: Grosset & Dunlap, 1969), vii.

43. Arthur Shulman and Roger Youman, *The Television Years* (New York: Popular Library, 1973), 6.

44. Donald F. Glut and Jim Harmon, *The Great Television Heroes* (New York: Doubleday, 1975), viii.

45. Vincent Terrace, *The Complete Encyclopedia of Television Programs, 1947–1976* (New York: A.S. Barnes and Company, 1976).

46. Tim Brooks and Earle Marsh, *The Complete Directory to Prime Time Network TV Shows: 1946-Present* (New York: Ballantine, 1979), ix. In the 1980s, they produced pocket-sized spin-offs of their larger book that concentrated on only the most popular series, or on particular genres.

47. Alex McNeil, *Total Television: The Comprehensive Guide to Programming From 1948 to the Present, 4th Edition* (New York: Penguin Books, 1996).

48. Lynn Spigel, *Make Room For TV* (Chicago: University of Chicago, 1992).

49. Richard Adler, "Introduction: A Context For Criticism," in Richard Adler and Douglass Cater, eds., *Television as a Cultural Force* (New York: Praeger, 1976), 1–16.

50. Adler, "Introduction," 6.

51. Adler, "Introduction," 13.

52. While there are several books and articles that predate *TV: The Most Popular Art* (including Raymond Williams' equally seminal *Television: Technology and Cultural Form*), I regard Newcomb's work as formative in the development of a humanities-based Television Studies in the U.S.

53. Horace Newcomb, *TV: The Most Popular Art* (New York: Doubleday Press, 1974), 59.

54. Newcomb, *TV*, 27.

55. Horace Newcomb, *Television: The Critical View* (New York: Oxford University Press, 1976), xv.

56. Newcomb, *TV*, 219.

57. Newcomb, *TV*, 220.

58. This may also partially explain the lag in the academic study of *past* television series and practices, which would not fully surface until the late 1980s. Significant historical works like William Boddy's study of the 1950s television industry, and Lynn Spigel's analysis of the domestic nature of early television, did not reach publication until the beginning of the 1990s. Similarly, the first academic anthology on sixties television, *The Revolution Wasn't Televised*, was only published in 1997.

59. Among the essays in the collection were Jane Feuer, "The Concept of Live Television: Ontology as Ideology"; Tania Modleski, "The Rhythms of Reception: Daytime Television and Women's Work"; Charlotte Brunsdon, "*Crossroads*: Notes on Soap Opera"; and Robert C. Allen, "On Reading Soaps: A Semiotic Primer." This collection also indicates how feminist theory and genre studies were coalescing around the soap opera as a particularly salient discursive formation at this time; four of the collections' eleven essays were explicitly concerned with soap operas.

60. E. Ann Kaplan, "Introduction," in Kaplan, ed., *Regarding Television: Critical Approaches—An Anthology* (Los Angeles: American Film Institute, 1983), xiii.

61. Boddy, "Loving a Nineteen-Inch Motorola: American Writing on Television," in Kaplan, 10.

62. The first such convention, held in New York in January of 1972, has acquired suitably mythical status amongst media fans in general. Over three thousand people attended (more than six times the projections), discussing the series, buying merchandise, and listening to presentations from *Star Trek*'s creators and actors, as well as from particularly active and prominent fans. This event, though greeted with bemusement to horror from the mainstream press, initiated the recognition of television fandom as an active cultural practice, and expanded the acceptable (or at least, possible) ways to be a television viewer.

63. Henry Jenkins, *Textual Poachers: Television Fans and Participatory Culture* (New York: Routledge, 1992).

64. Jenkins, *Textual Poachers*, 286.

6
Old Wine in New Bottles: Broadcast Rerun Syndication since the 1980s

> It all comes down to programming. . . . The Second Age of Television, then, is a new time in which the networks are joined by cable, syndication, VCRs, fourth networks, pay-per-view operators and marketers of backyard dishes in pursuit of the same audiences with essentially the same kinds of programs, give or take production values and styles. Old wine is filling many new bottles.[1]

As the previous chapters have shown, a constant rhetoric of innovation was emphasized during television's development that hid an equally constant reliance upon cultural repetition. As filmed programming came to dominate television at the end of the 1950s, the networks used their unparalleled powers to control the telefilm trade, gaining financial interest and syndication rights to virtually every prime time series they aired throughout the 1960s. When the government curtailed this power of the networks in the 1970s, the syndication market in off-network series fostered the development of nonnetwork stations and program distributors. As a generation of American television viewers began to make sense of their personal and cultural histories around the same period, the collected, recorded television of years past—readily available on virtually every broadcast channel—contributed to the construction of a national heritage centered on the experience of television.

Since that time, as new technologies like cable and the VCR flourished, broadcast television both expanded and adjusted, through the continued growth of independent stations, the development of the fourth, fifth, sixth, and *seventh* national commercial broadcast networks (Fox, UPN, WB, and Pax), and the erosion and ultimate removal of the Financial Interest and Syndication (fin-syn), and Prime Time Access Rules (PTAR). As deregulation has continued unabated, formerly antagonistic industrial forces have come together: Hollywood studios merge with broadcast networks (e.g., Viacom's 2000 union with CBS), broadcast networks invest heavily in cable networks (e.g., NBC's joint ventures Bravo, CNBC, MSNBC, and Court TV), and off-net sitcom distributors become corporate behemoths (e.g., Viacom). As Disney CEO Michael Eisner rightly quipped in the wake of his company's 1995 acquisition of Capital Cities/ABC, "there are synergies under every rock we turn over."[2] By the turn of the century, the television industry had thus reconfigured around its consummate product: the repeatable property, which not only included programs, but franchised program concepts (e.g., multiple incarnations of *CSI* and *Law & Order*, annual versions of *American Idol* and *The Real World*). Sparked by new technologies, new markets, and the new, burgeoning cultural sensibilities of the television heritage (as covered in the previous chapter), television has both expanded outward and "backward" since the eighties, claiming new terrain but filling it with familiar trappings.

This chapter and next trace how repetition, as manifested primarily in off-network syndication, contributed to the significant restructuring of television during the 1980s, 1990s, and early 2000s. In this chapter, I will focus on the broadcast (i.e., "traditional" over-the-air) syndication market of the 1980s through 1990s, when deregulation blurred the lines between media forms and industries, and new stations, new networks and new fictional first-run programming both flourished and failed. The 1970s FCC regulations which set up strict boundaries between network and nonnetwork programming and stations—the Financial Interest and Syndication Rules (fin-syn) and Prime Time Access Rule (PTAR)—are an important part of this story, as they increasingly came under attack from the networks and their allies throughout the 1980s and early 1990s, until wilting completely in 1995. While cable and satellite television were, in many ways, the key factor in these regulatory, industrial, and cultural reconfigurations, this chapter will primarily focus on the changes in the broadcast industry; Chapter 7 will examine cable's particular contribution to the shaping and experience of rerun television.

Booms, Busts and Barter

The structure of the syndication market has changed more rapidly in the past 25 years than at any point before. New media, new outlets, new players, and new forms of licensing have altered and expanded the expectations, practices, and goals of the entire industry. These changes have been felt most starkly in the sheer number of viable television outlets. During the early to mid-1980s alone, over 200 new independent stations came on the air in markets large and small across the country. Fueled in large part by government-fostered speculative financial markets—concomitant with the mythical belief that a license to broadcast is a license to print money—the number of independent stations doubled between 1979 and 1983, and continued to grow until 1985.[3] In such an environment, the appetite for programming only increased. Accordingly, network affiliates continued their quests for top-shelf syndicated fare, especially during the critical early evening access (7:00–8:00 p.m.) and late fringe (after 11:30 p.m.) periods where independent stations had become particularly competitive.

Four more broadcast networks have entered the fray since the late 1980s, greatly affecting the syndication market, but in somewhat contradictory ways.[4] While the amount of time available for syndicated programming on local stations has diminished with each additional network (including afternoon children's lineups variously programmed by Fox and WB), original series broadcast on these networks are now also sold in the off-net market; thus there are now seven venues through which programs technically become "off-network."[5] Adding to this plethora of programming, fictional first-run syndication finally returned to prominence in the late 1980s through late 1990s (after an effectual twenty-five-year absence), led by Paramount's upgraded house franchise *Star Trek: The Next Generation* (1987–94).

However, despite the rhetoric of endless financial opportunities and market invincibility suggested by these endeavors (and symptomatic of 1980s business culture in general), these expansions of commercial television could not be supported through the market alone, or at least the market as it was known. While programs were still "bought" and "sold," the terms under which deals were implemented were quite variable. This was, after all, the 1980s, when the very concept of "value" began to be fluid. Accordingly, the value of particular programming began to be measured not in money, but in the potential to attract money. Barter— an agreement in which programming is exchanged for advertising slots (i.e. "avails") instead of cash—has become a much more prominent and legitimate part of syndication trade since the 1980s, not only as a relief for cash-strapped stations during soft economic times, but also as a means of splitting a program's revenue stream into more flexible components. Under a typical barter arrangement, a station obtains the program in exchange for several minutes of advertising time, which the syndicator then sells to a national advertiser (as "national spot" advertising). The number of local advertising spots traded by the station varies from program to program (and market to market), but stations generally retain most of their ads, except during the most popular series (e.g., *Star Trek: The Next Generation* at its early 1990s peak), which come with a steeper price tag. Since barter's ascendancy, it has become the standard mode of dealmaking in syndication for all genres of programming, enabling multiple players (producers, distributors, advertisers) to, for example, reap variable revenues from *Seinfeld* throughout its billion-dollar-plus syndication cycles. In addition to barter, new licensing terms have also altered the exposure and flexibility of syndicated programming, and reruns in particular. The number of "plays" (how many times an episode could be run), the available time slots, and even the exclusive rights to a series were all made more negotiable in the 1980s, and have been ever since.

In broadcasting today, the rerun—whether off-network, off-cable, or off-first-run—is the nexus of a variety of revenue streams and industrial functions, all geared to maximize the returns on a familiar, stable property. Although the media and the market mechanisms may have changed, the programming itself has remained thoroughly predictable; in fact, save the odd minute or two shaved off to fit more advertising, it has often been completely identical to what had gone before. Just as in the earlier periods of television expansion in the 1950s and 1970s, rerun programming continued to lead the way in filling new schedules, promising a well-known slate of series and stars to attract viewers and advertisers. Perennial stalwarts like Norton, Lucy, Andy, Mary, Archie, Hawkeye, and Mr. Spock all continued to draw solid audiences throughout the 1980s, while, more recently, Sam, Homer, Roseanne, Tim, Kramer, Chandler, and Agent Mulder have joined them in the perpetual run of the television heritage. Similarly, the much-vaunted renaissance of first-run syndication and the rise of additional networks has occurred largely through unabashedly network-like, formulaic programming, recycling genres and stars (e.g., Suzanne Somers in *She's The Sheriff*), if not entire series (e.g., *The New Adam-12*). All in all, the past quarter century has seen a mix of abundance and monotony on television, as the amount of programming and programming outlets is larger than ever, but the variety of ownership and programming alternatives continue to be limited.

Unwanted Hours

Broadcasting became a much more cramped endeavor in most cities during the early to mid-1980s, as over 200 independent stations went on the air between 1979 and 1985. The number of independents doubled in many cities, while even small to medium-sized markets now had to absorb two or even three new stations. Though this was ostensibly the "free-market competition" the FCC and other policy and industry bodies had long crusaded for, the syndication market was still overwhelmingly tilted towards the networks, whether via national exposure on network time, or through the syndication clout of their O & Os, which could make or break a first-run or off-net syndicated series. Due to their enormous financial resources, networks and their O & Os, as well as a handful of powerful station groups like Tribune, Metromedia, Group W, and Gannett, essentially dictated the production of new first-run series, and the overall revenues of new off-net series. The sudden glut of new stations, many of which were owned by individuals, or even built on speculation thanks to relaxed regulations, thus created serious problems of supply in the program market. Where would all the necessary programming come from?

Again, first-run syndication functioned as the beacon of promise, the dream of nonnetwork "diversity" that producers and studios had always clamored for in earlier years. However, although it had registered a few long-term successes in the 1970s, like *The Muppet Show* and *PM Magazine*, first-run had hobbled into the new decade with only a few solid shows (e.g., *Donahue*, *Merv Griffin*). Accordingly, new off-network programming was still the more desirable, predictable choice of program directors. However, rising license fees and longer contracts for off-net series deterred many stations. Still, in lieu of serious, competitive first-run alternatives, off-net—particularly half-hours—continued to command the most attention and expenditure in the market.[6] For established independent stations, the most prominent off-net series scheduled in the prime-time access period had long been their peak performers, often beating anything new the network affiliates could offer. Moreover, as long as network affiliates were forbidden from airing off-network series during PTAR's access period, large-market VHF independent stations were virtually assured of acquiring the most popular rerun series, generally outbidding affiliates who could not afford to license the series if it could not run during that lucrative evening hour.

Throughout the 1980s, the most sought-after rerun series was without doubt Twentieth Century-Fox's *M*A*S*H*, the long-running CBS comedy-drama that instantly became the top-rated off-net program upon its release to local stations in 1979, a stature it would hold for over a decade. Though stations were initially skeptical about it in the 1976 rerun futures market (it had only been modestly successful in its first four seasons on CBS), it was soon regarded as a bargain compared to the prices paid for subsequent sitcoms like *Happy Days* and *Laverne & Shirley*, which commanded higher prices but failed to deliver consistent local audiences. In syndication, *M*A*S*H* was a juggernaut, "creaming" the competition no matter when it was scheduled, and earning millions for its syndicators, producers, and star Alan Alda, who had shrewdly acquired back-end profit participation in the series.[7] Ted James, a San Francisco entertainment industry financial analyst, called the series "clearly the most successful television property ever produced," while Alan Bell, program director at KTVU Oakland, claimed "*M*A*S*H* is a program with more legs than a centipede. It is absolutely unique. It's not possible to duplicate."[8] Fox admitted that it had undervalued the series on its first syndication cycle; it would not repeat that error the second time around. Thus, the asking price in 1983 (for the second run to begin in 1985) quintupled the original price, but most stations eagerly renewed anyway.[9] By the mid-1980s, *M*A*S*H* had become one of the medium's few evergreens, a series perhaps more ubiquitous than anything else on American TV at the time. Aside from *M*A*S*H*, however, the recent off-net pickings were relatively slim. Series such as *Happy Days, Laverne & Shirley, The Mary Tyler Moore Show,* and *All In The Family* had been among the most popular sitcoms of the 1970s, but were only moderate, fading successes as reruns in the 1980s, and especially in the shadow of *M*A*S*H*. Only *Three's Company,* distributed by D.L. Taffner, rivaled *M*A*S*H* in off-network popularity throughout the decade, although *The Jeffersons, Barney Miller, Taxi, The Bob Newhart Show* and *WKRP in Cincinnati* were also solid, if not spectacular, staples in particular medium-to-large markets.

While these long-running, late-1970s sitcoms began their off-net runs with solid ratings early in the 1980s, disaster loomed on the syndication horizon. The networks had hit a particularly fallow and uncertain period of programming, and were even more skittish about their prime-time schedules than usual. From 1980 through 1984, few new series lasted over two seasons, leaving only a handful of potential series with enough episodes to sell in syndication. After years of dominance during the 1970s, the sitcom form had tapered off in the early 1980s, and hour dramas filled the network schedules, including action series such as *Magnum, P.I.* (CBS) and *The A-Team* (NBC), and prime-time soaps like *Dallas* (CBS), *Dynasty* (ABC) and their assorted spin-offs or copycats.[10] While these long-form series performed very well for the networks—even prompting speculation in 1983–84 that the half-hour sitcom genre was dying—the move to "hours," (in the vernacular) coupled with the continuing fragmentation of local broadcast markets, created a time bomb in the syndication market. Hours historically fared well in the ratings during their first cycle, but fell precipitously thereafter; stations were wary of picking them up for long-term deals, and generally regarded many of the hour-long network hits of the 1970s (e.g., *The Six Million Dollar Man, Charlie's Angels,* and *CHiPs*) as fads with a short local shelf life. In the first half of the 1980s, however, more new off-network hours were being sold than at any period in the 1970s, and viable half-hour sitcoms were scant.[11] In 1986, when only three new, generally weakly-regarded off-net sitcoms hit the market (*Gimme A Break, Kate and Allie,* and *Double Trouble*), Dick Robertson, vice president of Lorimar Telepictures, remarked "[the sitcom shortage] is the only thing independents care about. It's that simple. These guys live and die on sitcoms."[12]

Despite notable exceptions like *Perry Mason, Star Trek,* and *The Rockford Files,* hours had always been hard sells in syndication. Their appeal was seen as limited to specific demographics, skewing too heavily towards children (e.g., *The Six Million Dollar Man*) or older adults (e.g., *Barnaby Jones*). Additionally, the serial form of popular network hours like *Dallas, Dynasty,* and *Knots Landing* was seen as a serious liability, as series with intricate, open storylines had never performed well in off-network syndication to that point. Worse, they took up 60 minutes of broadcast time—double the basic half-hour unit. A faltering half-hour could be relatively easily rescheduled or replaced, but a weak hour could be a serious problem.[13] In early jockeying for its *Cheers* and *Family Ties* on the futures market in 1984, Paramount shrewdly fed upon these concerns, touting research that showed that off-net half-hours consistently rated higher than off-net hours from 1978–83, and claiming that "half-hour comedies have been syndication's only long-running successes," noting their solid track record with *The Odd Couple*, *The Brady Bunch*, *Happy Days* and *Taxi*.[14] In addition, the rising production costs of many "flagship" series—exacerbated in the deficit-financed, style-conscious 1980s—priced several hours beyond most stations' reach. *Magnum, P.I.* garnered record fees for an hour when it first went on sale in the peak of its popularity in 1984, but its actual local performance in the late 1980s was less than spectacular, leaving most stations feeling burned. In 1986, Rick Feldman, the station manager of prominent Los Angeles independent KCOP, advised the studios and networks to reign in their up-front costs if they expected to profit in the back end. Citing ABC's glossy *Moonlighting*—a series the network actually owned—Feldman wondered how that network could possibly recoup its losses.[15] However, though local stations were reluctant to buy them, these, and other, hours eventually enjoyed a back end—but on cable (see Chapter 7).

Cashing in on the Television Heritage

The programming market is the product of human actions like any other. And like any other, it is shaped by its participants to fit particular priorities. When off-network hours were met with disdain and reluctance by stations, the demand for formulaic, stable, "good old" *half*-hours generated the widespread revival of just that: older half-hour sitcoms from the 1950s through early 1970s, many of which had been out of circulation for years. This phenomenon indicates precisely how repetition functions both within and between the areas of industry, policy, and culture. As the last chapter explored, off-net series marketed as "old favorites" were only viable because they had been legitimated as the television heritage, and thus, as American popular culture, in the seventies. Since that time, the television heritage has continued to engage issues of culture, industry and policy. Again, repetition largely functions in the name of innovation; the ostensible, familiar "old"—old series and films—used to legitimate and support the "new"—new stations and technologies. Accordingly, in the mid-1980s, the boom in new, ill-funded stations and the resistance to new off-net hours merged with the nascent television heritage to spark a syndicated revival of much older off-network series. The new stations needed affordable-yet-viable programming to fill their hours, but with the most desirable series and film packages already tied up with existing stations, they had to resort to the remainder pile of syndication: discounted old "favorites."

Series were regularly unearthed and repackaged in the 1980s with an explicitly nostalgic bent, plucked from the increasingly encyclopedic lore of "television land," despite having vanished, even from reruns, years before. Echoing their 1950s counterparts, several syndicators began to offer cut-rate packages of their older series. As early as 1981, Twentieth Century-Fox advised stations to "replay some of TV's favorite ratings" with its packages of film and television "classics," including *Batman*, *Planet of the Apes*, *The Jackie Gleason Show*. Meanwhile, Viacom announced *The Best of The Beverly Hillbillies*, a new package of an old favorite that would feature 58 episodes never seen in syndication.[16] Worldvision Enterprises formed an aptly-named Evergreen Programs division ("a treasure chest of programs") to push the little-seen 1960s series it had acquired, like *The Mod Squad*, *Combat!*, *The Invaders*, and *The Fugitive*, while MCA offered several of its late-1960s mystery series via its Encore Programs label.[17] Smaller distributors peddled series including *My Favorite Martian*, *The Real McCoys*, *The New Dick Van Dyke Show*, and *Mayberry R.F.D.*: all relaunches seemingly tailor-made for the struggling new UHF independents. Despite their apparent age, many less prominent 1950s series were revived as well. Avery Productions syndicated *The Golden Years of Vintage Television*, a package of excerpts from long-buried series including *Mama*, *This Is Your Life*, *Colgate Comedy Hour*, *Mr. Peepers* and *Space Patrol*. Some syndicators even touted these series as "first-run off-net," since they had been out of circulation for so long. Columbia Pictures Television even recharged its dormant Screen Gems brand and logo to sell their slate of past series including *Naked City*, *The Real McCoys*, and *Here Come The Brides*.[18] Even established and well-worn rerun series were able to participate in this booming nostalgia trend: in 1985, Viacom and Jackie Gleason announced a package of 75 "lost" *Honeymooners* episodes, none of which had been in syndication before.[19]

This trend peaked in 1985–86, as stations bucked the demands of syndicators selling new off-net series, and opted for a wide variety of past series; more series explicitly marketed as "vintage" or "classic" were sold that year than at any time before or since.[20] However, the key selling point for these series was not as much their ostensibly "classic" pedigree, but their price; most of them were offered at the cheapest possible rate for debt-ridden stations: straight barter.[21] Accordingly, for many of the newest independent stations, these series represented their only shot at familiar programming. Tucson's KDTU, for example, acquired series like *That Girl*, *Ben Casey*, *The Andy Griffith Show*, *The Mary Tyler Moore Show*, *The New Dick Van Dyke Show*, and *Eight Is Enough* for their prime-time schedule in 1985. In 1988, StarCast, a satellite music distributor for radio stations, even proposed an 18-hour vintage television format for struggling indie stations which would include series like *The Girl From UNCLE*, *The Many Loves of Dobie Gillis*, and *The Gale Storm Show*. That same year, Minneapolis independent station KLXI became "TV Heaven," featuring an all-classic lineup of series pitched to baby boomers and their families.[22]

The return of these series indicates how the television heritage and the economics of broadcasting worked symbiotically to determine the content of television. Had there not been an excess of stations and a related lack of viable new programming, it is quite likely that most of these series would have remained buried. Although a few of the revived series were hours, the half-hour sitcom dominated the selections; the genre is the crown jewel of television reruns, and had become such an expected component of American broadcasting that its effectual absence from recent network fare had to be filled in local syndication with the programs of the past. Thus, the television nostalgia wave of the 1980s was partially a by-product of industrial necessity, partially a result of the establishment of the television heritage in the 1970s, and partially a pointed appeal to an aging Baby Boomer audience.

"Off-Network" From Scratch

However, despite the nostalgic attraction of these "golden oldies," the primary objective of most local stations was still the acquisition of the most popular new off-network series. The rationale—which has held constantly throughout television history—was that stations could aspire to network-like status (and ratings) only by running programs most like contemporary network programs, i.e., the latest off-net hits. With only hours coming off the networks, and competition for popular half-hours tight, stations considered reviving the production of fictional first-run programming. This time the independents were more prepared financially than they had been in the 1970s. While their burgeoning numbers had intensified local competition, independents were also credited with expanding the television advertising market in general, and continuing the audience trend away from the networks and their affiliates.[23] In this environment, many stations and station groups sought to break their reliance on off-network programming, and saw the opportunity presenting itself in 1984. At an INTV panel in January of that year, Taft Broadcasting vice president Lucie Salhany called for new first-run programs, warning that "the future for off-network sitcoms is bleak... Our profit centers are dwindling and our program options shrinking. We can't let the networks and producers control [the future of] our independent stations." At the same panel, Barry Thurston, domestic syndication chief at network sitcom producer Embassy, disagreed, noting that the independent stations' most prudent options were still established television properties.[24] While he was clearly selling his wares, he was also giving a stark, yet accurate account of US television, as the vintage TV boom exemplified: familiarity sells. In addition, the highest-rated first-run nonfiction half-hours—Paramount's *Entertainment Tonight* and King World's *Wheel of Fortune*—played almost universally on network affiliates, not independent stations. Independents would have to generate other sources of programming, and their best bet at the time, as per the regime of repetition, was the new-but-strangely-familiar form of first-run sitcoms.

Accordingly, in September 1984, the thirty-two station New Program Group—formed from the major station groups Hearst, Gannett, Metromedia, Taft and Storer—announced the production of a new sitcom, *Small Wonder*, set to debut in first-run syndication in the fall of 1985.[25] Touting the series' network-level look and quality—longtime sitcom veteran Howard Leeds (*The Ghost and Mrs. Muir*, *The Brady Bunch*) was its creator and writer—the New Program Group aimed this series directly at the off-net sitcom drought. While many in the industry were skeptical, and critics mercilessly panned the series itself, *Small Wonder* successfully attracted a regular audience throughout its weekly 1985–89 run, even garnering enough episodes to sell as a weekday strip (as an "off-first-run" program).[26] After *Small Wonder* had gained interest and exposure in 1985, other series were quickly developed, and the mid-1980s saw 26 new first-run sitcoms reach production and distribution. Eleven sitcoms debuted in fall 1986 alone, resulting in an extra half-hour of nightly prime-time in many markets, as stations—including some network O & O's—experimented with a "checkerboard" approach, running five or more of the new series on weekdays in the same time slot. By the time the November sweeps were in, most of the series were performing adequately, resulting in the go-ahead for even more new series in 1987. With the off-net sitcom market still virtually nonexistent, with only *Mr. Belvedere* and *Who's The Boss?* debuting that fall, the demand for sitcoms seemed to warrant additional first-run production. Accordingly, at the 1987 NATPE, a record 82 first-run series were on offer—a 26% increase from the previous year.[27]

However, by the winter of 1987–88, both the first-run and independent station booms had begun to die down. The broadcasting market was now oversaturated with both stations and programming, and bankruptcies were increasingly common, as many stations and series—like so much 1980s real estate—had been built purely on speculation.[28] The stock market crash in October 1987 only exacerbated the situation. Although a handful of programs lingered for another season or more, and a few new series were even introduced as late as 1991, virtually all of these first-run sitcoms had vanished by the end of the 1987–88 season. While the financial shakedown of the industry and the glut of mediocre first-run offerings were certainly major factors leading to the first-run sitcoms' downfall, the primary reason was that network programming tastes had decisively shifted in the mid-1980s, and the market for new off-net sitcoms by the end of the decade had effectively reversed.[29]

In the wake of NBC's ratings blockbuster *The Cosby Show*, the networks returned to a sitcom-heavy lineup in the mid to late 1980s, and remained there for the next decade, filling the syndication pipeline with dozens of sitcoms. However, fictional first-run syndication did not disappear completely, as a new trend for action-adventure emerged, led by the unprecedented success of Paramount's *Star Trek: The Next Generation* in 1987. Many similar, genre-heavy series also found success in first-run syndication in *Trek*'s wake in the 1990s, including its sequel *Star Trek: Deep Space Nine*, *Babylon 5*, *Hercules: The Legendary Journeys*, *Xena: Warrior Princess*, *Forever Knight*, and *Highlander: The Series*. Ironically, most of these series were hours—precisely the format despised by local stations in the 1980s. The difference this time was a major resurgence of the action-adventure genre, which traditionally drew the highly sought young male audience.[30] Moreover, many of these series utilized either familiar texts (e.g., *Star Trek*, Greek mythology) or genres (space opera, melodrama), and ongoing narrative arcs to build audience loyalty. These shows attracted not only viewers, but *fans*, who, as the previous chapter discussed, built extensive subcultures around their favorite programs.[31] Successful series of this ilk thus functioned as nexus points for studios, the producers of licensed merchandise, and highly active fan communities.

While there were certain disadvantages to first-run syndication (including constantly shifting time slots and even channels in most markets), the upside for the studios was potentially great. Each series was produced and promoted through the studio alone, without the added filter of network control. Moreover, when a series accumulated enough episodes, it could be sold directly back into syndication as reruns, just as would a popular network series. The experience of Paramount's *Star Trek* franchise in the 1980s and 1990s deserves particular attention in this regard, as it illustrates how repetition and an awareness of the television heritage affected new production and distribution decisions at this time. The networks all passed on the new *Trek* in 1986, so Paramount put forward a substantial amount of money to produce 26 first-run episodes for first-run syndication. The risk was that not enough stations or advertisers would support the series, but the rewards were greater creative and marketing control, and 7 minutes of advertising time in each episode.[32] Paramount was prepared to abandon the project if it proved unsuccessful—the episodes would have simply been appended to the original *Star Trek*'s syndication package—but it ultimately succeeded as a network-quality series without a network. In turn, these first-run episodes ultimately became reruns, ripe for daily stripping; by fall 1999, four *Star Trek* series (including *Star Trek: Voyager*, which originally ran on UPN) aired in daily syndication in most markets.[33] Granted, *Star Trek* is a unique property, with a substantial built-in audience and a seemingly endless trail of merchandising to back up its television sales. As one of the most prominent series in the television heritage, the original *Star Trek* had been a rerun staple in nearly every market since the early 1970s. Its episodes had been viewed and reviewed dozens of times by millions of viewers, many of whom were ardent fans of the series. Though each new series has featured different characters and settings, they have successfully extended the *Trek* "universe," fostering nostalgia for the original premise as well as, not undeservedly, admiration for creator Gene Roddenberry's optimistic, if sometimes myopic, vision of the future.[34]

The Cosby Deal

Popular though the weekly action hours were, however, they were no substitute for a stripped, daily, proven off-network sitcom. Fortunately for stations, the networks had rediscovered the sitcom in the mid-1980s, and by the end of the decade, many newer series were primed for local syndication. These offerings included one of the most popular television series of all time, NBC's *The Cosby Show*, which became available for syndication through Viacom in fall 1986 (for a fall 1988 local debut). As the highly-touted "savior" of the sitcom genre—and the unchallenged number one series in the Nielsens—*Cosby*'s syndication came under much fanfare and expectation in 1986. By spring 1989, after it had run in local markets for a full season, however, *Cosby* had become one of the most controversial off-net programs in the history of syndication, and still remains the primary example of the excesses of the syndication market and the costs of overstated expectations of rerun success.

As *Cosby* became the top series on television in its second season, 1985–86, Viacom knew that its off-net sale could make syndication history. Network television had not been that dependent on only one specific hit sitcom since *I Love Lucy* 30 years earlier, nor, given stations' unsatiated desire for off-net sitcoms, had the market been that anticipatory about one's release to syndication. While similar hype was generated in the futures market of the 1970s, and would be duplicated again in the late 1990s around series like *Home Improvement, Friends,* and *Seinfeld,* the level of anticipation centered on what was, after all, only one series, was unprecedented. In October 1986, Viacom announced its terms. The series would be marketed like a first-run program, distributed via satellite and offered on a surprising cash-plus-barter arrangement. As described above, barter deals had been the saving grace of many syndicators and stations, as they enabled the former to sell national advertising on an otherwise lackluster series, and the latter to get programming for "free." In the 1970s and 1980s, barter had become the standard deal for first-run informational series like talk shows and newsmagazines, and for cut-rate, older series like the ones cited earlier which had been revived earlier in the decade. However, cash and barter terms had rarely been combined in the same deal for an off-network program; Viacom sensed that *Cosby* was no average off-net program, and upped the ante accordingly. In addition, in one of the most controversial aspects of the sales, the series would be sold on a per-market basis in a reserve-price auction; in other words, stations not only had to compete with each other, they had to at least match Viacom's calculated market value of the series. To raise expectations even more, Viacom planned to sell the series in market sequence: first New York, then Los Angeles, then Chicago, etc. This would guarantee big numbers and big publicity from the get-go. By sheer coincidence, as if to add an exclamation point to the proceedings, on the night that Viacom announced its terms (October 16, 1986), the series' first-run episode on NBC scored its highest-ever rating.[35]

From the beginning, the plan was met with skepticism and outright opposition. The stations in one major market, Tampa-St. Petersburg, passed completely on the series, bowing out of the process altogether rather than meet Viacom's reserve price. But after six months of high-stakes dealmaking, the series had been sold in 50% of the country, garnering record prices nationwide. The first sale, to New York's WOR, set the high-price tone early: $350,000 per episode, a New York market record. By April 1987, Viacom had already generated $100 million *over* its reserve prices.[36] By the time the series premiered locally in September 1988, it had generated over $600 million for its first syndication cycle; $4.2 million for each of the 149 episodes in the initial package. Significantly, almost all of the successful buyers—90%—were not independents, but network affiliates, who clearly feared that the ostensible *"Cosby* effect" could be used against them during the access hour. They paid dearly for the series, and ran it as a lead-in to the early evening local newscast, since they were still forbidden from running off-network series 7–8 p.m. Viacom, naturally, supported this all-or-nothing rationale; Donald Gillespie, a senior vice president, baldly stated that "we believe the program is the single show in syndication today that can change the competitive balance of power in favor of stations that have bought it."[37] After *Cosby* premiered, stations, syndicators, and industry reporters anxiously watched its ratings. The first sweeps indicated that it was performing better than what it had replaced, but not by much. The second revealed roughly the same data, and by the end of the third season sweeps, in May 1989, the judgment was official: *Cosby* had fallen well short of its hype, and was clearly not the blockbuster hundreds of stations had paid so much for.

Despite the syndication market's focus on only one series, *Cosby* was only the vanguard of an invasion of off-network sitcoms. Its NBC success had revived the moribund sitcom genre on the networks, and the prime-time schedules of the second half of the 1980s were filled with similar programs. This inevitably produced a veritable deluge of sitcoms debuting in off-net syndication: three in 1987, seven in 1988, and seventeen between 1989 and 1991, by which point industry observers wondered whether the market was again swamped with too-similar fare.[38] The arrival of the Fox network in 1987 only added to the boom, as the first of its series entered syndication in 1991, expanding an already crowded field from the Big Three. Accordingly, in stark contrast to just a few years before, off-network syndication was suddenly a buyer's market. In the wake of the *Cosby* fiasco, buyers were restless. Affiliates and O & O's were particularly burned on the *Cosby* deal, and generally opted back out of the off-network market, bypassing most new sitcoms coming on to the market in the early 1990s.[39] In addition, many stations decided not to renew their contract with Viacom for *Cosby*, and most syndicators— including Viacom—were more wary about how their series would be sold in the future. Given the disappointing returns, and a deepening economic recession, there would be less allowance for empty promises.[40] As Rick Lowe, the general manager of KOKI Tulsa commented, "*Cosby* taught us how to say 'no'."[41] But with dozens of off-network sitcoms coming into syndication in the 1990s, the terms of sale would have to be considered very carefully.

Cash to Barter

As the recession spread throughout the economy, programming was still sold by both barter and cash, though not without a great deal of concern. While barter would leave a station with more cash on hand, it would also sacrifice potential local advertising time to the national syndicator. Accordingly, the early 1990s saw a variety of syndication terms; the days of high-flying sitcom futures seemed to be over.

In 1990, Columbia offered the first off-Fox sitcom, *Married...With Children*, as a cash-plus-barter deal, holding only one minute of time.[42] Another highly popular series, Viacom's *Roseanne*, went on the market in 1991 in a more "traditional" deal, with no reserve price, and less barter time. Despite the recession, Warner Brothers successfully sold both *Full House* and *Murphy Brown* in 1991 on a straight cash basis. However, straight cash deals were becoming the exception as the recession wore on, as the lingering debt from the *Cosby* deal (and other questionable expenditures) depleted many stations' reserves. However, there proved to be one relatively consistent source of money in the industry: advertising revenue, which continued to grow throughout this period. Accordingly, barter increasingly became the standard form of transaction. Stations could acquire programs for less up front, and still have most of the advertising time to sell to local sponsors. Syndicators could capitalize on the national prominence of their series to attract national advertisers. Advertisers could be assured of more national spot exposure, at rates more amenable than those offered by the networks.

In 1991, Columbia took the unprecedented step of offering *Designing Women*, a then-popular CBS series, on a straight barter basis. A new off-net series had never been offered on straight barter before, but Columbia feared it would not recoup its costs if cash sales lagged, and put its faith instead in the relatively solid advertising market.[43] Other distributors with similar sales problems—such as Warner Brothers with *Family Matters*—adopted similar plans.[44] Hedging their bets, some distributors also offered a "pay-now-play-now" option whereby cash up front allowed a station to run a series for a year on straight cash, followed by all-barter for the rest of the term. Series like *Coach*, *The Fresh Prince of Bel-Air*, and *Evening Shade* were sold on variations of this plan with mixed results.[45]

The success of these sales and series, and the growing viability of basic cable as an off-network market (see Chapter 7), ensconced barter as the dominant form of syndication exchange by the mid-1990s, even after the economy had recovered and station revenues had improved. Where before they dealt with cash, and barter only secondarily, the usual deal for new off-net series by this point was—and still is—cash-*plus*-barter. This arrangement may have raised eyebrows in 1986 when Viacom first offered *The Cosby Show*, but a decade later it was standard.[46] At the time of *Cosby*'s off-net debut, the barter trade in new off-net sitcoms was nonexistent; by 1994, it was generating $100 million annually, even before the off-network launches of popular 1990s sitcoms *The Simpsons*, *Seinfeld*, *Coach*, *Home Improvement*, and *Friends*. Barter had grown so large so fast by the mid-1990s that speculation was growing that barter advertising revenues would eventually outpace network prime-time.[47] Barter deals may involve a less reliable source of revenue than cash up front, but one that's also far more flexible and potentially lucrative, indicating how the promise of televisual repetition was, in itself, seen as a sound investment. In other words, barter allows syndicators, stations, and advertisers to bet on the continuing *practice* of off-network syndication, rather than only on particular off-network programs.

Beyond the emergence of barter deals, which have expanded a series' effective long-term capital, syndication today takes place in a greatly expanded market. The addition of four *de facto* broadcast networks between 1987 and 1998 has bucked the predictions of the death of broadcasting in the face of competition from cable (although network audience share continues to dwindle). While it is possible to interpret the coming of Fox, UPN, the WB, and Pax this way, these new outlets aren't so much "networks" in the traditional sense but instead function largely as the programming outlet of their parent companies. At the times of their launches, three of these networks were subsidiaries of major vertically-integrated media corporations (Fox with News Corp., UPN with Viacom, and the WB with Time Warner), directly involved in the production and distribution of their properties. This relationship was the model for the future, as each of the old Big Three is now part of a larger media conglomerate (ABC with Disney, CBS with Viacom, and NBC with Universal). The legal barriers between studio and network, and, importantly, independent station and affiliate, have all come crashing down since the early 1990s, and the industrial and cultural borders between broadcasting, cable, film, and other media are getting less distinct with each passing day. The legal reconfiguration that produced this situation has been critical, as significant federal regulations, including PTAR and fin-syn, were undone through the changing status of off-network syndication and the official sanctioning of synergistic repetition.

The End of Fin-Syn and PTAR

As Chapter 4 described, the FCC implemented the Financial Interest and Syndication rules (fin-syn) and Prime-Time Access Rule (PTAR) to open up the programming marketplace on both ends: to expand the number of viable buyers for original prime time programming beyond the broadcast networks, and to allow more independent producers and distributors access to domestic and foreign syndication. The rules kept the Big Three broadcast networks from obtaining any vested interests in programs they did not produce, from syndicating any programs domestically, and, with few exceptions, from broadcasting in the 7–8 p.m. "access period" on Mondays through Saturdays. Independent stations and major studios credited these policies with making television more competitive and less network-dominated, while the networks consistently opposed them for creating an artificial barrier to competition. Adding to the networks' restrictions in the decade, a 1978 Justice Department consent decree limited their in-house prime-time production to only two-and-a-half hours per week.

However, during the 1980s and 1990s, all of these policies were challenged and ultimately disappeared, under the diminishing complaints of the rules' major supporters—studios and independent stations—and the concomitant rising discourses of deregulation from the networks. The FCC eventually repealed the rules after it decided that the broadcast networks—and over-the-air broadcasting itself—were only part of the overall media environment, and that it would not necessarily oppose the integration of the elements of this environment, which, by the early 2000s, included studios, networks, publishers, stations, cable and satellite system operators, software companies, and Internet service providers (ISPs), among others. The battles over fin-syn and PTAR were long and involved, fought with fierce lobbying, grandiose public posturing, boardroom maneuvering and internecine squabbles within the government and FCC. While it initially appeared that the rules would not survive the intense antiregulatory environment of the early 1980s, their eventual undoing came over a decade later, under a Democratic administration, and in a television environment rife with programming outlets, distribution windows, revenue streams, and utopian expansionist discourse. The cultural, industrial, and legal debates and strategies that ensued over the 15 years that led up to their evaporation indicate how televisual repetition functioned as a key form of productive and discursive capital. Again, although the rules were intended to produce diversity, it is striking how often critics and defenders alike ultimately drew upon the logic of repetition in justifying their positions.

Deregulation and the First Fin-Syn Battle, 1980–84

Even before Ronald Reagan became President in 1981, a deregulatory wave was spreading throughout the federal government. Most of the rules governing the airline industry had been removed in 1978, and the Carter administration's FCC, chaired by the pro-market Charles Ferris, was leaning in that direction for broadcasting. Ferris wanted to put his mark on the history of telecommunications by removing all barriers to the expansion of cable television, which would ostensibly expand the television programming market. In July of 1980, over the loud objections of broadcasters and motion picture studios (the National Association of Broadcasters (NAB), Motion Picture Association of America (MPAA), and Association of Independent Television Stations (INTV)), the FCC voted four to three to eliminate cable systems' signal retransmission and syndicated exclusivity limits, which had explicitly favored broadcasting over cable.[48] In his decision, Chairman Ferris extolled the virtues of this new, more "open" marketplace:

> The program supply market can now develop undistorted by this artificial regulatory scheme. It will adjust to a new reality where advertising rates will reflect both the distant signal as well as the local viewer, and the value of syndicated rights will account for viewers who can watch programs at times that are more convenient to them.[49]

These comments illustrate the terms with which deregulatory schema were articulated into conceptions of "liberating" television: the market could now be "undistorted," and programs made more "convenient" for viewers. As Thomas Streeter notes, however, and as this study has shown throughout, there is nothing "natural" about the television market—let alone television—that is somehow "liberated" by the "free market." Rather, television has always been molded out of hegemonic necessities.[50] In most other countries, until the 1980s and 1990s at least, these necessities centered primarily on the maintenance of national identity. In the United States, they have centered explicitly on commerce. Thus, under the discourse of the "American system," broadcasting in general, and television specifically, is "naturally" a "market."

Accordingly, in Chairman Ferris' comments and elsewhere, the "value of syndicated rights" looms as the key concept in this formation. Under Ferris and his successors, the FCC has argued that "unleashing" (to use their metaphor) the competitive forces of the marketplace would increase the value of syndicated programming and, concomitantly, television advertising rates, television financial markets, and television acquisitions. This basic logic has actually been borne out, as television continues to generate ever-increasing total revenues, despite recessions in the early 1990s and early 2000s. However, the original, ostensible public service mandate of PTAR and fin-syn, to foster genuinely new programming and innovation, has no necessary place in this logic. Instead, as befits a fundamentally conservative industry, and despite the occasional programming revolution (e.g., serialized prime-time drama in the 1980s, reality television in the 2000s), extant, already-aired programming has always been the ultimate prize, securing syndication license fees, advertisers, and viewers. Thus, under current telecommunications policy, the trade in repackaged reruns (or even potential reruns, in the form of dormant audiovisual libraries) from vertically-integrated corporations is, apparently, in the "public interest."

After the Reagan administration assumed office in 1981, the deregulatory philosophy already well under way in the late 1970s shifted into high gear. This was particularly the case at the FCC, under the leadership of avowed free-market zealot Mark Fowler, who espoused "*un*regulation" and sought to end public ownership of the airwaves. During Fowler's 1981–87 term as FCC Chair, several major telecommunications policies were curtailed or removed completely, including limits on ownership, station trafficking, cable fees, content regulation, and, most significantly, the repeal of the Fairness Doctrine in 1987.[51] However, Fowler was unable to topple one of the most far-reaching FCC television regulations: the fin-syn rules.

Throughout the early 1980s, in the wake of mounting cable deregulation and competition, the networks saw their chance to remove fin-syn in the favorable climate at the FCC, while the major studios and independent stations warned of absolute calamity should the rules be repealed. In the spring of 1982, the Coalition for Prudent Deregulation was formed in Hollywood to lobby for preservation of the fin-syn rules. Over the next year and a half, this group, made up of representatives of the MPAA, INTV, and other film and independent station interests, argued that, although the market was more competitive thanks to the rules, the networks were still clearly the dominant forces in television, and must continue to be curtailed. These pro-fin-syn forces contended that without the rules, the networks would simply revert back to the *de facto* extortion that prompted the regulation in the first place. INTV repeatedly claimed that independent stations' 1970s growth would have been impossible without fin-syn, and that if allowed back into domestic syndication, the networks would seek to shut independent stations out of the programming marketplace through favoritism to affiliates or program "warehousing": purposefully keeping a popular series out of the off-network syndication market in order to protect its affiliates.

The networks' rationale was twofold. First, they argued that the programming marketplace had expanded so much since the imposition of the rules in 1970—noting the growth of independent stations and cable networks—that there was little chance that they could monopolize it. Second, they reasoned that if they were willing to provide a prime time broadcast slot and a fair amount of the up-front costs of a series, they should also be able to obtain a share of the back-end syndication profits. Writing in a November 1982 *Broadcasting* op-ed, NBC general counsel Corydon Dunham framed the debate as between "free" and "pay" TV:

> Proponents of free TV believe that repealing the financial interest and syndication rules, as one immediate step, will enable more competition in the program supply marketplace and more investment in programming with more suppliers. This can only add to diversity, and creativity, for the television industry and the American viewer.[52]

"Pay" TV, i.e., cable, was brought into the fray because cable networks—most often financed or owned outright by the major studios—did not fall under the fin-syn rules, and could thus own and syndicate their programming, unlike the broadcast networks. More significantly, the discourse indicated by Dunham's remarks equates network economic freedom with "diversity," "creativity," and the public interest; "free" TV is thus constructed as part of a key American principle, liberty. Accordingly, the networks constantly cited the injustice of fin-syn, particularly in an era of rapidly escalating program license fees. "What is involved here strikes at the heart of our business," claimed James Rosenfeld of the CBS/Broadcast Group. "The effect of these rules is to squeeze the main artery of our program supply."[53] But how dire was the situation for the networks? The networks' public rhetoric was far from consistent on this issue. In 1983, drawing from published quotes, cartoonist Gil Eimer drew NBC President Grant Tinker with two heads, one telling NBC stockholders "we're going to do absolutely about as well in 1990 as we do now and it's going to be a dynamite business," while the other tells the FCC "free television is facing the greatest challenge in its many years of contributions to American culture and society."[54] Indeed, the networks' advertising revenue in the recessionary year of 1982 was $6.1 billion, a 381% increase since fin-syn had taken effect in 1971.[55]

As with his feelings about regulation in general, Fowler made no secret about which side held his favor, stating in April 1982, "our next step should be the institution of rulemaking proceedings looking toward the elimination of [the rules] ... the time for action has come."[56] In 1983, Notice of Proposed Rulemaking (NPRM) proceedings were officially commenced, with both sides filing statements on the issue. As befitting the Reagan administration's laissez-faire rhetoric, forces in the government lined up to agree with the networks' perspective, as the Federal Trade Commission, Department of Commerce, and even Department of Justice all filed positions supporting the repeal of fin-syn.[57] Drawn-out lobbying on this issue dominated the FCC's slate in 1983, and was ignited even further by various legislative gambits, most notably a transparently MPAA-friendly bill (HR 2250) sponsored by Los Angeles Democratic Representative Henry Waxman which would have banned any tinkering with fin-syn for five years, and an amendment to a fiscal 1984 Senate appropriations bill which would have barred funds from the FCC for anything related to the repeal of fin-syn. Both bills provoked indignant press conferences, and the further drawing of battle lines.[58] Undaunted, in August of that year, the FCC tentatively eliminated the financial interest aspect of the rules—leaving the syndication ban intact, but planning to "sunset" that as well by August 1990. However, after intense back-and-forth lobbying and front-page news throughout the fall of 1983, the FCC ultimately backed away from changing fin-syn, reportedly—and controversially—on the direct wishes of President Reagan himself, whose staff recommended a two-year moratorium on any changes in the rules.[59] Knowing that his FCC couldn't take down fin-syn without support from Congress or the President, Fowler instead directed the networks and the studios to resolve the dispute themselves. This kept them occupied for several years of accusatory rhetoric and perpetually stalled talks, with neither side willing to accept any compromises.[60]

In the meantime, however, the legal and hegemonic arguments for retaining fin-syn in its original form continued to diminish. The rules, and their corollary, PTAR, were premised on the scarcity of programming outlets. The networks' unparalleled domination of television programming and distribution was a demonstrable fact in 1970; but after nearly two decades of expanding programming outlets (independent stations, cable networks, and home video), this argument was more difficult to maintain. Granted, the "Three" were still quite "Big," and could still be said to effectively dominate the television industry. But as the networks' centrality had quantifiably slipped—prime-time audience levels dropping 16% between 1976 and 1985—the fundamental logic of fin-syn began to dissipate, at least as far as the FCC was concerned.[61] Although the antitrust elements of the rules as written were increasingly unfounded, billions of dollars were at stake for the winner of whatever ruling resulted, prompting a renewed war at the end of the 1980s.

The Second Fin-Syn Battle, 1988–92

The networks resumed their public grumbling about fin-syn before the 1988 general election, in anticipation of a new Congress and new FCC. Obliquely referencing Martin Luther King, NBC President Robert Wright claimed in June of that year that "the fresh breeze of deregulation hasn't blown much over the networks."[62] The studios, independent stations, and their allies once again formed a coalition in the spring of 1989 as a response to what they perceived as increased network lobbying. However, there was no action pending on the issue in either the FCC or Congress, with new Commission chair Alfred Sikes preferring to let the two sides sort it out, and Capitol Hill particularly reluctant to revisit the issue.[63] This time, the networks tried to paint themselves as the conciliatory side, tacitly agreeing with each other to concede the syndication ban if it would mean some kind of compromise on the financial interest aspect of the rules. Indeed, as journalist Bob Woletz remarked, with the 1978 consent decree—which capped network prime-time production—due to lapse soon, and fin-syn still vulnerable, the prospect of "transforming a net cost into a lifetime annuity"—i.e. obtaining back-end rights and/or vested interest in series they aired—arguably prompted the burst of network mergers and buyouts in the second half of the decade, as GE purchased NBC's parent company RCA, broadcaster Capital Cities merged with ABC, and Loews, Corp. chairman Laurence Tisch acquired CBS.[64]

In January 1990, the beginning of the end of fin-syn was finally set in motion, as the nascent Fox Broadcasting Network petitioned the FCC for an eighteen-month waiver of the rules. In many ways, Fox was poised to be the ultimate child of deregulation, its entire development arguably premised on the eventual repeal of fin-syn and a host of other owner-ship restrictions. In the mid-1980s, media mogul Rupert Murdoch, the chairman of Australia-based News Corp., purchased both the Twentieth Century-Fox motion picture studios and the Metromedia station group, one of the largest station groups in the country, with VHF independent stations in major markets. Combining the two assets in the name of vertical integration, Murdoch and Fox CEO Barry Diller launched the Fox Broadcasting Network in November 1986 with the late-night *Joan Rivers Show*. Although this initial offering was not successful per se, it helped legitimate the longstanding idea of a fourth commercial broadcast network. However, when Fox's two-night prime-time schedule debuted in the spring of 1987 (including its early trademark hit, *Married...With Children*), it marked the would-be network's first serious foray into "network" broadcasting, though Fox was not an official network at that point (or since). By limiting their prime-time programming hours, Diller and Murdoch had brought their enterprise just to the brink of becoming an FCC-defined network. By the time they delivered their petition in 1990, they had gathered 124 affiliates and were broadcasting nine prime-time hours. While Fox had long surpassed the affiliate threshold in the Commission's definition of a broadcast television network, they had not yet reached the limit of 15 prime-time hours. Their petition cited the goal of 1970s broadcasting policy as developing more viable outlets for broadcasting, thus improving the competitiveness of the market, and ostensibly serving the public interest through a greater diversity of programming. Fox argued that a fourth major network was precisely what the policies hoped to encourage, but that in order for them to stabilize, they needed more consideration and nurturance than the rules would allow. However, they would sooner give up their plans for a network than divest their considerable financial interest and syndication rights in their series. In their petition, they sought a redefinition of the term "network" which would be based not on number of affiliates or broadcast hours but on some other economic measure.[65]

The response to Fox's request from the usual sides in the fin-syn battle was confused, signaling a new turn in the issue. After all, Fox was now a multimedia conglomerate with both a motion picture studio *and* an ostensible television network, as well as numerous holdings in publishing, broadcasting, and cable television. If the networks came out opposed to Fox's request, would that render their stance against the rules hypocritical? Similarly, how could the coalition of studios and independent stations oppose the petition, as Fox was the primary example of a successful "nonnetwork" broadcast endeavor, something the major studios and independent (i.e., not affiliated with the Big Three networks) station groups had sought and benefited from?[66] In May 1990, the FCC decided on a compromise, which allowed Fox to expand its weekly prime-time programming to eighteen-and-a-half hours, but forbade it from acquiring any financial interest in new programs for a year.[67] Soon after the Fox waiver was granted, the Commission was faced with a rulemaking proceeding on fin-syn again, after the deadline for the studios and networks to come to an agreement had passed. Due primarily to the Fox waiver, the sentiment was growing that the rules would not last for long in their current state; long-time commissioner James Quello publicly stated that "the networks are going to get some degree of relief."[68]

This relief was going to come through a reconsideration of the financial interest aspect of the rules, and several plans were offered, from groups ranging from the National Telecommunications and Information Administration (NTIA) to the Writer's Guild of America. While these plans differed considerably in the details, one central tenet was agreed upon: the networks should be allowed—in principle—to negotiate for financial interest in any series that they broadcast. This agreement was a major victory for the networks, and the most viable option for most producers, who were faced with a softening syndication market due to the recession and the surfeit of off-network programs. By exchanging a negotiated percentage of back-end interest in a series for higher license fees up front, producers could develop their programs with less worry about recouping their costs, sharing the long-term risk with a network. Similarly, the networks would be more likely to develop marginal series they had acquired an interest in, perhaps purchasing and airing enough episodes to support a subsequent syndication run, rather than canceling faltering series early in their runs. This compromise illustrates how the real goal of both producers and networks was not "up front" revenue but rather in the more lucrative back end, where televisual repetition beckoned. As Woletz remarked in 1988, when the networks were still seeking a way to crack fin-syn, network broadcasting functioned primarily as a "way-station en route to the real market," syndication.[69]

For several months in 1990–91, the Commission weighed the various proposals about how to deal with fin-syn. Commissioner Sherrie Marshall, following the NTIA plan, favored a "two-step" negotiation process whereby a network could bargain for financial interest in a series only after it had come to a deal on the license terms for the initial network broadcast run. Chairman Sikes and Commissioner Quello wanted an outright repeal, which would be phased in over a three-year period, allowing the networks to bargain for financial interest in a greater percentage of their series each year.[70] As the vote deadline approached, freshman Commissioner Andrew Barrett stepped from the sidelines to put forward a compromise plan that allowed greater financial interest overall, but still retained much of the current restrictions on ownership and syndication.[71] Despite opposition from the networks and both Quello and Sikes, when the votes were cast in April, the Barrett plan won, three votes to two, with Commissioners Marshall and Duggan joining Barrett in the majority. Not surprisingly, both traditional sides of the fin-syn battle opposed the new rules—the networks claiming that they barely made a dent in the original rules, and the studios blasting the provision that allowed the networks back into foreign syndication—and immediately filed lawsuits preventing their implementation.

The Barrett plan failed because it was a bad compromise, too close to the original rules to please the networks, and too liberal towards the networks for the studios and independent stations. The only real winner was Fox, which once again eluded the definition of a network and thus the rules in their entirety. President Bush was disappointed with the outcome, and the commissioners themselves reported a great deal of "bad blood" after their year of trying to fashion a deal.[72] While these new, "Barrett" rules were on hold while the issue was tied up in court, they did prompt some speculation about the networks' next strategy. The prize of financial interest and back-end syndication rights was so valuable that at least one network, NBC, was reportedly considering scaling back its prime-time schedule to 15 hours so that it could join Fox outside the purview of the rules, effectively becoming a "non-network network."[73] A March 1992 University of Miami poll even found that 42% of network affiliates expected their networks to scale back prime-time hours to escape the new rules, a prospect they were not necessarily opposed to, as it would allow them to obtain syndicated programs during the newly freed nightly hour.[74] Even while the new rules were in limbo, the opportunities for synergy they dangled—by placing complete freedom from fin-syn just outside of the reach of the Big Three networks—indicate how forces in the industry were jockeying for position in anticipation of repeal.

In November 1992, the United States Court of Appeals officially struck down the new rules. The judges were particularly harsh on the FCC commissioners in their decision, intimating that the compromise was merely a ploy to get the network and studio lobbyists out of their offices.[75] The original rules went back into effect, and the Commission was left to start over. However, with a new administration coming into power after the election of Bill Clinton, there would be immediate changes in the process.

The End of Fin-Syn and PTAR, 1993–95

As the Clinton administration took over, Commissioners Sikes and Marshall resigned, leaving Barrett, Duggan, and, as acting chair, Quello, the most ardent opponent of the rules. In a move designed to put a seal of finality on the issue before a new set of commissioners could come into power, on April 1, 1993, Quello and Barrett voted to simply "gut" all of the financial interest components of fin-syn, and to phase out the syndication limits over three years.[76] By this point, all the studios could do was delay the sunset of the rules by forestalling the end of the Justice Department's consent decrees against the networks. While Justice had lifted the decree in early 1992, the studios and their legislative allies had filed suit to keep the decrees in place. Finally, in November of 1993, Judge Manuel Real formally lifted the consent decrees, removing the last legal barrier to the end of fin-syn, which was now due to completely expire in November 1995.

The new FCC, chaired by consummate Clinton Democrat Reed Hundt, came into office concerned with "reregulating" some key aspects of telecommunications, but fin-syn was clearly not one of them. Instead, they sang the praises of the new competitive, diverse free market in television, and even accelerated the demise of fin-syn by two months, to September 1995.[77] In anticipation of the post-fin-syn world, investors and media corporations clamored for television assets. In September 1993, Viacom set its sights on Paramount Communications, but soon found itself in a high-stakes bidding war with Barry Diller and his QVC cable home-shopping empire. Although the price seemed steep, Viacom ultimately prevailed by the spring of 1994, bringing Paramount and all its programming capital under its already wide umbrella; the combined Viacom-Paramount television library alone had over 14,000 hours of programming.[78] Similarly, in October 1993, Paramount and Warner

Brothers separately announced plans for new broadcast television networks to debut in January 1995. With fin-syn out of the way, the line between networks and studios was effectively erased; as of this writing, all six major broadcast networks are part of larger multimedia corporations. Disney purchased ABC in 1995, Viacom acquired CBS in 2000 (and, with UPN, technically operates two broadcast networks), and NBC merged with Universal in 2003.

As fin-syn was removed, so was the other key element in the syndication-based regulations of the 1970s, the Prime-Time Access Rule (PTAR). In the 1970s and 1980s, independent stations were unanimous in attributing their growth to this rule, which kept network and off-network programs off of all network affiliates in the top 50 Nielsen markets during the 7–8 p.m. "access hour." Even while fin-syn was being eroded, PTAR had been seen as unassailable, in large part because network affiliates had rebounded in the 1980s with the first-run game show juggernauts *Wheel of Fortune* and *Jeopardy!*, which faced off with *M*A*S*H* reruns on the dominant independent station in virtually every market in the nation throughout that decade. Affiliates were generally reluctant to open up this half hour to the networks, even if it meant the possibility of obtaining off-net reruns.

However, seeing that action on fin-syn was imminent, in April 1990, Orlando CBS affiliate WPCX petitioned the FCC to eliminate PTAR. Citing the 1987 decision to revoke the Fairness Doctrine on the grounds that the "scarcity" argument—i.e., the longstanding premise that broadcasting channels are a scarce public resource—was no longer applicable, the station's petition asked the Commission to declare PTAR a violation of stations' First Amendment rights.[79] Later that year, Disney and the Meredith Corp. broadcast group filed similar petitions. Rich Frank, the president of Walt Disney Studios, argued that the rule had not fostered its intended program diversity, but had instead reduced the access period on network affiliates to "a crater of quiz shows and tabloid television" like syndicated hits *Wheel of Fortune* and *A Current Affair*.[80] However, though then-Chairman Sikes was interested in revisiting PTAR—reportedly as a favor to former FCC chairman Richard Wiley, now a lawyer for Disney—the remaining commissioners were not, openly preferring to wait until the petitions worked through the federal court system before being forced to act on them.[81] Unlike with fin-syn, action on PTAR was not immediately in the cards, even after the comparably more harmonious Clinton FCC took over. Accordingly, the petitions languished in the justice system for four years until early 1994, when WCPX took theirs to the US Court of Appeals. An FCC spokesperson admitted that the Commission had been "ducking" PTAR, claiming, "we are not obligated to respond unless the court directs [us] to."[82]

Soon after the court took up the petition, it did just that, directing the FCC to proceed with a Rulemaking. In April 1994, the FCC announced it was revisiting PTAR, and sought public input. Tipping its hand to warn the rule's proponents, the Commission said it would consider "the continuing need for such a provision in view of changes in the television programming marketplace."[83] Clearly, it would be an uphill battle to retain the rule. "It's quite clear that things are quite different," Chairman Hundt told reporters, underlining the diminishing prospects of the rule's retention.[84] While network affiliates and major off-network distributors were already preparing for the end of the rule by tentatively exploring program licensing during the access hour (see below), first-run distributors and independent stations were less than ecstatic. As INTV President Jim Heglund ruefully remarked, "Big 3 affiliates will hog the best off-net shows. We'll pay higher prices for lesser quality product and end up delivering lower lead-in audiences to the Fox, WB and Paramount networks. So much for fostering diversity."[85] On July 28, 1995, after weighing both sides over several months of testimony and thick economic reports, the FCC voted unanimously to repeal PTAR, effective August 30, 1996. Chairman Hundt, explicitly linking PTAR with fin-syn, claimed that "[the FCC] should be for real competition, not lining one industry's pockets at the expense of another's."[86]

More Wine, More Bottles, Fewer Vintners

As both fin-syn and PTAR disappeared into the pages of broadcasting history, the resultant reconfigured television emerged. Traditional boundaries between producers, studios, and networks began to blur considerably, if not dissipate altogether. The removal of the rules prompted the real ramifications of long hypothetical questions. Would the networks choose to produce the majority of their prime time programming in-house? Or would they also produce programs for cable, syndication, and even other networks? Would studios tie their networks to unpromising series, with their eye on the syndication back end? Would the networks play favorites, opting for an in-house or parent company series over one in which they didn't have as large a financial stake? This last question loomed particularly large. *Variety*'s Brian Lowry noted in 1995 that the networks would now "face a double whammy as suppliers—not only losing money broadcasting a failed series but on deficits from production as well."[87] At a Hollywood Radio and Television Society luncheon in September 1997, ABC Entertainment president Jamie Tarses sheepishly admitted that, all else being equal, she would most likely schedule a series from parent company Disney over one from an outside studio: "yeah, I'd pick the Disney show . . . if that circumstance ever came up, that would make life easier."[88] Indeed, a few of the early post-fin-syn network productions failed spectacularly, reviving complaints about network oligopoly.[89] However, enough have survived—and even flourished, like CBS Productions' *Dr. Quinn, Medicine Woman*, and NBC

Studios' *Will and Grace*—to indicate that the networks will certainly continue to develop and produce, or at least command a significant interest in, most of their prime-time programs.[90]

With PTAR and fin-syn gone, the television industry now rides the rerun through multiple incarnations and revenue streams. In such an environment, the television heritage established in the 1970s has become, since the 1990s, an efficient vehicle for program licensing and unprecedented industrial synergies, accelerating the cultural and historical legitimation of more recent series, and bolstering their "evergreen" stature in off-network syndication. Consider how many recent network series have been widely hailed (and incessantly hyped) as all-time classics. High-rated post-1990 network series such as *The Simpsons*, *Northern Exposure*, *Seinfeld*, *Frasier*, *The X-Files*, *ER*, *Ally McBeal*, *The West Wing* and *CSI* have all been touted as "groundbreaking," and of having zealous fans; even lower-rated series such as *Twin Peaks*, *Homicide: Life on the Street*, *NewsRadio*, and *Alias* are discursively constructed as "cult favorites," lending an air of hipster distinction to their legacies.[91]

The consolidation on both sides of the market, with buyers and sellers morphing together in tangled bundles of corporate ownership, has both deepened and accelerated this process. With the boundaries between producers, networks, studios, and even stations now almost completely blurred, successful series are treated as long-term projects, ripe for continuous recirculation and repackaging. News Corp's August 2000 acquisition of Chris-Craft is a landmark of media synergy in this regard, as it brought together a film studio (Twentieth Century-Fox) a broadcast network (Fox), and several major-market broadcast stations (the combined Fox and Chris-Craft stations), including duopolies in four top-ten markets (New York, Los Angeles, Dallas-Fort Worth, and Phoenix).[92] On the buying side, News Corp, together with its fellow station lords (Tribune and Viacom in particular), exerts a powerful influence on the off-network syndication market, packaging terms for series and advertising rates across their entire station ranks, including split runs on their duopoly stations.[93] As sellers, these very same corporations (or rather their corporate siblings, like Twentieth Television) set the terms by which series are produced and syndicated. This consolidation has become so complete that NATPE itself has become more of a "pre-up-front market for media buyers" than a marketplace for selling programming to stations.[94] Moreover, programming decisions at stations across the country are increasingly no longer local, but corporate. Accordingly, many distributors and station groups no longer attend NATPE, their decisions long made by the convention's January date. As *Broadcasting*'s Steve McClellan put it, NATPE is, increasingly, "a bit of an anachronism."[95]

Despite this unprecedented consolidation, however, the long-term prognosis for broadcast syndication is far from certain. There may be fewer buyers and sellers overall, but there are also many more potential outlets for first-run programming in general, including not only the Big Four networks, but also the WB and UPN, first-run syndication, and, as the next chapter will explore, cable networks. Moreover, each of these sources has also converted successful first-run series into viable reruns suitable for broadcast or cable syndication.[96] With so many "proven," and "familiar" programs vying for syndicated attention, true hits are relatively rare. As *Variety*'s Melissa Greco quipped, in such an environment, "squeaking out 100 episodes of a sitcom no longer guarantees a syndie windfall."[97] This problem of diminished returns has become particularly acute in the off-net sitcom trade, where the glut of network series in the 1990s has largely failed to deliver long-term success in rerun syndication. Although sitcoms are still the standard-bearer of rerun syndication for a variety of reasons, their diminishing success on the networks has spilled over into lowered expectations in syndication. While there are well over a dozen off-network sitcoms in syndication as of this writing, the off-net ratings are still dominated by *Friends*, *Seinfeld*, and *Home Improvement*, each of which has run on local schedules since the mid to late 1990s. Despite stations' continued demands for long-term rerun sitcoms, only a scant few have survived the network sitcom drought of the turn of the century, as one-hour dramas and reality series dominated the top of the ratings in network prime-time.[98] As a result, most of the recent off-net sitcoms in syndication today entered the market as high-priced network hits—often sold very early in their network runs—but fell from favor precipitously in syndication (e.g., *3rd Rock From The Sun*, *Dharma and Greg*, *The Drew Carey Show*).[99] Citing network, syndicated, and cable fare, many in the industry have even pointed to an oversaturation and subsequent exhaustion of comedy on television. As one anonymous network executive told *Variety*'s Josef Adalian in 2001, "Comedy's broken right now. People are getting bored with the landscape of sitcoms that all look the same."[100]

This last comment points to the ultimate problem media industries have always faced. Despite the consolidation and control won by a few mega-corporations since the mid-1990s, they still cannot control the most decisive factor in their bottom lines: the audience's tastes. Audience preferences shifted decisively around the turn of the century to two program forms that have complicated the logic of repetition built up by decades of rerun syndication. First, sixty-minute dramas attracted reliable mass audiences on almost every network. While many of these have been "procedural"-based crime shows with largely self-contained episodes (e.g., the *CSI* and *Law & Order* franchises on CBS and NBC, respectively), series with a high degree of serial narrative have also been relatively popular (e.g., *The West Wing*, *Buffy the Vampire Slayer*). As popular and acclaimed as they may be in their network runs, however, neither dramatic form has historically fared well in rerun syndication. Second, and arguably more significant, has been the much-vaunted rise of event-laden reality series such as *Survivor, The Bachelor,* and *American Idol,* which have shaken up the networks' previously unquestioned faith in scripted television. Reality series have been leveraged virtually entirely on the front end, designed for immediate impact on network ratings, with unknown, unprofessional talent, and unpredictable pseudo-narratives. While this genre has been attacked for its ostensible loosening of the medium's content and professionalism (e.g., its use of non-union cast and crew), it has also undeniably been the most successful programming trend of the century thus far. It remains to be seen, however, whether it can be as successful in rerun form. The only significant venture thus far in this direction—CBS' all-too-anxious decision to strip reruns of the just-completed first season of *Survivor* as counter-programming against the 2000 Summer Olympics—was an unmitigated failure.[101]

With several network-level sources for off-network fare, twenty-first century off-network broadcast syndication is thus more like a desperate front-end grab for quick ratings, rather than a longer-term relationship between station, rerun, and viewer. Accordingly, since the late 1990s, in an effort to boost the profitability of particular series, sitcoms have typically been "double-run": aired twice daily (often in both early and late fringe times), thus burning through episodes at double the clip of traditional stripping. Series may air even more frequently in the same market on duopoly stations, where the two jointly-owned stations split the same series in different dayparts. However, despite these substantial changes in standard industry practices, the most significant impact on television since the 1980s has come not from over-the-air broadcasting, but from cable, and its primary competitor, satellite. The next chapter will examine how the culture and industry of cable and satellite have factored decisively in maintaining—and enhancing—televisual repetition.

Notes

1. Les Brown, "Five Tumultuous Years," *Channels Field Guide '87*, p. 9.

2. Qtd. in Wayne Walley, "The colossal combos," *Electronic Media*, 7 August 1995, p. 3.

3. Although there were a few network affiliate additions during this period as well, the overwhelming majority of new stations were independents. In addition, the FCC abolished the antitrafficking rules in station sales, which allowed virtually unlimited station buying and selling. Ownership limits were still in place, though relaxed considerably, but as William F. Baker and George Dessart describe, stations could be bought one day and sold the next, "swept up into the maelstrom of stock speculation, mergers, and leveraged buyouts." William F. Baker and George Dessart, *Down The Tube* (New York: Basic Books, 1998), 27.

4. Technically, the four newcomers—Fox, UPN, the WB, and Pax—are not "networks" according to the FCC's definition. As ruled after the Fox-inspired

dealing leading to the repeal of the financial interest and syndication rules in the early 1990s, a "network" must broadcast more than 15 hours of prime-time programming a week. Though Fox did program 16 hours in the 1990–91 season, it has never exceeded 15 since then, and shows no signs of further expansion; the other three are nowhere near that mark.

5. As of this writing, however, no Pax-originated series has yet been sold on the off-network market as reruns.

6. According to Dean McCarthy, director of program services at the Harrington, Righter and Parsons station representative firm, off-network programs constituted 80% of the total syndication market in 1981. "NATPE 1981," *Broadcasting*, 9 March 1981, p. 60.

7. "Back-end" arrangements such as Alda's are contract clauses that could have only arisen in an era of cultural repetition, guaranteeing a percentage of a series' syndication profits, rather than its initial network run. The term also refers to syndication profits in general; "up front," refers to cash paid or received at the beginning of a production, sale, or contract

8. Qtd. in Earl C. Gottschalk, Jr., "S*M*A*S*H," *Channels of Communication*, February/March 1982, p. 47; "Mustering out 'M*A*S*H'," *Broadcasting*, 28 February 1983, p. 40.

9. A few stations in Connecticut, Nebraska, Illinois and Georgia protested the steep asking price of the 1979–83 seasons, and unsuccessfully sued Twentieth Century-Fox for breach of contract in 1983. "Fox price increase for 'M*A*S*H' draws protests, lawsuits," *Broadcasting*, 31 October 1983, p. 61.

10. Eight of the top-ten series of the 1982–83 and 1984–85 season were hours, while only one sitcom, *Kate & Allie*, finished in the top-ten in 1983–84. Compare this to 1973–74, when sitcoms claimed five of the top-ten spots, or 1993–94, when seven sitcoms ranked in the top-ten, and thirteen sat in the top twenty. Alex McNeil, *Total Television* (New York: Penguin Books, 1996), 1152, 1156, 1161.

11. "NATPE 1981," 60.

12. Qtd. in "Independent television: the good gets better," *Broadcasting*, 6 January 1986, p. 62.

13. Cognizant of this, Metromedia even considered retooling *Dynasty* so that it could be sold as half-hours instead of hours. "Cable sitcoms making their way into syndication," *Broadcasting*, 8 July 1985, p. 75.

14. "Warm-up," *Broadcasting*, 4 June 1984, p. 7; Advertisement, Paramount Television, *Broadcasting*, 31 October 1983, p. 35. Oddly, Paramount chose to ignore the unique success of its own one-hour syndication staple, *Star Trek*, in making this claim.

15. Rick DuBrow, "Back-end blues," *Channels of Communication*, June 1986, p. 73.

16. Twentieth Century-Fox Television, advertisement, *Broadcasting*, 7 December 1981, pp. 16–17; *The Best of the Beverly Hillbillies*, Viacom, advertisement, *Broadcasting*, 25 January 1982, p. 75.

17. Evergreen Programs, Inc., advertisement, *Broadcasting*, 15 March 1982, p. 9; Encore Programs, advertisement, *Broadcasting*, 27 August 1984, pp. 20–21.

18. "Independent programing: more than just movies," *Broadcasting*, 30 September 1985, p. 60.

19. The episodes consisted of kinescopes of *Honeymooners* sketches culled from *The Jackie Gleason Show* and edited to conform to a half-hour length. Fifty "new" episodes aired on Showtime in the fall of 1985, before being syndicated with an additional twenty-five for the following year.

20. According to *Broadcasting*, "the description 'older' is universally shunned by syndicators in favor of the term 'classic' or 'vintage'." "New life in old TV shows," *Broadcasting*, 18 March 1985, pp. 54+. 1985, not coincidentally, was also the year Nick at Nite, the most prominent rerun-based cable network, debuted. See Chapter 7, and Derek Kompare, "I've Seen This One Before: The Construction of 'Classic TV' on Cable Television," in Janet Thumim, ed., *Small Screens, Big Ideas: Television in the 1950s* (London: I.B. Tauris, 2001), 19–34.

21. One entire firm, the DFS Program Exchange, had been founded in the 1970s on the straight barter trade of child-oriented afternoon programs like *Rocky and Bullwinkle, Yogi Bear, The Brady Bunch, and Bewitched*.

22. "Oldies format, for TV," *Broadcasting*, 11 April 1988, p. 102–103.

23. "Independent television: the good gets better," *Broadcasting*, 6 January 1986, pp. 61–64.

24. "Original programing answer to product shortage, INTV hears," *Broadcasting*, 23 January 1984, pp. 74+.

25. Hal Erickson, *Syndicated Television: The First Forty Years, 1947–1987* (Jefferson, NC: McFarland & Co., 1989), 317–318.

26. *Small Wonder* arguably succeeded due to its combination of freshness and familiarity. The plot was lifted from the typical mid-1960s "fantastic" sitcom, most notably the short-lived *My Living Doll* (CBS 1964). In *Small Wonder*, an inventor builds a robot in the guise of an 11-year-old girl, who becomes a part of his family, despite the fact that she's 10 times smarter and stronger than any human, and speaks only in a low monotone. As no doubt expected by the series' admirers, each episode revolved around the robot Vicki being nearly found out by nosy neighbors and various authority figures. While a first-run syndicated sitcom was considered innovative per se in 1985, *Small Wonder's* strength was its formula, enabling it to blend in with both the television heritage (or at least the wing holding *Bewitched, I Dream of Jeannie*, and *My Favorite Martian*) and whatever slate of off-net sitcoms it found itself next to.

27. "First-run programing fueling syndication market," *Broadcasting*, 19 January 1987, pp. 106+.

28. "Suppliers say the face tough couple of years ahead," *Broadcasting*, 11 January 1988, p. 39.

29. "Half-hour sitcom glut no laughing matter," *Broadcasting*, 23 November 1987, pp. 49+.

30. In one of the more misogynistic assumptions of the television industry, a male-heavy audience is generally more valued by advertisers than a female-heavy audience; this is why the networks are willing to sell the proverbial farm to obtain exclusive rights to National Football League games.

31. There were several attempts to cash in on established series, stars, or properties at this time, including some of the series already mentioned, and *War of the Worlds, Friday the 13th: The Series, The New Adam-12, The New Dragnet, The Untouchables,* and *Kung Fu: The Legend Continues.*

32. During their first runs, both *The Next Generation and Deep Space Nine* were the only fictional first-run series with a barter split favorable to the syndicator rather than the station; while the stations could sell 5 minutes, Paramount got seven.

33. Paramount had even bolstered the rerun appeal of *The Next Generation* early in its run in 1988 by offering stations a package of the previous season's episodes to air adjacent to the current season's.

34. Given the decidedly cool response to the latest series, *Star Trek: Enterprise* (which premiered on UPN in 2001), and feature film (*Star Trek: Nemesis,* 2002), however, the *Star Trek* franchise's long-term future is, as of this writing, much more tenuous than it seemed to be in the late 1990s. However, other *Star Trek* spin-offs (notably novels and video games) continue to sell well, and its episodes have effectively made the transition to acquisitive repetition, via DVD box sets (see Chapter 8).

35. "Cosby in syndication: cash plus barter," *Broadcasting*, 20 October 1986, p. 29.

36. "The 'Cosby' numbers in syndication," *Broadcasting*, 27 April 1987, pp. 58+.

37. "'Cosby': Off-network's biggest deal ever," *Broadcasting*, 12 September 1988, pp. 76–78.

38. "Sitcoms in syndication: Too much of a good thing?," *Broadcasting*, 29 May 1989, pp. 48–50.

39. "It's a buyer's market for off-network sitcoms," *Broadcasting*, 4 December 1989, pp. 94–95.

40. Viacom was forced to abandon a 1989 plan to "sweeten" the renewal of *Cosby*—this time on a cash-only, per-episode basis—with the addition of the weaker spin-off, *A Different World*, after it found few takers; only 5% of current *Cosby* stations accepted the plan. Marianne Paskowski, "'Cosby' renewal plan set," *Electronic Media*, 1 October 1989, p. 1; "Viacom, clients playing hardball over 'Cosby'," *Broadcasting*, 13 November 1989, p. 40.

41. Qtd. in Cheryl Henton, "An enviable situation," *Channels*, 17 December 1990, pp. 36–38.

42. However, even among a crowded field, *Married...With Children* was in demand from independents *and* affiliates, because of Fox's waiver from the fin-syn rules (see below). Technically, the series was "not" an off-net program, because Fox was "not" a network. Therefore, affiliates could freely run the series in the access period. "More access for the Bundys," *Broadcasting*, 14 January 1991, p. 56.

43. "CPT sells 'Designing Women' on barter basis," *Broadcasting*, 13 May 1991, pp. 35–36.

44. Geoffrey Folsie and Joe Flint, "The new all-barter off-network: no cash down, ads later," *Broadcasting*, 2 December 1991, pp. 3–4.

45. Mike Freeman, "What price comedy? Tracking off-net trends," *Broadcasting*, 16 November 1992, pp. 30+. MTM was unable to sell *Evening Shade* in broadcasting at all, and instead reached an agreement with cable's Family Channel in 1994.

46. Wayne Walley, "Barter craze entrenched in syndication," *Advertising Age*, 13 June 1994, sec. S, p. 18.

47. Steve McClellan, "Barter boom continues in off-net," *Broadcasting & Cable*, 4 April 1994, p. 27.

48. The signal retransmission rule, which had been modified several times throughout the 1960s and 1970s, limited the number of distant broadcast stations a cable system could "pull in" to a local market. Similarly, the syndicated exclusivity rule allowed both stations and program distributors to require "exclusive" licenses to broadcast a series in a particular market, thus keeping imported cable channels—specifically the new "superstations"—from running popular series, in competition with local stations.

49. Qtd. in "FCC now all but out of cable business," *Broadcasting*, 28 July 1980, p. 25.

50. Streeter, *Selling The Air*, 163–216.

51. Although the Fairness Doctrine was officially repealed by his successor, Dennis Patrick, the groundwork for its undoing was crafted by Fowler.

52. Corydon Dunham, "Eliminating financial interest and syndication rules: the network side," *Broadcasting*, 1 November 1982, p. 15.

53. Qtd. in "CBS closed-circuit on syndication and financial interest rules," *Broadcasting*, 1 November 1982, p. 26.

54. Gil Eimer, "The battle of the networks rerun$, or the legend of fin-syn," *Channels of Communication*, January/February 1984, p. 41.

55. "Annual Volume of Advertising in United States," *Television Factbook* 1979, 1990, p. 77-A, p. C-332.

56. Qtd. in "FCC under gun on financial interest," *Broadcasting*, 14 June 1982, p. 31.

57. "Syndication, financial-interest comments: high-stake rulemaking," *Broadcasting*, 31 January 1983, pp. 28–32. However, the Department of Justice did

not back the elimination of the syndication aspect of the rules, as it conceded that the networks could too easily revert back to their original, pre-fin-syn strategies of favoritism and "warehousing" of series.

58. Among the opponents of repeal were NATPE, the primary organization for syndicators, and stars like Alan Alda and Larry Hagman, who claimed that it was in the public interest to keep the networks at bay, but who privately had pocketed millions in profit-sharing from their respective series *M*A*S*H* and *Dallas*. Supporting repeal and the networks, unsurprisingly, was the entire New York congressional delegation. "NATPE acts to stir up grass roots support for bill," *Broadcasting*, 25 July 1983, p. 93; "FCC set to make its move on financial interest," *Broadcasting*, 1 August 1983, pp. 19–20.

59. Reagan was always under suspicion from network executives who feared that his loyalties to the film industry prevented him from fulfilling what otherwise would fit well within his free-market philosophy. Rumors abounded of a September 1983 "briefing" in the Oval Office, during which Fowler was ordered, in no uncertain terms, to leave fin-syn alone. Such explicit directives from the executive branch are illegal, but the matter was never pursued through the courts. However, according to *Broadcasting*, Fowler was "pained" and taken aback by the President's reluctance to repeal fin-syn. "Ganging up on the networks re fin-syn," *Broadcasting*, 7 November 1983, pp. 31–35.

60. CBS pulled out of the initial round of talks early in 1984, offering this explanation: "After lengthy negotiations, it is clear that it will not be possible to arrive at a definition of 'financial interest' acceptable to both sides. For this reason it has been agreed that additional negotiation will not be productive." Qtd. in "Latest monkey wrench in fin-syn," *Broadcasting*, 20 February 1984, pp. 35–36.

61. Steve Behrens, "Going soft: the emergence of a buyer's market," *Channels Field Guide '87*, p. 16.

62. Qtd. in "Wright continues to push to lose finsyn, rep rules," *Broadcasting*, 6 June 1988, pp. 29–30.

63. One unnamed congressional aide quipped to *Broadcasting* that the issue was a "fight between the rich and the wealthy." Qtd. in "MPAA forms coalition to preserve fin-syn rules," *Broadcasting*, 24 April 1989, pp. 30–31.

64. Bob Woletz, "On to 1990: can the next fin-syn war be averted?," *Channels of Communication*, February 1988, p. 83.

65. "Fox waiver petition may be open sesame for fin-syn revision," *Broadcasting*, 29 January 1990, pp. 19+.

66. "Falling into place over the Fox petition," *Broadcasting*, 12 March 1990, pp. 45–47.

67. In the wake of this decision, Fox grew to sixteen prime-time hours in the 1990–91 season, but since then has stabilized at fifteen hours, running three hours on Sunday and two on every night the rest of the week. In a move to both placate affiliates and run a tighter ship, the network has always ceded

the 10:00–11:00 p.m. hour to local stations, thus allowing them to run syndicated programming, including reruns of off-Fox series like *The Simpsons* and *That 70s Show*.

68. Qtd. in "Fin-syn talks fail, FCC takes over," *Broadcasting*, 18 June 1990, p. 19.

69. Woletz, "On to 1990," p. 84.

70. The Quello-Sikes plan was also intended to normalize Fox as a network, by changing the definition to over one-hundred affiliates or over fourteen prime-time hours, both milestones Fox had already passed.

71. The Barrett compromise included the following elements: the networks can acquire financial interest and syndication rights in any non-prime time programming; the networks can acquire financial interest and syndication rights in outside-produced prime-time series in accordance with a "two step" plan which separates the initial series licensing and negotiations for back-end interest by at least thirty days; the networks can syndicate outside-produced prime-time programs in foreign syndication markets; "in-house" productions or co-productions are limited to 40% of the prime-time schedule; the networks can produce programming for first-run syndication, but those series must be distributed by a third party; the rules apply to networks with more than fifteen hours of prime-time programming to affiliates reached by more than 75% of US television homes; the rules will be reviewed on June 15, 1995.

72. "FCC's fin-syn surprise: everybody knocks it," *Broadcasting*, 15 April 1991, pp. 37–38; "New fin-syn rules disappoint white house," *Broadcasting*, 22 April 1991, pp. 32–33.

73. "Going dark at 10," *Broadcasting*, 6 May 1991, pp. 20–21.

74. Joe Flint, "Fin-syn may lead to prime time cut, affiliates say," *Broadcasting*, 2 March 1992, p. 30.

75. In their decision, the judges wrote that

> The impression created is of unprincipled compromises of Rube Goldberg complexity among contending interest groups viewed merely as clamoring supplicants who have somehow to be conciliated. The possibility of resolving a conflict in favor of the party with the stronger case, as distinct from throwing up one's hands and splitting the difference, was overlooked.

Qtd. in Harry A. Jessell, "Appeal court vacates rules," *Broadcasting*, 9 November 1992, p. 5.

76. Harry A. Jessell, "Networks victorious in fin-syn fight," *Broadcasting & Cable*, 5 April 1993, pp. 7+.

77. A former industry lawyer, Hundt was a longtime associate of Vice President Al Gore, and had worked for Ted Turner during his unsuccessful bid for CBS in the late 1980s. Though he would not reveal his position on fin-syn immediately after his confirmation in November 1993, he clearly stated to reporters his philosophy of high-tech, free market development: "The FCC has a great chance to set economic policy in an industry that's so

important...we must get the economic growth that the telecommunications business can provide." Qtd. in Dennis Wharton, "Hundt gets ready for FCC post," *Daily Variety*, 24 November 1993, p. 1.

78. Geoffrey Foisie and Christopher Stern, "Paramount, Viacom say 'I Do'," *Broadcasting & Cable*, 20 September 1993, pp. 14–16.

79. "PTAR challenged at FCC," *Broadcasting*, 23 April 1990, p. 89.

80. Qtd. in Bill Carter, "Disney seeks to expand market for reruns," *New York Times*, 10 December 1990, sec. D, p. 9.

81. Dennis Wharton, "Sikes' PTAR plan getting little support," *Daily Variety*, 22 May 1992, p. 3.

82. Qtd. in Doug Halonen, "WCPX-TV pushes FCC to ax PTAR," *Electronic Media*, 14 February 1994, p. 3.

83. Qtd. in "FCC to consider PTAR," *Television Digest*, 4 April 1994.

84. Qtd. in Chris Stern and David Tobenkin, "FCC moves on prime time access rule," *Broadcasting & Cable*, 24 October 1994, p. 7.

85. Qtd. in "Q & A with Jim Heglund," *Electronic Media*, 9 January 1995, p. 12.

86. Qtd. in "FCC clears way for network progr. between 7 and 8 p.m.," *The Entertainment Litigation Reporter*, 15 August 1995.

87. Brian Lowry, "Changing Channels," *Daily Variety*, 8 March 1995.

88. Qtd. in Michael Schneider, "Littlefield knocks 'bad' series repeats: panel hashes out show ownership," *Electronic Media*, 15 September 1997, p. 2.

89. One of the more controversial, and embarrassing, in-house failures, was NBC Productions' *Union Square*, which debuted in September 1997 in prime-time's choicest time-slot (8:30 on Thursday, between the red-hot sitcoms *Friends* and *Seinfeld*) to universally scathing reviews and allegations of financial favoritism. The series' failure added to the perception that NBC was coasting on its successful Thursday-night lineup, and NBC Entertainment president Warren Littlefield, the chief architect of the network's prime-time schedule, was removed from the company in September 1998.

90. The networks even produced and sold several "in-house" productions to other networks during the mid to late 1990s. As early as 1993, ABC Productions had sold a short-lived series (*Class of '96*), to Fox as a midseason replacement. However, a more significant milestone in broadcast history was made in September 1994, when CBS began airing *The Boys Are Back*, produced by ABC Productions, marking the first time a series produced by one of the Big Three had aired on another. The following year, NBC began running CBS Entertainment's *Caroline in the City*, which ultimately ran for four seasons. By the early 2000s, however, network-owned programming was the rule rather than the exception, prompting a push to revive fin-syn in some form. Several independent studios, including Carsey-Werner-Mandabach and Sony (who did not own a network) formed

the Coalition for Program Diversity in January 2003 to critique network control. They noted that, in the 2002–03 season, CBS had controlling interest in 90% of their prime-time programs, Fox had 85%, ABC had 76%, and NBC had 55%. Bill McConnell, "Over our dead bodies," *Broadcasting & Cable*, 6 January 2003, p. 1.

91. I am not suggesting that each of these series are, or will even become, evergreens. Rather, the television heritage provides a discursive resource that the series' owners can use to promote their series as all-time favorites. Moreover, as Chapter 8 will explore, the addition of DVD box sets has provided an additional form of ostensible cultural and industrial permanence; with the exception of *Ally McBeal*, each of the series listed here has seen release in this format since 2000.

92. Steve McClellan, "Fox in the UPN House," *Broadcasting & Cable*, 21 August 2000, p. 4. Although the fate of UPN itself was very much in doubt at the time, after Viacom's takeover of CBS (and remains somewhat tenuous as of this writing), News Corp insisted it wanted the netlet to survive, and did not change the affiliation of these large-market stations away from UPN. The Chris-Craft purchase also put News Corp over the FCC's 35% cap (i.e., the limit of how much of the total US TV audience could be reached by one owner's stations), at 40%, and helped prompt the FCC to raise the limit in 2003, despite heated public and political opposition.

93. For example, *Seinfeld* ran on both of News Corp's Los Angeles stations, KCOP and KTTV, in the early 2000s.

94. Joe Schlosser, "More than just syndication," *Broadcasting & Cable*, 29 January 2001, p. 8.

95. Steve McClellan, "Rewriting the calendar," *Broadcasting & Cable*, 31 December 2001, p. 14.

96. Indeed, long-running UPN and WB programs coming onto the off-net market in the late 1990s were even sold on their novelty and "unfamiliarity" to audiences, given their low ratings against the other networks. Chris Pursell, "New off-net yucks mean big bucks," *Variety*, 23 August 1999, p. 27.

97. Melissa Greco, "News Corp's power play," *Variety*, 10 February 2003, p. 27.

98. For example, the only new sitcom to debut in off-net in Fall 2003 was *The King of Queens*.

99. It became standard practice during the comedy boom of the second half of the 1990s to market sitcoms in their second season, instead of the customary fourth or fifth seasons. The idea was to capitalize as rapidly as possible on the current flavor of the month. As Scott Carlin of Warner Brothers Domestic Television Distribution stated, "When a show is hot on the network and looking like it's going to go the distance of four years or more, there's a feeling on both sides that there's no time like the present." Qtd. in Cynthia Littleton, "'Nanny', 'Moesha' step out," *Broadcasting & Cable*, 12 May 1997, pp. 31–32.

100. Josef Adalian, "TV sitcom train jumps laugh track," *Variety*, 26 February 2001, p. 1.

101. That said, a proposed reality television cable channel, financed in part by several former reality contestants, plans to feature reruns of series such as *Survivor, Big Brother*, and *The Amazing Race*. In addition, as I complete this book, Viacom has announced the May 2004 release of the first season of *Survivor* as a DVD box set.

7

TV Land: Cable and Satellite as Boutique Television

[Cable] has not revolutionized the basic corporate structure of television. It has been integrated within it.[1]

Over the past two decades, repetition—and the specific role of off-network syndication—has expanded beyond the traditional broadcast spectrum, due to the restructuring of the television industry in the wake of continued deregulation and market expansion, and the interrelated development of technologies that have augmented the television experience. In the early years of the twenty-first century, TV is clearly "more" than it was 50, 30, or even 10 years ago; there are many more viewing options, thanks to the deployment of cable and direct broadcast satellite (DBS) distribution systems and program services; the widespread adoption of domestic video production and playback devices (i.e., videocassette recorders (VCRs), DVD players, and related equipment); and emerging broadband/Internet applications. While there are certainly new media and program forms (e.g., electronic programming guide (EPG) interfaces, reality television), all of these seeming innovations and expansions have benefited most from the medium's continued reliance on the televisual past, whether in the form of off-net, off-cable, or off-first-run reruns of fictional series, or in the recombinant uses of fictional and nonfictional audiovisual fragments, as in cable series like VH-1's *I Love The 80s*, MSNBC's *Time and Again*, or A&E's *Biography*. As this study has shown, a media text's cultural and industrial durability in repetition has been a primary design feature of many forms and entire genres since the industrialization of publishing in the nineteenth century. In television terms, a series'—or to use the vernacular of the media industry, a "property's"—propensity for repetition is an essential element in the overall viability of the studio, producer, distributor, network, station, and even fan.[2] In short, American television—both as an industry and as a culture—needs repetition.

Since the 1970s, the key technological, industrial, legal, and cultural field in the expansion of televisual repetition has been cable and satellite television, or what the FCC refers to as the multichannel video programming services.[3] As indicated by their histories, and more specifically by the discourses surrounding them, cable and satellite television systems have always been perceived and promoted as "different" than traditional broadcasting. Indeed, since cable and satellite channels do not fall under the same FCC strictures as broadcast stations, they are legally entitled to this difference, however it may be defined. Whether described in the language of fear and destruction (e.g., as the death-knell of over-the-air broadcasting, a once-prevalent image which still persists in some circles), or hope and revolution (e.g., as the aesthetic and/or social redeemer of television), cable and satellite have clearly functioned as somehow exterior to broadcasting, as precisely "*not* TV," to borrow the catchphrase of one popular cable network. While cable and satellite systems, technologies, services, networks, and programs have matched these distinctive descriptions at times, they have also drawn extensively from established forms, practices, and texts. Indeed, on the whole, as Thomas Streeter argues, cable and satellite have not provided so much an alternative to television, but rather an expansion of its dominant logic: repetition.[4] Cable has mostly provided "more" of what broadcast television has always delivered: more comedies, more dramas, more sports, more talk shows, more music, more language, more violence, more nudity, more religion, more channels, more personalities, etc.

This discursive clash (i.e., repetition as innovation) has deep roots in the history of cable in the United States. There was nothing all that "new" about cable technology by the time it began its period of greatest growth in the late 1970s. As a physical means of transmitting and receiving television signals, cable had been in use since the 1940s, practically as long as network television broadcasting itself, with the same coaxial cables, signal amplifiers, microwave relays, and the like which also supported traditional broadcast television.[5] Originally tied more explicitly to over-the-air broadcasting (as "community antenna television" (CATV) until the late 1960s), cable television developed steadily at the margins of television throughout the 1950s and 1960s, providing retransmission (i.e., straight-up repetition) of distant broadcast signals from cities to surrounding rural areas and, more controversially, to other cities. According to Brian Winston, cable's primary function at that time was the improved reception of existing broadcast signals, a factor that remains important in attracting and maintaining customer subscriptions to this day.[6] Despite this fairly mundane function, however, cable boosters also held out the promise of a "new," "alternative" television system parallel to but outside the control of the Big Three networks and broadcast stations. As Streeter recounts, the promise of these utopian, "blue sky" discourses enabled cable television interests and supporters to erode government restrictions in the 1970s, and articulate a system of specialized, nonbroadcast channels that fully blossomed in the 1980s and 1990s.[7]

With over 300 nationally broadcast cable networks by the early 2000s, these discourses have become a kind of reality, even if the skies have not been quite as blue as promised along the way. However, it is important to acknowledge the genuine innovations, forms and expanded parameters fostered by cable- and satellite-based programming over the past 30 years. Programming forms including music videos, public access, continuous news, several varieties of nonfiction, and long-form fictional television were all developed or enhanced via cable networks. Cable programs and networks have genuinely provided a greater range of diversity and novelty than was ever presented over broadcast networks and stations. Nevertheless, Winston's phrase "improved reception of existing broadcast signals" still best describes how cable predominantly functions in the current media environment.[8] Like the independent stations before them—while cable networks have loudly exclaimed the rhetoric of innovation—they have most often thrived on the stuff of repetition, offering schedules filled with past film and television: in short, reruns. From the original cable "superstation," WTBS, to the latest niche channel, such as TV One, extant films and television programs have been cable's bread and butter.

Moreover, as a key component in the consolidation of the entire media terrain into vertically- and horizontally-integrated, thoroughly-synergistic corporations, cable has functioned to insure the viability of programming beyond the cultural and industrial capabilities of broadcast stations, adding not only a few more links in the profit chain, but also an array of practices designed to promote and program series in ways that broadcasting alone could not. The concept of "improved reception" thus takes on an added layer of meaning for viewers, for in presenting familiar programming, cable networks do not merely run it; they strip it, promote it, repackage it, and recombine it. Accordingly, the experience of rerun series on cable is presented as aesthetically "more" than it was over broadcasting. For example, some series are presented in digitally restored or even "uncut" forms. Other series are presented in daily blocks of two or more, encouraging hours of immersive viewing of one particular program. On some channels—notably Viacom's Nick At Nite and TV Land—programs are even periodically run in "marathons": days-long blocks of continuous episodes of one series, or similar series, in themed parts of the schedule. These devices, and others, constitute cable's *distinctive repetition*, whereby repetition does not only reign; it is refined and focused, capitalizing on both the television heritage, and viewers' expectations of repetition. In other words, with cable, it is increasingly not enough to simply present the familiar over and over again, as in broadcasting; the familiar must be made unique and remarkable.

Given that strategy, the relatively miniscule ratings of cable networks relative to their broadcast counterparts are beside the point. Their appeal is directed at specific, loyal audience segments, rather than the mass audience; their viewers come to expect particular kinds of packaging and a more unique viewing experience.

Thus, cable networks function as television *boutiques*: venues offering a limited array of products for specialized audiences. Channels like BET, Bravo, TV Land, the Sci-Fi Channel, Boomerang, Lifetime, the Hallmark Channel, Trio, and Spike TV are designed to capture particular audiences (and thus, particular advertisers) designated by age, gender, sexuality, ethnicity, and interest. They build their brands through the acquisition and promotion of programming appropriate to their image. While virtually every cable boutique, including TV Land, also runs original first-run programs, reruns generally form the core of their identity, especially when they are seeking to establish themselves with audiences and advertisers. As with broadcasting, a popular, familiar rerun is thus the lifeblood of cable. However, once a cable brand is established, it is not necessarily stable. Just as clothing boutiques must continually update their couture, cable boutiques must constantly monitor their ratings for apparent shifts in their audience's tastes. Sometimes, the brand remains the same, but its content is refreshed, as when Court TV removed reruns of *Homicide* in favor of *The Practice*. Other times, the entire brand is shifted, as with FX's shift from a female to a male target demographic, or another network's similar, three-stage movement from older-skewing, down-home country as The Nashville Network (TNN), to 18–34 frat-boy hijinks as Spike TV, "the first network for men." In short, cable boutiques chase their desired viewers (or at least the ratings-derived numerical representations of ostensible desired viewers) with the most appropriate programming they can obtain.

This chapter traces how, in the name of "alternative" television, and in the distinctive forms of exclusive boutiques, cable has effectively extended broadcasting's familiar regime of repetition, and has fostered the ongoing consolidation of the media industry. I will first explore how cable networks first developed and related alongside the existing broadcasting policies and interests in the 1960s and 1970s, focusing in particular on the first cable boutiques: the "superstations." Then, I will trace how cable expanded in the 1980s, largely via the boutique model of networks like Lifetime and (especially) Nick At Nite. Finally, I will examine the cable boutique's role in the integration of television into "one world" of content in the 1990s and 2000s.

Superstations: Broadcast to Cable

At the beginning of cable's conspicuous arrival in mainstream policy and discourse, it was pronounced to be anything but familiar. Streeter describes the "blue sky" rhetoric of cable television executives, legislators, and communications activists in the 1960s and 1970s as sincerely advocating innovative programming, community services, and interactive systems which were to enable activities ranging from home shopping to grass-roots democracy. In utopian discourses that would be repeated nearly verbatim around the Internet in the late 1990s, cable was promoted as a socially beneficial technology that could—on its own, apparently—improve the condition of the nation, an especially pressing concern in the wake of the social upheaval of the 1960s. Ralph Lee Smith's 1972 *The Wired Nation*, originally presented in *The Nation* magazine, described this theoretical new television in glowing terms. "Television can become far more flexible, far more democratic, far more diversified in content, and far more responsive to the full range of pressing needs in today's cities, neighborhoods, towns and communities," he wrote, but he also noted, prophetically, that "the easy availability of... nationally prepackaged material could inhibit creative local programming."[9]

Those concerns were well-placed, as cable system operators were generally not concerned with providing local access or even producing their own local commercial programming, but in importing programs from other sources: mostly broadcast signals from other cities, or, in a few scattered circumstances in the 1950s and 1960s, uncut feature films from specialized services. However, the FCC effectively "froze" the industry in the 1960s via the 1965 *First Report and Order*, which essentially banned cable systems from operating in the top one hundred markets, precisely because of concerns of repetition. The rule was issued because local broadcasters were opposed to distant signal importation, i.e., the unauthorized transmission of broadcast signals on cable systems. They had legitimate reasoning at the time, as cable systems paid neither the stations for such retransmission, nor the program distributors for royalties on the programs they sent over their wires. Moreover, stations argued, cable was an unfair "back door" into markets by distant broadcasters, adding competition for viewers and advertisers and negatively impacting their market standing. A series of court challenges to cable systems were mounted in the late 1960s on precisely these grounds. In each of them, however, the Supreme Court ultimately ruled that, while the cable industry was liable to federal regulation in principle, cable companies were *not* liable to pay royalties for the programming they carried.[10]

Over the late 1960s, however, this "community antenna" rhetoric, with its image of distant reception of over-the-air signals, shifted to a "wired" discourse of "cable," which suggested original transmission and (more significantly), *connection*, rather than only reception. With this new image, the cable industry, along with friendly policymakers and activists, were able to advance a convincing discourse of cable's unique potential contributions to society.[11] Largely as a result of this discursive push, the

FCC, which was less inclined than ever to favor established broadcasting interests at this point, passed new cable rules in the early 1970s. Their 1972 *Third Report and Order* removed the ban on distant signal importation, and thus allowed cable into the lucrative top 100 markets. However, as first articulated in earlier rulemakings, the FCC did require some local origination of programming. While the industry opposed and grumbled about the various public access and governance requirements of the rules, they began expanding into the nation's cities.

In his 1995 dissertation, Eric R. Guthey argues that the 1972 rules contained the seeds of their own destruction, which helped pave the way for greater distant signal importation and, more significantly, satellite distribution, later in the decade.[12] The rules contained "contradictory policy objectives," which were ripe for repeal or simply unenforceable. One of the most significant rules concerned limits on the importation of distant signals. While the new rules did allow them, *contra* the earlier, strictly pro-broadcasting philosophy, they also contained an "anti-leapfrogging" mandate, which was meant to placate local broadcasters. "Leapfrogging" referred to a cable system bypassing a local broadcast program source, such as a network affiliate or an independent station, in favor of a similar source from a distant origin, such as a larger market. The rules' must-carry provision mandated that at least four local broadcast signals must be carried by the cable system, but the antileapfrogging component assured that local stations would not be unfairly passed up. Because of this provision, however, virtually every cable system within 300 miles of Atlanta was mandated to carry UHF station WTCG, since no other independent stations were available. As the only independent station in a fairly large geographical area, WTCG, via its legendary owner Ted Turner, thus consolidated its hold on the best available syndicated programming.[13] In the wake of the 1972 rules, cable operators sought to make peace with broadcasters by promoting the WTCG experience, which suggested how cable systems could expand the range of broadcast stations. At the 1974 INTV convention, INTV president Roger Rice claimed, "cable can make an independent a regional station rather than just a local station."[14] At this time, WTCG and a few other large-market independents, including WGN in Chicago and KTVU in San Francisco, were already regional channels (in the South, Midwest, and West Coast, respectively) on cable due to microwave retransmission. However, the line of sight and signal boosting limits of microwave transmission could only extend their signals so far; KTVU was carried throughout the mountains and valleys of northern California and Oregon, while WTCG extended across most of the southeast. However, the reach of these stations, and the growth of national cable distribution altogether, may have stopped at this point were it not for the simultaneous development of the satellite communications industry.

Satellite communications had been developing in the United States since the late 1950s, under the public corporation COMSAT. As another communications alternative to established systems and technologies, satellites also carried their own blue sky discourses. Guthey notes that after the 1963 invention of the geosynchronous satellite—which could orbit at an altitude of 22,500 miles and match the rate of the Earth's rotation, thus appearing to be "fixed" in the sky—"satellite technology joined cable as the *deus ex machina* of the broadcast reform movement."[15] However, as it had with cable, the FCC essentially blocked satellite distribution of domestic television for most of the 1960s and early 1970s, until the 1972 "Open Skies" ruling fostered the private development of satellite services, and opened the doors for satellite distribution of television programming. In anticipation of a national cable viewership, Time Inc. launched its commercial-free premium service of feature films and special events as Home Box Office (HBO) later that year. However, satellite receiver dishes were a tightly controlled technology, and cable's antileapfrogging provisions were still intact until 1975, thus HBO, like WTCG, was only a regional service (via microwave links in the northeast) for its first three years. Shortly thereafter, the FCC licensed smaller, 4.5-meter television receive-only (TVRO) dishes, or "earth stations," which made satellite reception much more affordable for individual cable systems to obtain.[16] In 1977, 500 earth stations were in use by television stations and cable systems; by 1984, there were over 5400 in operation.[17] The rapid development of satellite transmission and reception in the late 1970s was the critical spur to the cable television industry, as it greatly facilitated national distribution. As Streeter writes, "what brought cable to the point of takeoff, in sum, was not cable itself, but the possibility of cheap networking via satellites."[18]

On the very same day that the FCC approved the new TVRO dishes— December 20, 1976—WTCG began satellite distribution, becoming the first cable "superstation."[19] Boosting the development of satellite television even further, in October 1978, following chairman Charles Ferris' faith in technology and the free market, the FCC endorsed an "open entry" policy, which allowed for the virtually unlimited satellite distribution of television signals.[20] WTCG immediately changed its advertising rates to reflect a national, rather than local audience. Within a year, its call letters had changed to WTBS, reflecting a change in the name of its parent company (to Turner Broadcasting System). It was still technically a local broadcast station, but owner Ted Turner was focused on the national market. Within months of the open entry ruling, satellite carriers nationwide began retransmitting the signals of three other stations: WGN Chicago, WOR New York, and KTVU San Francisco. Unlike WTCG/WTBS, however, these others were "reluctant" super-stations. They were faced with significant competition for advertising in their home markets already, and could not afford to simply adopt a national mode of address.[21]

The term "superstation" suggests that these channels were more than mere stations. However, "mere stations" was essentially what they were: typical local independent stations, but with a national reach. Despite some surface differences, reflecting their regional or national audiences, all of the superstations were programmed exactly like textbook-independent broadcast stations, with old films, off-network reruns, cartoons, and sports filling their schedules. This is a far cry from Turner's congressional testimony in 1976, when he claimed that his superstation would "produce its own programs," and "not just [run] 'I Love Lucy' and 'Gilligan's Island' for the 57th time."[22] The reference to these particular familiar (and much-maligned) rerun series is ironic on a few different levels. Although the FCC repealed the syndicated exclusivity, or "syndex," rules in 1980, ostensibly allowing superstations to run whatever they could afford, older series like *I Love Lucy, Gilligan's Island, Father Knows Best* and *Leave It To Beaver* were especially important to their overall success. According to Sidney Pike, WTBS' director of television operations in the 1980s, older series were both cheaper to acquire—particularly in light of syndicators' increased license fees based on the superstation's quasi-national reach—and less likely to be duplicated in local markets, due to their age.[23] These series thus capitalized on the television heritage to offer distinctive, if not particularly innovative, programs. While WTBS ran *Leave It To Beaver* and WGN *The Cisco Kid*, local stations were far more likely to air more recent fare like *Happy Days* or *M*A*S*H*. By the time the nostalgia trend had hit the broadcast syndication market in the mid-1980s, the superstations had already staked part of their identities on vintage reruns. Thus, while repetition had already been a part of television since the 1950s, and although there was little difference between the superstations and independent stations, the former were able to hook into the discourse of the "new," via cable, to foster their own sensibility of distinctive repetition.

At the beginning of the 1980s, despite a decade of ardent cable discourses, the local-cum-national superstations were still among the most popular nationwide cable channels. The premium channels HBO and Showtime had carved out a niche with a mix of recent Hollywood films, live music and sporting events, and a handful of original productions, but the new, all-sports channel ESPN was just getting by. Pay channels that featured sexually explicit programming, however, were faring quite well, indicating that the discourses about cable providing distinct alternatives to broadcast television were sometimes accurate.[24] But other services came and went throughout this period. From 1979 to 1981, while the cable penetration rate steadily expanded from 19% to 28% of all U.S. households, and the number of nationally distributed cable channels doubled, from 19 to 38, there was little stability among cable networks beyond the superstations and a few premium channels. The prognostications and opinions on cable varied considerably, largely due to this relative paucity of programming alternatives. Commenting in an overview of new television technologies in the conservative magazine *Across The Board* in 1981, ABC Video Enterprises cable programming developer (and former network program chief) Michael Dann proclaimed that "not since the automobile has America had an invention which will so change people's lives. That's exactly what cable will do."[25] *New York Times* columnist Russell Baker was more skeptical, presciently observing that "[cable] threatens to divide among 180 channels material already inadequate for thirteen channels."[26] However, the promise of new economic television frontiers ultimately outweighed the general ambivalence toward the programming, and cable developers regularly launched new channels throughout the first half of the 1980s.

National advertisers—essential for programming support—remained wary, however, and with good reason. Channels that provided anything other than generalized fare, uncut movies, or porn had yet to attract steady, sizable audiences. Moreover, the actual audience measurement standards for cable TV were far from standardized or reliable, with Nielsen and Arbitron frequently coming up with contradictory results. Accordingly, major advertisers continued to place their bets with the Big Three broadcast networks, who, despite the additional competition from independent stations, PBS, and now cable, still accounted for over 80% of the prime-time television audience in the early 1980s. ABC, CBS, and NBC took in a combined $6 billion in advertising revenue in 1982, 30 times basic cable's relatively paltry $204 million (two-thirds of which went to Turner's WTBS and Cable News Network (CNN)).[27] Industry boosters cited the "magic" penetration rate of 33% as the point at which ad rates would increase, but the advertising was slow to come, even after cable reached 40% of households by the end of 1983. As a result, several prominent cable services—like CBS' bold, high culture-oriented CBS Cable—went under, while others were forced to merge to survive.[28] Thus, despite the continued promises of economic expansion via cable (the new "blue sky" of the 1980s), the actual expansion of new programming outlets was fairly tenuous at this time.

However, the success of the superstation model had inspired at least three new basic cable channels: the USA Network, the Christian Broadcasting Network (CBN), and The Entertainment Channel.[29] While these channels had no over-the-air broadcasting component, they effectively operated as de facto independent stations, particularly in regard to off-network reruns. In 1981, Joel Chaseman of the Post-Newsweek station group referred to this as "a disturbing pattern ... abundance without diversity. The channels are filling up with the same old programming ... "[30] This "same old programming" was lucrative for channels like USA and CBN in particular. While the latter was somewhat ambivalent about its reliance on familiar, "wholesome" off-net series like *Ozzie and Harriet*, granting that such reruns had helped them gain audiences and advertisers but insisting that they would eventually program more original series, USA heavily promoted its array of off-network series with themed dayparts and events.[31]

By the second half of the 1980s, largely on the vitality of the super-stations, CNN, and USA, basic cable networks were in a better position to garner viewers and programming. Fifty per cent of households sub-scribed to cable by early 1987, while 61 basic cable networks contended for audiences. Having settled on a firmer financial ground, cable could now begin to encroach on what was up until then the sacrosanct territory of the local broadcaster: new off-network syndication. From this point forward, cable would become a legitimate competitor for television properties, and not just another market "below" or "after" broadcasting.

Off-Network, On Cable

As the broadcast syndication market deepened its veneration of the elusive off-net half-hour sitcom in the mid 1980s, top cable channels such as USA, CBN, and Lifetime saw "a window of opportunity" to obtain some recent, but relatively neglected off-network programs: the much-maligned hours.[32] In the wake of NATPE 1987, the situation was dim for the distributors of recent hour series such as *St. Elsewhere*, *Cagney and Lacey*, and *Simon and Simon*, who received only slight interest for their series from local broadcasters. Local stations' tastes had shifted more decisively toward off-net sitcoms and first-run talk shows, leaving little room for hours. MCA, the producers of the expensive and faddish *Miami Vice*, were particularly worried that they would not be able to sell their series in syndication, as it was not only an hour, but also an increasingly dated hour.[33]

However, cable networks were interested in these series because they sought familiar, popular programming, and could afford to take a chance on the hours. They not only had large gaps of time to fill on their schedules, but also had an increased advertising revenue and subscriber base, and could thus meet distributors' prices. Accordingly, audience-favorite USA was the primary customer of off-network hours in the mid to late 1980s, licensing male-skewing action-oriented series such as *Airwolf*, *Riptide*, and *Miami Vice*. While the handful of broadcast stations that had actually pursued these series were upset at this "reversed" syndication sequence—i.e., going to cable first, rather than to broadcast—the hours were a boon for both the buyers (the cable networks) and sellers (the program distributors). By 1988, it had become a standard procedure in the syndication market to bypass local stations entirely, and shop off-net hours directly to the cable networks. USA, Lifetime, and the Family Channel (formerly CBN) functioned as the de facto "Big Three" of off-net hours at this time, paying up to $200,000 an episode for a particular series. While this figure was far short of what the typical off-net sitcom could garner in broadcast syndication, it still represented a sizable sale to only one buyer (as opposed to dozens or hundreds). As Pat Fili, senior vice president of programming at Lifetime pointed out, "It's a lot easier to sell to us than to 100 different stations."[34] For example, in their largest program outlay to that time, USA acquired exclusive six-year syndication rights to *Murder, She Wrote* in 1988 for $30 million, a deal that marked the first time a top-ten network series had bypassed broadcast syndication completely in favor of cable.[35]

The off-net hours not only garnered high fees up front for their distributors; they were also popular with cable audiences, meeting and surpassing their buyers' expectations. The Family Channel, Lifetime, and USA all ran their plum off-network hours in prime time, and these series were the highest-rated programs on each of the channels. These reruns were so successful that a network-like competition for prime time ratings even developed between these three channels at the end of the 1980s.[36] However, the most significant result of the successful adaptation of the off-network syndication market to cable was the use of reruns to shape and bolster cable networks' identities. This enabled them to further differentiate themselves from their competition with well-chosen series that matched their target audience, i.e., to function as television boutiques. Lifetime was particularly pleased with its acquisitions throughout the late 1980s and early 1990s, which included the critically acclaimed dramas *Cagney and Lacey*, *LA Law*, *Moonlighting*, and *thirtysomething*, all of which appealed to its target audience of "upper-scale, loyal" adult women. The network even credited its much-improved ratings in 1988 to *Cagney and Lacey* alone.[37] The Family Channel (formerly CBN) opted for an appropriately family-oriented slate, acquiring *Beauty and the Beast*, *Father Dowling Mysteries*, and *The Waltons*. Meanwhile, USA pursued a young male audience, and highlighted the action and gunplay of its *Airwolf*, *Miami Vice*, and *The Equalizer*.

The acquisition, scheduling, and promotion of these series indicate that off-network programming, and not original productions, formed the foundation of some of the most popular and powerful cable networks. The discourse of the television heritage, as activated via off-network reruns, had enabled these networks, and others, to shape their core identities around extant, familiar programs, attracting audiences to something distinctive, yet also "safe." Functioning as branded boutiques, these networks still offer unique spaces known for particular kinds of television.

Rerun Nations: Viacom's Nick At Nite and TV Land

However unique these cable boutiques are, like all contemporary brands, they also function as key financial components of their parent corporations. Accordingly, the wave of consolidations that has united studios, media companies, cable multiple system operators (MSOs), and cable networks in an unprecedented agglomeration of industrial synergies since the 1980s has also contributed to the rapid development of off-network properties on branded cable networks. One of the most important corporations in this regard is Viacom. Created from divested CBS syndication and cable assets in anticipation of the fin-syn rules in 1971, Viacom used its slate of off-network evergreens—including *I Love Lucy*, *The Andy Griffith Show*, *The Beverly Hillbillies*, and *The Twilight Zone*—to propel its growth into one of the primary syndicators of U.S. television in the 1970s and 1980s. By 1986, Viacom had expanded its cable interests, acquiring the MTV Networks (cable networks MTV, Nickelodeon, Nick At Nite, and VH-1) and the remaining half of Showtime/The Movie Channel from Warner Amex; obtained controlling interest of faltering film studio Orion Pictures; and produced the most successful series on network television, NBC's *The Cosby Show*. At the time, Alan Kassan, a media industry analyst with First Manhattan Corp., called Viacom "the prototype for what a modern media company should look like, in terms of vertical integration." Journalist Meryl Gordon was no less sanguine, commenting, "what we're talking about here is synergy with a capital *S*."[38] As expansive as the company was at that point, it would grow even more after National Amusements chairman Sumner Redstone took it over in 1987. Viacom merged with Paramount Communications in 1994, creating a mega-corporation with abundant synergies across the board through cable, theme parks, home video, and retailing.[39] Redstone claimed at the time that "if there were a right time for this entertainment giant to be born it's right now."[40] Still not content with its vast holdings, Redstone's "giant" eventually acquired its original corporate parent CBS in 2000.

Aside from MTV and its sibling channels, which have dominated much of the televised youth culture for over 20 years, two of the primary avenues of "capital-S-Synergy" at Viacom have been its interlinked Nick At Nite and TV Land cable networks, the preeminent rerun-based cable television boutiques. Launched as a tentative foray into prime-time programming by the children-oriented Nickelodeon network in the summer of 1985, Nick At Nite soon developed into a space quite distinct from that channel's daytime schedule of children's programming. Two decades later, it is a staple of virtually every basic cable lineup in the United States, as is its spin-off channel, TV Land, a 24-hour all-rerun channel that launched in the spring of 1996. Drawing from the growing cultural validity of nostalgia (and the television heritage in particular), and capitalizing on the relatively inexpensive costs of older sitcoms, each channel has acquired the cable syndication rights to dozens of different off-network reruns throughout their histories, from *The Honeymooners* to *Roseanne*.

While Viacom's continued corporate pursuit of exploitable, repeatable rerun properties is certainly significant in political economic terms, what makes both Nick At Nite and TV Land particularly important for television (and for television studies) is what they *do* with all those reruns. The networks' active, exhibitionist construction of vintage television, or, in Viacom's trademarked phrase, "classic TV," is the original rerun television boutique on cable, and has inspired many similar endeavors from other networks. The very "TV-ness" each channel has presented serves as a key example of the shift towards distinctive repetition that developed on cable television at the end of the twentieth century. Unlike independent broadcast stations, Nick At Nite and TV Land are no mere rerun venues; they are methodically constructed *shrines* of the television heritage, where past programs are immersed in a stylized array of promotional material and intertextual associations. Through their selection of programs and aesthetic framing, Nick At Nite and TV Land have foregrounded the historical construction of "television," producing a compelling blend of decades, televisual styles, and memories. In short, they are television-themed television boutiques, and reflexively function as a kind of "living history," the television heritage incarnate.

The channels' self-aware treatment of the television heritage has taken on many guises since Nick At Nite's inception, but has always centered upon the idea of the channels as the primary homes for reruns on television. After experimenting with a few older reruns acquired in the mid 1980s "classic TV" boom, Nickelodeon formally launched Nick At Nite in 1985 to attract the baby boomer parents of its daytime viewers, with slightly older-skewing but still child-friendly series. Nick At Nite's initial mode of address, echoes of which still remain, harked exactly back to the boomers' nostalgic TV neverland of the late 1950s, with colorful space-age shapes, bouncy pre-program bumps and promos ("Hello out there from TV land!," "Your home for classic TV!"), overenthusiastic announcers' voices, mascots, and music reminiscent of the era (or at least the pastel-laden 1980s version of the fifties). This iconography of TV dinners and Raymond Loewy cocktail tables was consistent with discourses of the fifties nostalgia already in circulation at this time, and was particularly appropriate considering that virtually the entire Nick At Nite schedule consisted of black and white programs like *The Donna Reed Show* and *My Three Sons*, which all originally aired circa 1958–1963. However, these design elements became somewhat incongruous as more recent programs were added to the schedule in the late 1980s and early 1990s. Several popular 1960s and 1970s series were acquired at this time, including *The Dick Van Dyke Show*, *The Lucy Show*, and, in a massive, $40 million deal in 1992, the exclusive rights to 650 hours of MTM programs, including *The Mary Tyler Moore Show* and *The Bob Newhart Show*.[41] After obtaining these series, as well as the cable rights to all-time rerun champ

I Love Lucy, Nick At Nite slightly shifted its mode of address. The playful retro feel was retained but the jokey, fifties "TV dinner" sensibility was toned down. Instead, programs were openly highlighted as "classics," with Nick At Nite acting as faux-portentous guardians of history by "preserving our television heritage."[42] A few years later, as their schedule focused more on the 1970s (e.g., *The Brady Bunch, Happy Days, The Partridge Family, Welcome Back, Kotter*), Nick At Nite adopted a suitably "groovy" tone befitting the seventies nostalgia of the 1990s. Since that time, Nick At Nite has continued to adapt to the prevailing winds of retro and nostalgia, adjusting their lineup and iconography as necessary. Accordingly, their early 2000s lineup has centered on the 1980s (apparently the TV neverland of Generation X parents), and includes the likes of *Cheers, The Cosby Show, Family Ties, Full House*, and *Roseanne.*

TV Land, launched in the spring of 1996, has expanded the ethos of Nick At Nite into a 24-hour schedule, running more series over a wider swath of the television heritage, and notably scheduling dramas and adventure series instead of only sitcoms. With a larger conception of the television heritage, TV Land's overall brand design has functioned differently than Nick At Nite's. While Nick At Nite has always tended to emphasize a particular historical era of television on their schedule (with appropriate imagery), TV Land has packaged their lineup as a kind of all-purpose TV museum, usually associating series by genre rather than era. On TV Land, a schedule might consist of *The Munsters, Sanford and Son, Gunsmoke, Fantasy Island, All In The Family*, and *Cheers*, meaning that a viewer could experience comedies, dramas, and adventure series from the first four decades of television in a few hours without changing the channel. In addition, TV Land has occasionally offered original non-fiction programs that explore particular series (e.g., behind the scenes of *The Dick Van Dyke Show*) or issues (African-Americans on television) via retrospective interviews and appropriate images and clips. Similarly, repackaged archival interviews from *60 Minutes* and *Entertainment Tonight* (whose video libraries are conveniently owned by Viacom) have provided a further degree of historicity, in the compilation/talking-head documentary style that has been common on cable networks since the late 1990s.[43]

No matter which periods or genres of television their programs have referred to, or of the particular modes of presentation, Nick At Nite and TV Land have functioned as decidedly postmodern spaces of cultural history: collections of sounds, images, and personalities which have fostered a generalized (albeit particularly flavored) television heritage, rather than only an engagement with specific programs. Decades, representations, characters, genres, and plots blur right into each other, resulting in a multimediated *pastness*, rather than a more specific sense of "the past." The channels have drawn from and expanded viewers' television memories along these lines by rewarding them with an array of promotional devices designed to foster participation in the television heritage. Marathon blocks of episodes (e.g., a "Mary-thon" of *The Mary Tyler Moore Show*, a "three-hour tour" of *Gilligan's Island*) are often scheduled on each network, allowing viewers to immerse themselves in a single series for several hours, or in the case of TV Land's occasional "Fandemonium" weekends, days. Other themed events have linked the television heritage with the calendar (Nick At Nite's "summer block party," which ran a three-hour block of episodes from five different series airing each weeknight in the summer; e.g., "Monkee Mondays," "Bewitched Bewednesdays," "Sgt. Joe Fridays," etc.), or even television's own clichés (as in Nick At Nite's "Very Very" and TV Land's "Box Set" blocks, which consisted of episodes from different series, but with familiar sitcom plots; e.g., amnesia, snowstorms, disastrous parties, lottery tickets, troublesome relatives, etc.).

Each network has also consistently run series of 30-second thematic promos that play off the television heritage with bits of trivia related to particular genres, series, and characters. For example, during the mid 1990s on Nick At Nite, a series of promos called, appropriately enough, "Our Television Heritage," drew viewers' attentions to recurring sounds and images on particular series (e.g., the "Major Nelson Howl" on *I Dream of Jeannie*, the "Reuben Hair Shift" on *The Partridge Family*), foregrounding the pleasures of recognition generated through televisual repetition. That is, you would only understand references to, for example, "the Unger leap," and "Hiya," if you were already familiar with their prominence on *The Odd Couple* and *Rhoda* (respectively). Similarly, a 1999–2000 series of promos on TV Land with the catchphrase "Times change, great TV doesn't," used clips from old series with new, ironic dialogue overdubbed, so that Uncle Bill (of *Family Affair*) tells his nephew and niece, Jody and Buffy, that he wants to get a nose ring, and *Dragnet*'s Joe Friday raps to an audience about police work. The gap between now and then is humorously amplified in these short bits of television, which have reveled in the televisual constructions of the past, the present, and our modes of understanding the differences between them. While each channel has run hundreds of promos from a wide range of sensibilities over their tenures, their significance to the overall boutique design is crucial, arguably greater than that of the programs themselves.[44] Just as a striking logo, catchphrase, or perceived sensibility propels boutiques and brands in contemporary capitalism, these promos have helped establish Nick At Nite and TV Land as *the* "homes of classic television," with all the attendant consumer expectations.

As the primary rerun television boutiques, Nick At Nite and TV Land have clearly been premised on viewers' prior experiences of televisual repetition. The television heritage, or, more specifically, these networks' particular versions of its discourses, has consistently been activated and reinforced through each network's selection of series, scheduling devices, and promos, which have all encouraged semiotic associations not only among the series each channel is currently running, but also outward to a broader conception of "television" itself. An annual TV Land awards ceremony was even inaugurated in 2003, honoring viewers' all-time favorite television series, characters, and actors, thus further enshrining their television heritage in formal honors. As seen throughout Nick At Nite and TV Land, and particularly encapsulated in the TV Land Awards, the carefully maintained designs of the networks suggests that the television heritage is a quite particular set of references (i.e., centering on the most repeated series, plots, characters, and/or aesthetic sensibilities) that can be simultaneously communicated as "timeless" entertainment, camp/retro refashioning, and cultural history. While these viewing positions may differ (even if they do overlap at points), they have also clearly attracted enough of the appropriate demographic groups to enable each network to thrive.[45] By encapsulating particular genres and eras (e.g., "Cop Shows," "Comedies," "the "Fifties," "the Seventies") as retro-packaged bundles of televisual style, Nick At Nite and TV Land have produced a particularly effective boutique of the television heritage, as well as two of the most reliable of Viacom's cable networks. They are the archetypal television boutiques, and have provided a clear model for the creative deployment of distinctive repetition, inspiring a broad range of similar channels in their wakes.

Ready-Made Identities: Boutique Channels in the 1990s and 2000s

The success of the Nick at Nite/TV Land rerun boutique model strengthened the bond between off-network syndication and cable network branding. The deals that first brought older and more recent off-net reruns to cable in the 1980s were standard business a few years later. Many broadcast stations, however, were troubled with the success of off-net cable syndication by this time, and contended that its continuing growth would ultimately sabotage the broadcast side of the market.[46] In addition, broadcasters also worried that some programs would be overexposed on cable through repetition, and would thus be a less attractive prospect in the new "off-network-off-cable" market. Despite these reservations, however, the trajectory of the market was clear by the end of the 1980s: basic cable was an increasingly vital component of the off-network syndication market, and off-network syndication was clearly fundamental to basic cable's viability. The only major difference since then has been more of degree than of kind, profoundly shaped by the ongoing economic and technological shifts. In a digital mediascape that boasted over 300 basic and premium cable networks at the beginning of the twenty-first century, channels must function more than ever before as distinctive locations that become known for particular kinds of content; i.e., as boutiques.

Moreover, unlike in the seller's market of the 1980s, content is now abundant in this environment, with a relatively wide variety of viable programming for all dayparts and audiences coming from networks, syndication, basic cable, and premium cable origins. While individual series still matter, as the owners of the cable rights to *Seinfeld* would certainly testify, audience fragmentation has expanded the feasibility of a broader range of content. Accordingly, while traditional reruns remain important, they are a diminishing part of the overall cable picture. The codes of repetition established by off-net reruns have, however, been applied by all cable boutiques, regardless of programming. While the rerun-and-retro design of Nick At Nite and TV Land has not been duplicated in full anywhere else, its general approach to distinctive repetition persists in other cable networks who have focused on producing or acquiring branded properties keyed to their boutique identities. Lifetime is "television for women," while Spike TV is "the first network for men." Trio offers "pop, culture, TV," but HBO presents its critical-darling originals as somehow "not TV." Whole channels are dedicated to the mystery, science fiction, and western genres; several channels now exclusively feature animation. On all of these networks, regardless of the particular genre, niche, or sensibility of the boutique, the fact of repetition not only justifies the programming; it actively structures its presentation.

During the economic and technological expansion of cable networks and systems in the second half of the 1990s (in the wake of major physical upgrades in most markets), off-network fare was still the most highly valued rerun form. Cable networks routinely bid not only for hours, but also for the more expensive half-hour sitcoms. As explored in the last chapter, despite high demand in broadcast syndication at this time, a glut of off-net sitcoms helped the market absorb this demand to an extent. Again, Turner, now a subsidiary of Time Warner, was the most aggressive buyer in this market, obtaining the lucrative cable rights to more recent (and more expensive) off-net series like *Seinfeld*, *Roseanne*, *The Drew Carey Show*, and *Friends*, while refreshing its afternoon lineup with 1980s–1990s sitcoms like *The Cosby Show* and *The Fresh Prince of Bel-Air*.[47] Turner's goal was essentially to wrest the primary off-net market away from broadcast stations, to turn cable (and TBS and TNT in particular) into the primary off-net venue. As Bob Levi, vice president of Turner Entertainment Networks, stated in 1995, "we want to get our hands on sitcoms that are in their first syndication cycle," rather than wait until a series has been airing on local stations for several years.[48]

Several other cable networks have shared Turner's appetite for more recent sitcoms, including BET, Lifetime, USA, and WE (Women's Entertainment).[49] Stations, still the primary avenue for most big-ticket syndication, pursued only the top-rated series (e.g., *Roseanne*, *Murphy Brown*, and *Home Improvement*), passing by many "middling" sitcoms like *Major Dad*, *Evening Shade* and *Wings*, which were all hastily acquired by cable networks in their first syndication runs in the mid 1990s.[50] By the late 1990s, with cable networks flexing their new economic muscle, most eager off-net distributors had worked out previously unthinkable "split exclusivity" deals for their programs, selling them to both stations and cable networks. Under these arrangements, stations would typically get a limited exclusive run for a few years, followed by cable exclusivity, as with 1998 sales of Eyemark's *Caroline In The City* with Lifetime, and Columbia Tri-Star's *Seinfeld* with TBS.[51] However, for new off-net hours, which are not normally stripped any more by stations, the usual arrangement since the late 1990s has been for a simultaneous split exclusivity, whereby cable networks get unlimited weekday runs while local stations have a limited weekend run. This enables the cable network to use the series as a boutique property while also granting the local station the right to the series as popular fillers in otherwise difficult timeslots (e.g., weekend afternoons and late nights). More recently, exclusivity has become even more negotiable on cable, as the same series is sometimes sold to multiple cable networks, in complex deals involving particular dayparts, episodes, and/or entire seasons. For example, TNT split the rights to the second cable syndication cycle of *NYPD Blue* with Court TV in 2001, ceding prime-time runs, but gaining runs at any other time of the day.[52] Similarly, Nick At Nite and Oxygen split *Roseanne* between them in 2003.[53] The loss of exclusivity may seem somewhat ironic given the glut of content in the market. Particular boutiques still have particular uses for particular programs, however, and may cede singularity for a reduced price.

Regardless of how a program is acquired, though, all boutiques use strategies of distinctive repetition to acquire and build their own television heritages. For example, the Sci-Fi Channel has regularly used various themed programming blocks to air their reruns, including a biannual *Twilight Zone* "Chain Reaction" marathon that lasts two to three days. In addition, they have presented distinctive versions of series like *Babylon 5* and the original *Star Trek*, running the former in the widescreen glory it was denied in its initial syndication run, and running all 79 episodes of the latter with scenes long deleted for syndication, plus 20 minutes of new interviews and commentary from the series' creators, cast, fans, and scholars.[54] Starting in 2002, TechTV branched out from their computer-centered schedule to run the 1960s marionette adventure series *Thunderbirds* with added text commentary (adding a further level of distinction), and a late-night block of anime. While these series would seem to differ greatly from the channel's usual lineup of hi-tech advice and reviews, their "geek-hipness" factor has attracted enough of their target audience to justify these acquisitions. Even original series produced for a particular cable network can quickly become an established, distinctive rerun property through judicious repetition and repurposing.

HBO's signature series (e.g., *The Sopranos*) are run repeatedly across its multiplexed channels during and between seasons, fostering and amplifying the presence of the series in its public profile. In addition, as on Nick at Nite and TV Land, promos and program bumpers link HBO's programs together as one distinctive package.[55]

While reruns are sold to cable networks on the promise of their fit with the boutique network's identity, this does not necessarily happen. Sometimes the fit between boutique and program is near perfect, and can be maintained for years, as with Nick At Nite/TV Land and *All In The Family*, the Sci-Fi Channel and *Star Trek*, and Lifetime and *The Golden Girls*. More often, however, boutiques must constantly monitor their programming to maintain the image they wish to project. This has especially been the case with post-1980s off-net hours, which, due to their complex serial narratives and segregated genres, present the risks and benefits of a greater degree of distinction than do the relatively broad-appealing half-hour sitcoms.[56] Despite the boutiques' surge toward recent sitcoms in the second half of the 1990s, hours have remained their primary rerun vehicle. Hours typically draw a narrower, but more committed audience than sitcoms, providing a more refined instrument to reach a particular audience demographic. However, because sales are made well before the series begin their rerun cycles, even well-regarded, demographically solid hours may fall from favor during or even before their cable runs. *Ally McBeal*, for example, was a red-hot network series in the late 1990s, and a seeming no-brainer for acquisition. Once it had decisively faded from the zeitgeist, however, it did not perform anywhere near its initial expectations a few years later for FX. Nevertheless, series that fail on one boutique may still be desired by another in a subsequent syndication cycle. *Homicide: Life on the Street* was not an adequate match for Lifetime's ostensible audience, but suited Court TV well for several years. Similarly, FX was disappointed by the long-term performance of *The X-Files*, but that did not deter the Sci-Fi Channel and TNT from acquiring it for their needs in a nonexclusive deal in 2002.

The mixed success of reruns on cable—where repetition *per se* reigns, but particular hits are more difficult to come by—indicates how reruns may stay the same, but boutique identities are fluid. Reruns help solidify a channel's image, but usually not for the long term. For example, Fox's FX began its existence in 1994 in the mold of Nick At Nite and USA: as a light, somewhat retro-leaning general audience channel, with a schedule filled with vintage Fox-produced off-net series, such as *Hart To Hart*, *Mission: Impossible*, *Nanny and the Professor*, and *Batman*. Faced with stagnant interest from cable systems and viewers, FX changed their image a few years later, replacing their whimsical logo and iconography with a "harder" bold-faced green and black look, and dumping their vintage schedule in favor of more recent (and more male-skewing) Fox products like *The X-Files* and *NYPD Blue*, as well as the all-time evergreen

M*A*S*H. These additions "elevated the profile" of FX in the late 1990s, according to its vice president Mark Sonnenberg, which allowed it to devote more resources to new programming as well as top-drawer reruns.[57] Over the next several years, they introduced a variety of original series throughout their schedule, diminishing the role of off-net reruns in their overall image. Since 2001, they have moved into what could be called "HBO territory," with several explicit, yet critically acclaimed, scripted series, including *The Shield* and *Nip/Tuck*. While FX still relies on repetition, it has increasingly defined its brand not as much through familiarity as through *difference*; that is, by offering material considered outside the bounds of "normal" broadcast television, or what cable ostensibly promised in its "blue skies" years ago.[58]

FX's movement from vintage rerun to original series boutique has been mirrored in other cable networks. Lifetime's slate of original, female-skewing ensemble dramas commands solid ratings, and has enabled them to relegate their reruns to daytime and late-night hours. Similarly, since 2002, USA has capitalized on the critical and audience support of their *Monk* and *The Dead Zone* to extend their original series production. While other networks have had a spottier track record of original scripted production (e.g., A&E, TNT), the more established basic-tier networks still clearly trend toward increased original production of both scripted and nonscripted series, and, concomitantly, a reduced reliance on off-net reruns. The overall reason given for this movement has been the diminishing long-term ratings of off-net series on cable.[59] In the current environment, it may be more efficient to generate a new series than to continue reviving an old one. Moreover, it may also be more lucrative in the long run, as successful new series, even from cable, may eventually become successful rerun properties: USA's *Monk* set television history in the summer of 2002, when it became the first made-for-cable drama to become repurposed as an ostensibly first-run network show on ABC.[60]

One Big Pot?

Cable's aggressive pursuit of initial syndication cycles and original productions has further narrowed its difference with broadcasting. No longer satisfied with getting syndication hand-me-downs, cable's now dominant share of television audiences and advertising revenues has given it the clout to compete not only for prime reruns, but also for prime projects from top-drawer studios and talent. The most decisive factor in this shift, particularly since the regulatory free-for-all opened up in the mid-1990s, has been the sheer fact of consolidation: cable networks, program distributors, broadcast networks, and even broadcast stations are increasingly owned by the same few parties; the "poles" of the market, whether buyer and seller, or broadcast and cable, are no longer as distinct as they once were. MTV, VH-1, Nickelodeon, Spike TV, and all their multiplexed spin-offs (e.g., M2, Noggin, TV Land) are all owned by Viacom, which also owns Paramount Pictures and its extensive film and television libraries, including *Happy Days, The Brady Bunch, Cheers,* and *Star Trek*. Similarly, the Turner channels (Cartoon Network/ Boomerang, CNN, TBS, TCM, TNT) are part of the massive Time Warner empire, whose assets also include AOL, HBO/Cinemax, the WB network, the entire Warner Bros film and television library, and a nearly unparalleled collection of popular trademarks, ranging from Batman to Bugs Bunny.

As described in the last chapter, consolidation has had an enormous impact on broadcast syndication, with the entire nation's programming virtually determined by two companies, Fox and Tribune, who control powerful stations in the largest markets. Consolidation has similarly affected cable boutiques, as corporations seek to maximize returns on program properties across their integrated studios and cable networks. All the major networks have repeated (or rather, "repurposed") programs, program materials, and concepts between their broadcasting and cable operations, as when ABC Family reruns ABC's *The Bachelor,* NBC airs episodes of Bravo's *Queer Eye For The Straight Guy,* or MTV's *Video Music Awards* cross over with CBS' *Big Brother*. In addition, some particularly successful properties, like Viacom's *Star Trek* universe and Time Warner's DC Comics characters, migrate among even more of a corporation's subsidiaries, and show up in a wide array of films, television shows, books, software, and other media.

On the surface, consolidation has resulted in rather obvious synergies like the examples just cited, or as seen in a spate of cable syndication deals in the mid 1990s that sent a few Fox and WB-owned rerun properties to their respective cable boutiques. However, despite great consolidation, the media industry is still more complex than the cold logic of horizontal and vertical integration would indicate. Fox's sales of *NYPD Blue* and *The X-Files* to its in-house cable boutique FX were met by lawsuits from producer Steven Bochco and actor David Duchovny, who claimed that their series were not sold at fair market value in order to maintain Fox's synergy. Similarly, *M*A*S*H* producers Alan Alda and Gene Reynolds complained that their well-worn evergreen series was being drastically overexposed on FX, which ran it six times a day for five years around the turn of the century. Several years later, however, in an effort to stave off such perceptions of in-house, "sweetheart" deals, *CSI* and *Law and Order: Special Victims Unit* were sold to their corporate siblings TNN and USA (respectively) for close to $1.5 million an episode, above their likely market value.[61] In 2003, Warner Brothers sold its *Gilmore Girls* to Disney's ABC Family, rather than any of its own boutiques. While some properties certainly continue to circulate in-house, boutiques will always seek the best fit for their brand, and distributors for their show, even if it means going "outside" the corporate family.

There are many pathways to distinctive repetition in cable television. Although I have argued in this chapter that the acquisition of established properties has been one of the most prominent, I do not wish to suggest that this will always be the case in the future. Repetition may be a constant facet of industrialized culture, but its particular function and application is constantly changing. While film and/or television reruns have been historically critical in virtually every successful entertainment-oriented cable boutique's development, their importance has demonstrably lessened once successful original programming is established. At that point in a channel's development, the television heritage shifts again, for once it no longer has to rely upon the umpteenth rerun of *The X-Files*, it may relegate it to a 2 am time slot, or cease running it altogether, in favor of its own branded show. If that new series is successful, however, it may still one day become one of the established old guard of the television heritage, and ride repetition onto a new boutique. Or perhaps even a new television platform, as broadcasting and cable are no longer the only viable venues for televisual repetition. The next chapter will explore how repetition has extended from the circulation of programs on television to the circulation of tangible television objects—i.e., home video tapes and discs—directly to consumers.

Notes

1. Thomas Streeter, "Blue skies and strange bedfellows," in Lynn Spigel and Michael Curtin, eds., *The Revolution Wasn't Televised: Sixties Television and Social Conflict* (New York: Routledge, 1997), 236.

2. Repeat viewing, video trading, the production and use of annotated episode guides, and spin-off production are all key practices in contemporary media fandom. See Matt Hills, *Fan Cultures* (New York: Routledge, 2002); Sara Gwenllian-Jones and Roberta Pearson, eds., *Cult Television* (Minneapolis: University of Minnesota Press, 2004); Henry Jenkins, *Textual Poachers: Television Fans and Participatory Culture* (New York: Routledge, 1992); Kurt Lancaster, *Interacting with Babylon 5: Fan Performances in a Media Universe* (Austin: University of Texas Press, 2001); Camille Bacon-Smith, *Enterprising Women* (Philadelphia: University of Pennsylvania Press, 1992).

3. For the sake of clarity, I will generally use the term "cable" in this chapter to refer to the channels and services offered by both cable and satellite systems.

4. Thomas Streeter, *Selling The Air: A Critique of the Policy of Commercial Broadcasting in the U.S.* (Chicago: University of Chicago Press, 1996), 180.

5. Streeter, "Blue skies," 226–227.

6. Brian Winston, *Media Technology and Society—A History: From the Telegraph to the Internet* (New York: Routledge, 1998), 308–309.

7. Streeter, "Blue skies." It is also interesting to note that the development of Direct Broadcast Satellite (DBS) in the 1980s and 1990s was discursively

fueled, in large part, by offering a "better" alternative not only to traditional television, but also to cable.

8. Winston is much more emphatic on this point than I am: "The cable channels have almost totally failed to alter the established genres and forms of television broadcasting in any significant way, never mind add to them." Winston, *Media Technology*, 318.

9. Ralph Lee Smith, *The Wired Nation* (New York: Harper Colophon, 1972), 8, 28.

10. The 1968 Fortnightly v. United Artists Television decision ruled that a West Virginia cable system had not violated existing copyright law in its retransmission of television signals from stations in Pennsylvania, Ohio, and West Virginia. The 1974 Teleprompter v. CBS decision upheld the earlier precedent, noting that while cable systems had expanded their origination of local programming in the intervening years, they still fell short of functioning in a "broadcast" capacity:

   > By importing signals that could not normally be received with current technology in the community it serves, a CATV system does not, for copyright purposes, alter the function it performs for its subscribers, as the reception and rechanneling of these signals for simultaneous viewing is essentially a viewer function, irrespective of the distance between the broadcasting station and the ultimate viewer.

   Fortnightly Corp. v. United Artists Television, Inc., 392 US 390, US Supreme Court, 1968; Teleprompter Corp. v. CBS, 415 US 394, US Supreme Court, 1974.

11. Streeter "Blue skies," 225–226.

12. Eric R. Guthey, "The Legend of Ted Turner and the Reality of the Marketplace" (Ph.D. diss., Emory University, 1995), 279.

13. Guthey, "The Legend of Ted Turner," 279–281. Around the same period, Turner's acquisition of Atlanta's major league baseball and basketball franchises also assured a ready source of popular, royalty-free programming for WTCG.

14. Qtd. in "INTV and CATV: a you-scratch-my-back-I'll-scratch-yours proposition," *Broadcasting*, 11 February 1974, p. 26.

15. Guthey, "The Legend of Ted Turner," 289. Guthey also writes that "the new players who really transformed the broadcasting and telecommunications industry were no innovative, individual entrepreneurs possessed of vision and daring-they were heavily capitalized and politically powerful aerospace defense contractors such as Hughes Aircraft, Lockheed, and General Electric, operating with staggering federal subsidies for research and development in rocket and satellite technology." "The Legend of Ted Turner," 291.

16. HBO got RCA to discount its transponder space on the Satcom satellite, and even helped cable systems acquire cheap earth stations. Guthey, "The Legend of Ted Turner," 297.

17. Winston, *Media Technology*, 299.

18. Streeter, *Selling The Air*, 177.

19. Despite the diminishing federal regulations, Turner still had to resort to a legal fiction in order to secure satellite transmission of WTCG. In December 1975, he formed the Southern Satellite Systems (SSS) retransmission company, and sold it to an associate for $1.00. At the time broadcasters were forbidden from owning satellite retransmission carriers. When WTCG sought its satellite transmission, there was SSS to provide the signal. In anticipation of the move, Turner had even obtained inexpensive transponder space and had fostered the interest of cable system operators nationwide. Guthey, "The Legend of Ted Turner," 300, 309–311.

20. On Ferris, see "Grounded against future shock," *Broadcasting*, 19 March 1979, p. 48.

21. "The state of the superstations," *Broadcasting*, 23 July 1979, p. 29. By 1983, 90% of WTBS' audience lay outside its home metropolitan area, compared with only 48% of WGN's, and 30% of WOR's. Sidney Pike, "Superstation programming," in Susan Tyler Eastman et al, eds., *Broadcast/Cable Programming: Strategies and Practices* 2nd Edition (Belmont, CA: Wadsworth, 1985), 307–308.

22. Qtd. in Guthey, "The Legend of Ted Turner," 247. In his critique of the entrepreneurial myth surrounding Ted Turner, Guthey argues that, far from being a "rugged maverick," Turner was simply taking advantage of both WTCG's unique position of strength in the Atlanta market, and the growing deregulatory wave in government in the 1970s. As Guthey writes, despite his "aw-shucks," "little guy" performance in front of the House Communications Subcommittee in July 1976, Turner was effectively "preaching to the choir," as "the entire federal regulatory apparatus" was moving towards an "open door" policy of reconfiguring television beyond broadcast interests. "The Legend of Ted Turner," 250. As Harry Shooshan, the chief counsel and staff director to the House Communications Subcommittee at the time, remembers, Turner was not as much a pilot as a passenger: "the wave was created by cable, by HBO, by the Open Skies ruling, and by a host of other regulatory changes.... Turner got his surfboard out early and rode it all the way to the shore." Qtd. in Guthey, "The Legend of Ted Turner," 238.

23. Pike, "Superstation programming," 312.

24. Broadcasting remarked, "observers of human nature may note that Escapade subscribers outnumber Bravo's by more than four to one." "Cable's programming cornucopia in the sky," *Broadcasting*, 3 May 1982, pp. 48+.

25. Qtd. in Randall Poe, "Narrowcasting," *Across The Board*, June 1981, p. 7.

26. Qtd. in Poe, "Narrowcasting," 11.

27. Julie Talen, "Satellite Networks: The Great Programming Shakeout," *Channels of Communication 1984 Field Guide to the Electronic Media*, pp. 15–16.

28. For example, the joint cable ventures of ABC and Hearst Publishing purchased the Cable Health Network late in 1983 and joined it with their

similarly-ailing Daytime to form Lifetime, which launched in February 1984. Similarly, ARTS merged with RCA's The Entertainment Channel to become Arts & Entertainment (A & E). The "merging" solution was still an option as late as 1990, when two nascent comedy channels—MTV's HA! and HBO's Comedy Channel—joined forces to become Comedy Central.

29. The Entertainment Channel featured several former network series that had not been picked up for syndication due to their early cancellation and lack of episodes, including *The Associates, Paul Sand in Friends and Lovers, Skag* and *When Things Were Rotten.*

30. Qtd. in "Cable programing gets its own convention," *Broadcasting,* 12 October 1981, p. 38.

31. "Special Report: Cable TV," *Broadcasting,* 22 October 1984, p. 80+.

32. John Motavalli, "Cable enters the mix," *Channels,* February 1988, p. 54.

33. "MCA pulls Miami Vice from syndication," *Broadcasting,* 16 February 1987, p. 29–30.

34. Qtd. in Sharon D. Moshavi, "Cable no longer second-class citizen at NATPE," *Broadcasting,* 21 January 1992, p. 78.

35. "'Murder, She Wrote' to appear on cable," *Broadcasting,* 8 February 1988, p. 102.

36. For example, in the fall of 1988 at 9 p.m. weeknights, USA ran *Miami Vice,* Lifetime ran *Spenser: For Hire,* and CBN ran *Remington Steele.*

37. Rich Brown, "Off-net hours find good home on cable," *Broadcasting,* 29 June 1992, pp. 26+; Harvey Solomon, "Off-net hours: life after cable," *Channels Programming Handbook 1989,* p. 48.

38. Meryl Gordon, "Fast Company," *Channels of Communication,* April 1986, pp. 24–29.

39. Geoffrey Foisie and Christopher Stern, "Paramount, Viacom say 'I Do'," *Broadcasting & Cable,* 20 September 1993, pp. 14–16. Following on the heels of successful endeavors by Disney and Time Warner to open retail shops filled with licensed merchandise, the corporation also opened the Viacom Store on Chicago's Magnificent Mile in the fall of 1996. Despite its array of expensive goodies related to Viacom properties such as MTV, Nickelodeon, Nick At Nite, and *Star Trek,* however, the store failed to generate numbers which would warrant an expansion as a chain, and closed in 1998.

40. Qtd. in "Ready to take on the world," *Broadcasting & Cable,* 20 September 1993, p. 20.

41. Steve Coe, "Nick's big deal is the cat's meow," *Broadcasting,* 13 July 1992, pp. 22–24.

42. In a public relations move that seemingly combined the two sensibilities, Dick Van Dyke was even appointed "President of Nick At Nite" at the same

time. It was obviously a continuation of the jokey theme—a TV King for TV Land—but it was also an acknowledgment of the cultural ascendancy of television and the formation of the television heritage, as one of its all-time great comic actors became the public figure of its archives. Van Dyke appeared in ad campaigns promoting the "new" Nick At Nite throughout 1992, and sat on the channel's advisory board, helping to pursue a variety of promotional and cultural projects centered on "classic TV." Allison Fahey, "Van Dyke to lead Nick's move from 'campy' to 'classic'," *Advertising Age*, 4 May 1992, p. 46; Joanne Lipman, "Nick At Nite Uses Chairman to Make Pitch," *Wall Street Journal*, 2 July 1992, sec. B, p. 6.

43. This mode of presentation in itself is an increasingly significant form of televisual repetition, which is explored more fully in the book's conclusion.

44. For an intriguing exploration of the importance of these microsized "bits" of television, see Megan Mullen, "Surfing through 'TV Land': Notes toward a theory of 'Video Bites' and Their Function on Cable TV," *The Velvet Light Trap 36*, 60–68.

45. While neither consistently ranks among the top-ten basic cable networks in terms of audience size, they have succeeded as their rerun-laden independent stations did before them: low programming costs, reasonable advertising rates, and a stable, consistent audience.

46. Qtd. in Solomon, "Off-net hours," 49.

47. John Dempsey, "Seeking fresh sitcoms, TBS signs 'Coach' for '97 season," *Daily Variety*, 5 July 1995, p. 7; John Dempsey and Cynthia Littleton, "TBS wins battle over 'Seinfeld'," *Daily Variety*, 14 September 1998, p. 1.

48. Qtd. in Dempsey, "Seeking fresh sitcoms," p. 7. Turner's pursuit of successful rerun properties has always prompted its acquisition strategies. WTBS superstation was successful enough to prompt second and third Turner cable networks: Turner Network Television (TNT) in 1988, and Turner Classic Movies (TCM) in 1993. Turner's pursuit of MGM/UA in 1985, while hardly anomalous in the no-holds-barred conglomeration of the period, almost brought the company down, but Turner was able to sell off pieces of the corporation (its production facilities and name), in order to hold on to what it was really after: the MGM/UA film and television library, which included films like the James Bond and Pink Panther series, and TV programs like *The Man From UNCLE*, *Gilligan's Island*, and *Fame*. In the 1990s, Turner continued to acquire broadcasting and film properties, with the clear intentions of developing new cable outlets for these extant programs. In 1991, Turner bought animation studio Hanna-Barbera, and turned around within a few months to launch the Cartoon Network, an all-animation basic cable network filled with Hanna-Barbera and MGM titles. Similarly, in 1993 Turner acquired a package of three hundred recent Paramount features to bolster its cable networks, and, in 1994, obtained Hollywood film financiers/studios New Line Cinema and Castle Rock Entertainment. Soon after, Turner itself was acquired by Time Warner, which united its holdings with the Warner Brothers film and television libraries, production facilities, and broadcast network, in addition to a

multitude of other holdings in print, motion picture, and electronic media. As TBS vice president Scott Sass stated in 1994, "our strategy in the 1980s was gathering a lot of copyrights...now, we're after new, quality, killer copyrights." Qtd. in "TBS plots new growth off its new Hollywood studios," *Electronic Media*, 23 May 1994, p. 36.

49. Like the earlier unwanted hours, however, most of these series most likely would not have been syndicated at all were it not for cable. For example, around the turn of the century, USA ran a daily block of what could best be called "Must See TV" leftovers; i.e., the hapless, short-lived series such as *Something So Right*, *Boston Common*, and *The Single Guy*, which were intended to fill in the gaps on NBC's red-hot Thursday night schedule between *Friends*, *Seinfeld*, and *ER*.

50. TBS was the first cable network to ink such a deal, when Buena Vista sought a cable license for its sitcom *Empty Nest* to help offset the relatively lackluster response to the series from stations. Significantly, the broadcast and cable syndication windows were merged with this deal; Buena Vista guaranteed local stations exclusive rights during the series' first off-net year, while TBS would start running it during its second year out. "Cable playing bigger role in sitcom deals," *Broadcasting*, 30 September 1991, pp. 25–26; David Tobenkin, "'Evening Shade' goes to Family Channel," *Broadcasting & Cable*, 2 May 1994, p. 28; Rich Brown, "Cable casts growing shadow in syndication," *Broadcasting*, 26 January 1993, pp. 36+.

51. John Dempsey, "Syndies rattle the windows: cablers and stations more willing to share shows, risks," *Variety*, 15 June 1998, p. 23; "'Seinfeld's' got plenty of nothing," *Broadcasting & Cable*, 21 September 1998, p. 74.

52. John M. Higgins, "Split shift for Blue," *Broadcasting & Cable*, 30 April 2001, p. 16.

53. Chris Pursell, "Cablers ink 'Roseanne' off-net pact," *Variety*, 6 March 2000, p. 57.

54. Although noted fandom scholar Henry Jenkins did not appear in *Star Trek: The Special Edition*, fellow "fanademic" Constance Penley did, commenting on the Kirk/Spock relationship in a few interview segments.

55. Indeed, one 2003 promo even featured digitally-excised characters from every HBO series milling around at an upscale cocktail party, as if to suggest that Tony Soprano (*The Sopranos*), Carrie Bradshaw (*Sex and the City*), and Nate Fisher (*Six Feet Under*) lived in the same reality via HBO.

56. For an account of how daily viewing of an off-net prime-time serial differs from experiencing it in its original network run, see Laura Stempel Mumford, "Stripping on the Girl Channel: Lifetime, thirtysomething, and Television Form," *Camera Obscura* 33–34 (Spring 1994 – Winter 1995): 167–190.

57. Qtd. in Ray Richmond, "Cable's net worth: pay TV finds pillars in off-net dramas," *Variety*, 12 January 1998, p. 108.

58. Allison Romano, "Can The Shield fix FX?," *Broadcasting & Cable*, 11 March 2002, pp. 16+.

59. See John M. Higgins, "Rethinking the off-net market," *Broadcasting & Cable*, 30 September 2002, p. 20; Allison Romano, "Off-net and off-the-mark," *Broadcasting & Cable*, 21 October 2002, p. 11.

60. *It's Garry Shandling's Show*, originally produced for Showtime in the late 1980s, was actually the first made-for-cable series to make this jump, as it also ran on Fox from 1988 to 1990.

61. John Dempsey, "Cablers prepare for rerun race," *Variety*, 26 March 2001, p. 28.

8
Acquisitive Repetition: Home Video and the Television Heritage

> Strangely enough, everything will be done in order to turn "flow" culture into a "lasting" commodity, or at least a product that may be used several times over....[1]

The last two chapters have examined how televisual repetition has become a particular brand of culture, in the wake of the television heritage that has developed since the 1970s. Broadcast and cable syndication markets developed in response to these concerns, and series were increasingly crafted with the back end firmly in mind. Boutique television (on both broadcast and cable channels) fostered extensive framing and branding techniques, creating distinctive spaces for televisual repetition. Although the changing concept of the television heritage successfully secured these transmitted spaces, the television industry had far less success in exploiting the most significant new medium of the 1980s and 1990s: home video. While TV-related merchandise ranging from published episode guides to collectible plates had been effectively marketed during this period, the programs themselves remained, for the most part, only available through television; that is, through over-the-air, cable, and satellite broadcasting. Home video's primary medium, VHS tape, was portable, permanent, and easily accessible to most consumers, and while particularly well suited for film distribution and exhibition, it was incompatible for the mass distribution of entire television series. However, the rapid adoption of Digital Versatile Disc (DVD) technology at the end of the 1990s prompted a reconception of television on home video. The enhanced technical standards and new industrial practices developed for the new format allowed for the delivery of hours of television to consumers in small, tangible packages that also happened to look rather nice on a bookshelf.

The rapid development of television on DVD—becoming standard less than five years after the format's debut—should be seen in the context of the array of changes that affect how the medium is, and will be, financed, produced, distributed, experienced, and linked with the rest of the culture. For the past two decades, the domestic set has been transforming, in fits and starts, from an analog, low-definition receiver of broadcast signals to a digital, high-definition, customizable multimedia portal, incorporating hundreds of channels, an augmented audiovisual range, and a greater capacity for interactivity. New technologies, business models, regulatory structures, programming forms, and modes of viewing increasingly mesh with the old, with widely varying, and often unpredictable results. Accordingly, it is impossible to gauge exactly what "television" will be in another decade or so (let alone by the time this book is released). However, it is clear that the centralized, mass-disseminated, "one-way" cultural institution that has held sway since the middle of the twentieth century is largely ceding to a regime premised instead upon individual consumer choice, and marked by highly diversified content, atomized reception, and customizable interfaces. While the development of boutique cable channels described in the last chapter is certainly a key part of this transition, their use of distinction is likely only a harbinger of an emerging media environment in which programming will be the result of direct viewer decisions (limited by corporate offerings, of course), rather than advertiser-supported general transmission.

These changes around television are also part of a larger conceptual shift across all media, as the aesthetic, technological, industrial, and cultural boundaries between previously discrete forms (text, film, broadcasting, video, and sound recordings) are increasingly blurred, challenging established practices and paradigms. As I have suggested throughout this study, technology, industry, and culture are not autonomous domains: each is shaped by the other in particular ways, helping construct particular media forms and practices in particular contexts. While repetition has long been one of the standard practices of media production and distribution, its specific application has varied considerably over time, and between different media forms and regimes. For television, changes in its practices of repetition began in the mid-1970s, as the previous chapters have discussed. The television heritage and the development of cable boutiques fostered the cultivation of the televisual past as a ready source of cultural and industrial capital. One additional mid-1970s event factors large in the development of televisual repetition: the introduction of home video.[2] Home video devices—in particular videocassette recorders (VCRs), but also video cameras (camcorders), laserdisc players, Digital/Personal Video Recorders (DVRs/PVRs), and Digital Versatile Disc (DVD) players—may differ in their specific functions, but they all have in common the primary innovation of video technology: the ability to selectively play back prerecorded programs.[3] In addition, and just as significantly, most of these devices can also record incoming audiovisual signals onto the fixed media of tape or disc. Whether playing or recording, however, video devices are physically and culturally connected to television sets, forcing television—as both a technology and cultural form, to borrow Raymond Williams' description—into a complex new relationship that foregrounds its function as an audiovisual display device, rather than its more established role as a dominant modern cultural institution. This link destabilizes the direct presentation of scheduled television events, and enables people to use their personal media technology to create or access programming on their own terms, rather than stay locked to the fare and schedule dictated by the broadcasting industry.[4]

However, despite the ubiquity, unique qualities, and speed of acceptance of home video, and its critical importance to late twentieth-century media culture, it has been sorely understudied in the academy. Several important articles, collections, and books were published in the wake of the initial video expansion in the late 1980s and early 1990s, but as the devices became part of everyday life, scholarly interest in this area waned, and has been almost nonexistent when compared to the more established fields of film and television study, or even to recent emerging concerns like new media and the Internet.[5] This is unfortunate but not surprising given the dominant impression of home video as a "neutral" media tool. The VCR, for example, has sat in the public and academic imaginary largely as it does in our living rooms: quietly next to the set. However, each of these sleek boxes, ranging from the first VCR to the latest PVR, are not mere enhancements of media; they are *reconceptions*, profoundly altering our relationship with dominant media institutions, and with media culture in general. They are explicitly designed upon the premise of mediated repetition, and have thus added a significant new dimension to the concept of the rerun, and to the very concept of the media text.

While home video has been physically connected to television at the level of technology and everyday culture, it has ironically not been as critical to the television industry itself. Instead, the VCR has functioned largely as the primary domestic extension of the film industry, rather than as a supplement to television. As Frederick Wasser explores in his 2001 study of the relationship between home video and Hollywood, while the film industry first viewed the VCR with suspicion, it has since become its most crucial technology, fostering new markets for their products, and even providing the majority of their revenue since the late 1980s. By contrast, television's primary goal, at least in the United States, has always been selling potential audiences to advertisers, rather than selling programs directly to consumers. Accordingly, while there certainly were thousands of television-based titles released on home video during the last quarter or so of the twentieth century, they have been a decidedly marginal cultural form relative to both television, and to the film-centered home video industry.

The industrial and technological changes of the late 1990s and early 2000s considerably altered these relationships, as the boundaries between media producers and distributors all but vanished in the age of consolidation, and the VCR largely gave way to the DVD player. As the last two chapters discussed, all six U.S. commercial broadcast networks are now part of larger mega-media corporations, and are as much sellers as they are buyers of cultural products. This has facilitated the synergistic "horizontal" exploitation of media properties across different forms and venues, enabling new revenue possibilities. Digital Versatile Disc (DVD) technology, introduced in 1997, has been especially critical in this regard. With much higher resolution sound and image than VHS tape, random access capability, a smaller size, and, most significantly, a larger storage capacity, the DVD has rejuvenated the home video industry, and has finally enabled television to achieve what film had by the mid-1980s: a viable direct-to-consumer market for its programming.

This final chapter investigates the culmination of televisual repetition: the DVD box set, a multiple-disc package containing an entire season's worth of episodes from a particular television series. First introduced by Fox with the release of the first season of *The X-Files* in the spring of 2000, the box set is a nexus point of twenty-first century media change, incorporating high technology, corporate consolidation, user convenience, and commodity fetishism. It extends the reach of the institution of television into home video to an unprecedented degree, and functions as an intriguing aesthetic object in its own right. It fulfills the decades-long relationship between television and its viewers, completing the circle through the material purchase—rather than only the ephemeral viewing—of broadcast texts. DVD box sets have become the ultimate bearers of televisual repetition, placing television programming in a more direct, repetitive, and acquisitive relationship with its viewers. I will examine how the distinctive physical and cultural qualities of the DVD box set have brought television's home video practices more in line with those of film, and have fostered an ideal of acquisitive repetition based on individual television viewers (or more specifically, fans) rather than stations, networks, or advertisers. DVD box sets are not only television-related merchandise; they function culturally (and increasingly, industrially) *as* "television."

Home Video as a Publishing Industry

In *The Capitalization of Cultural Production*, Bernard Miége describes three models of cultural production.[6] Two of these, publishing and flow, correspond with the film and television industries. Under the publishing model, firms produce media material for sale directly to consumers. Book publishers and record labels are the archetypal publishing firms, as they generate income by the sale of media in the form of tangible objects. As Chapter 1 described, the film industry has functioned as a publisher, as it has always made its products available to viewers on a paid admission basis (i.e., one ticket, one screening), even after it had begun raising revenue through sales to television stations and networks in the 1950s. Although Sony, the manufacturer of the original consumer VCR, the Betamax, initially promoted home video in the 1970s as a means to record television programs (i.e., to capture broadcast flow), home video has also functioned predominantly as a form of publishing. Since the legal challenges to the domestic video market died down in the early 1980s, viewers have rented or purchased tapes or discs for home use, with the revenue split among retailers, wholesalers, distributors, and producers. Hollywood was initially uncertain about home video, as it had been with television in the 1950s, for upsetting their established business model, but it has since merged the new technology (and its concomitant modes of viewing) into its operations not only with minimal turmoil, but with increasing reliance.[7] Once the exclusive province of theatrical distributors and exhibitors, feature films are now routinely made available directly to consumers as tangible, obtainable home video objects (i.e., VHS tapes and DVD discs). Video releases initially generated only ancillary revenue for Hollywood studios, but since the late 1980s, domestic U.S. video sale and rental revenues have consistently outpaced domestic box office grosses. By the early 2000s, annual video revenue regularly doubled the take at the box office.[8] Accordingly, home video, rather than theatrical exhibition, is now Hollywood's primary source of profits.

The home video version of a theatrical film release is now an expected cultural artifact, its appearance taken for granted. The phrase "I'll just wait for the video" is a commonsense expression of this sentiment, indicating how effectively the film industry has used the consumer publishing model in adapting to the challenge of a new technology. In reexamining this history, it is important to note that the successful cultural and industrial confluence of film and video was facilitated by the symmetry between individual films and individual home video objects. Drawing on existent cultural relationships between readers and books, and listeners and sound recordings, a single film almost always fits on a single tape or disc, taking up about as much space as a trade paperback book, or, in the case of laserdisc and DVD, a single LP or CD. Tapes and discs are thus spatially congruent with existing fixed media forms, fitting easily into typical domestic settings on shelves, entertainment centers, and coffee tables. Accordingly, they are usually placed next to books and recorded music both at home, and in retailers, emphasizing their similarity as tangible media objects. Since the film industry was already adept at publishing, delivering specific titles to specific places for specific audiences, releasing their products on home video was thus not as disruptive a practice as they first feared, despite the major differences between public and private film-viewing experiences. Films on video are still marketed as individual texts, and around familiar theatrical elements: stars, genre, release dates, auteurs, and "high concept." Home video has been, in part, a successful domestic repetition of theatrical film.

While the publishing model connects producers and consumers more or less directly (through the sale and rental of media texts), the flow model is premised on an exchange carried out completely within industrial bounds: between producers, broadcasters (and cablecasters), and advertisers. The syndication market examined in this book has historically functioned according to this model, with producers selling programming to broadcasters, who then sell access to hypothetical viewers—i.e., time within programming on their widely distributed channels—to advertisers. Actual viewers/consumers are irrelevant in the flow model, represented only by the statistical fictions of ratings and demographic data. Their ostensible role is to sit back and passively receive the programming and advertising sent out by stations, networks, and sponsors. As Eileen Meehan points out, unless you are directly participating in the ratings sample, your choice of programming is superfluous to the economic relationship between producers, broadcasters, advertisers, and the providers of ratings data.[9] In addition, while the publishing model treats media texts as discrete objects, the flow model is premised instead on the aggregate experience of broadcasting over time. Accordingly, television has long urged viewers to "stay tuned" in order to boost contact with advertisements across their schedule and regardless of program. While individual television episodes have a particular duration, and television series eventually cease production after a finite number of episodes, televisual flow itself never ends: there is always "more" television. This principle has been seen not only in the linkage of programs on an individual night of viewing, but also in promoting the entire network or station line-up, in attracting viewers to new fare in the future, and, most significantly for the current transition to home video, in sustaining interest in particular series for as long as possible, even long after that series has ceased production. Flow has been essential to television economics from the smallest local station to the most established cable boutique. As Raymond Williams famously claimed, "the fact of flow" is "the central television experience."[10]

Despite the centrality of flow to the business of broadcasting, however, licensed consumer products tied to particular broadcast programs have also been sold ever since radio emerged as a national medium in the 1920s. While these products have been varyingly successful, they have been only ancillary revenue sources, based on familiar characters and situations; they have not been copies of the actual broadcast texts themselves.[11] However, the VCR's recording function—designed and promoted by hardware manufacturers like Sony, who recognized a growing consumer desire for flexible broadcast schedules in the 1970s— exists precisely to harness broadcast flow, to produce copies of it for later viewing.[12] In capturing flow in this manner, domestic video recording complicates the broadcasting model in two ways that expand the role of the viewer beyond their ostensible duty as hypothetical eyeballs.

Timeshifting, i.e., recording programs for later playback, destabilizes the relationship between advertiser, broadcaster, and viewer, separating the scheduled time from the viewing time. Accordingly, as advertisers and broadcasters fear, commercials are likely to be skipped on the eventual viewing of the recorded program.[13] However, timeshifting alone is generally only a postponement of broadcast flow; once watched, it is likely that recorded programs are not watched again. The actual acquisition of recorded programs is a less prevalent, but arguably more significant home video practice, whereby viewers assemble a collection— or more appropriately, an archive—of television from recorded broadcast flows. As detailed by Kim Bjarkman, video collectors regard television flow as available not only for ephemeral viewing but also for permanent safekeeping. In fact, they often consider themselves better caretakers of programs than producers or broadcasters, preserving the flow of broadcasting into tangible texts that can be collected, organized, maintained, and traded.[14] While the film industry, due to its successful adaptation of home video, has generally been successful in shepherding its collectors into renting or purchasing officially released video objects, the television industry, having built their business around the sale of time rather than of physical objects, has not been historically oriented towards such exchanges. In lieu of "officially-released" television on home video, unauthorized television collecting (via VHS) has flourished, albeit on the margins of television culture, with very little impact on the business of television. Even early on in the home video era, however, the fact that viewers like these wished to preserve their favorite television shows on video suggested that a *potential* market existed for commercially released (i.e., officially published) home video copies of television series. Accordingly, the owners and producers of television programming have established a small presence in the home video market. While television programs have been released on home video since the early 1980s, the dissonance between the flow and publishing models, coupled with the significant limitations of VHS technology, have complicated these attempts.

Unlike a film, which is nearly always experienced as one unbroken text, most fictional television is serial, presented in separate episodes. As the scheduling and advertising practices of television have long indicated, series are designed primarily for optimum modularity, adhering rigidly to specific formulas regarding program length (e.g., 30 or 60 minutes), daypart (daytime, prime-time, "fringe"), genre (sitcom, drama), and frequency of viewing (daily, weekly, annual). This has historically facilitated broadcast flow, standardizing the delivery of particular audiences to advertisers around particular genres and times, thus stabilizing television advertising markets, and establishing television brands for continued exploitation as continuing series and as reruns. This formularity has also fostered the episodic form of television production and distribution, built around "seasons" of 13 to 26 episodes (the current standard season order for most prime-time programs on U.S. network and cable television). However, in a home video culture that has defaulted to a feature film, 2-hour program length—it is no coincidence that most blank consumer VHS tapes run exactly this long—individual television episodes are too short for one tape, while entire seasons, let alone series, much too long. While a typical Hollywood film currently runs just under 2 hours, a full season of a typical 30-minute Hollywood sitcom, without commercials, is the equivalent of nearly eight and a half hours. The available options for dealing with this issue on videotape have had to sacrifice either thoroughness, by releasing only particularly significant episodes (e.g., *The Best of The Honeymooners*) or physical space (by filling up retailers' and consumers' shelves). Each of these options has been problematic. For example, while the popular drama series *The X-Files* was a likely candidate for VHS release, its signature convoluted narrative arc complicated possible "best of" configurations. In addition, at 202 episodes and nine seasons, a complete release of *The X-Files* on VHS (with the standard two episodes per tape) would take up over 100 cassettes (10 feet of horizontal shelf space), more than all but the most dedicated viewers (let alone retailers) would likely obtain for completion.

In addition, as this book has examined, the flow model has assured that television programs have been ubiquitous on television itself in the form of reruns. Popular as well as obscure shows have long found syndicated homes on stations and cable networks. From the standpoint of the television industry, this combination of seriality and repetition has ensured that television series are distributed *on television*, generating syndication and advertising revenue across the schedule and through-out the years. Accordingly, rerun syndication has also functioned as an effective argument against the marketing of programs on home video. Why would a studio release a series on home video that was already widely available on television? Conversely, if such a release were success-ful, would that negatively impact the program's future syndication value? When this market uncertainty is factored with the difficult distribution decisions outlined above, it is no wonder that the home video presence of series television has been a much more circumscribed endeavor than rerun syndication. For example, while *Seinfeld*, one of the signature series of the 1990s, has been a solid rerun staple in local and cable television, generating well over $1 billion in rerun syndication fees, it has yet to be released on home video in any form.[15]

Although a relative few television programs have long been available on home video, they have never commanded a significant market share, primarily due to the factors discussed above. The contrast between television and film on home video is stark: while the majority of extant feature-length Hollywood films released during the sound era have found their way to tape or disc at least once, the number of television series made available on home video represents only a tiny percentage of the output of the American television industry. This marginalization has been compounded by the fact that "television" has not been a common category in most video rental and sales outlets. Home video has long been industrially structured and culturally promoted as "film," with the vast majority of tapes and discs in the market drawn from theatrical features, and the very iconography of video retailing redolent with stereotypical Hollywood imagery.[16] Accordingly, the medium-specificity of television ceased to function as a viable genre in video rental stores and retailers, and its programs were generally folded into established cinematic genres.

Despite these significant barriers, however, television series have still been released to home video. According to Sam Frank's *Buyer's Guide to Fifty Years of Television on Home Video*, hundreds of different television series had been made available on commercial home video in the United States by the end of the century.[17] Most of these programs have had only small-run releases on niche distributors like Shokus, which specializes in little-seen series in the public domain from the 1950s and 1960s, or through mail-order clubs like Columbia House, which serviced relatively small market niches without having to win over retailers. Most significantly, virtually every series made available on home video during this period was only ever released in individual episode or incomplete collected configurations; only a scant handful were ever released in totality on VHS or laserdisc.[18] However, the introduction of DVD technology at the turn of the century provided a critical spark to the expansion of television on home video, due to several interrelated factors: the rapid, exponential growth of the DVD market, the unique properties and distinction of the technology itself, and the successful creation and exploitation of cult audiences. The culmination of these factors has been the season box set, the video object that successfully converted broadcast flow to published text, and finally crystallized television, and its repetiton, into a tangible form.

The DVD Effect

While we may often refer to the shiny boxes and tiny devices that we call "technology" as "revolutionary," they are ultimately only the physical manifestations of developments within existing social, industrial, and cultural formations. As Brian Winston states, "[T]here is nothing in the histories of electrical and electronic communication systems to indicate that significant major changes have not been accommodated by preexisting social formations."[19] Despite the ostensibly neutral science of the laboratory, technologies are social, produced from and entering into established contexts that facilitate particular uses while curtailing others. Accordingly, it is certainly significant that the key media technologies of the past 50 years, ranging from analog audiotape to the personal computer to digital high definition video, have all centered on the issue of information storage and reproduction, helping foster the move away from "live" media forms, and towards the collection and repetition of existing texts. As Miège argues, these developments "may be essentially characterized as a confrontation between the publishing model and the flow model.... The stakes involved are considerable."[20]

As media industries have required increasing amounts of revenue from extant products in order to survive, and as media users have favored media that provide accessibility, flexibility, and choice, new technologies have facilitated changes in the modes of media production, distribution, exhibition, and consumption. Since the introduction of home video, cable networks, and video game systems to mid-1970s homes, domestic media consumption has expanded alongside new media technologies, incorporating not only the cultivation of new niche demographics (e.g., boutique channel viewers, video gamers), but also viable markets for the continued distribution of "old" texts in "new" configurations, including, most prominently, cable networks (as discussed in the last chapter) and home video. Although it wasn't the first home video technology, or even the first significant use of the optical disc format, DVD technology has reenergized this process of continual expansion and adoption. Accordingly, it is not only a "spin-off" or upgrade from VHS, but rather the first significant media format of the twenty-first century, and a major development in the history of media repetition.

The venerable VHS cassette has been around since 1976, a geological tenure in electronic media terms. Although efficient as short-term storage and playback media, VHS cassettes are also relatively bulky, and prone to dust collection. Like all forms of magnetic tape, VHS tape is also vulnerable to stretching, jamming, and image and sound drop-outs. Moreover, VHS tape is a poor long-term storage medium, with a relatively short lifespan. As a tape ages, the magnetic particles flake off, thus reducing fidelity, and polluting VCRs with the resultant dust. Nevertheless, since the demise of the domestic version of Sony's Beta format in the mid-1980s, VHS has been the only major format for domestic video playback and recording. While a significant upgrade, Super VHS, was introduced in 1987, and smaller formats were developed to shrink the size of camcorders, none of these have challenged VHS' command of the market. A major reason for VHS' market longevity despite its considerable drawbacks has likely been that its two predominant uses—the rental of feature films and the timeshifting of television programs—are all short-term activities. While video rental stores have had to manage their inventories carefully to balance high initial demand for new releases with a varied selection of older titles, most consumers have not had to similarly deal with a large amount of aging

VHS cassettes. Indeed, the bulk of VHS revenue has come primarily from rentals, rather than from purchases. For those "videophile" consumers most interested in acquisition and high fidelity, the only viable alternative to VHS at the consumer level was laserdisc, which maintained a slim hold on the high end of the home video market in the 1980s and 1990s.

This situation held sway until the spring of 1997, when DVD technology was introduced after years of development and delay. Since then, the DVD player has supplanted the VCR as the most quickly adapted electronic appliance in history. Despite a global recession in the early 2000s, DVD players have been on an exponential growth curve. As of this writing, they are present in over half of U.S. households, a landmark reached in less than half the time it took the VCR.[21] As a "must-have" technology, DVD received all the press, and increasingly, all the retail space, in the early 2000s, with VCRs and VHS tapes pushed to the margins in major retail outlets like Best Buy, Borders, Circuit City, and Amazon.com. Like the vinyl LP in the early 1990s, the VHS tape is an endangered species.

For the purposes of media reproduction and storage—i.e., high-fidelity repetition—DVD technology is not only "new"; it is also demonstrably "improved." Even the disc itself, and, more importantly, its packaging, have decided aesthetic advantages over their VHS counterparts. The DVD extends the 20-year reign of the slim, shiny 5-inch circle of the compact disc (CD), signifying the long-delayed arrival of video in a familiar, convenient digital format, and implying it will do for home video what the CD has done for home audio.[22] Similarly, the DVD case appears to be the logical merger of the VHS sleeve and the CD jewel box, with the height of the former and the width of the latter. However, unlike the open-bottom cardboard sleeve that provides minimal protection to VHS tapes, the plastic Amaray DVD "keepcase" offers snug security, effectively protecting the disc and presenting a clean surface, while taking up even less space on the shelf.

The state-of-the-art outward appearance of DVD is reflected in the technical specifications of the format itself. Optically encoded with binary data rather than the physical manipulation of magnetic particles, DVD reproduction is clean and vibrant against the fuzzy and muddled look and sound of VHS. This factor alone generated the initial "early adapter" boost from cinephiles, who appreciated a home presentation of films that was finally much closer to theatrical glory, with finer detail, deeper contrast, a wider color spectrum, a cinematic aspect ratio, and multiple-channel sound. In addition, the "random access" feature of DVD content has fostered an array of additional textual materials: stylish interactive menus, behind-the-scenes documentaries, theatrical trailers, audio commentaries, photo galleries, cast and crew biographies, storyboards, deleted scenes, and hidden "easter eggs."[23] Moreover, even when all of these enhancements and additions are factored in, DVDs offer a much smaller package than either VHS tape or laserdisc. Several hours of high-fidelity audio and video signals can be held on one side of a DVD, tripling (or better) VHS' storage capacity while simultaneously improving upon its audiovisual quality. Thus, an entire film, and all of its additional material, can easily be experienced in high-fidelity glory without changing the disc or even getting up from the couch.

DVD has sparked a new approach to the video distribution of feature films, as the upgraded audiovisual quality and inclusion of extra materials has raised the cultural status of video releases both within Hollywood and in general. While discs still serve as functional copies of an original text, the additional features included on most DVDs amplify various elements of their central text, thus producing new media experiences.[24] Simply put, watching a DVD of a feature film is a distinct experience from watching it in any other form, be it in the theater, on television, or on videotape. The uniqueness of this experience has been exploited by the media industry, with most feature film releases containing more material than can be experienced in one sitting. Indeed, it could be argued that DVDs, rather than theatrical prints, contain the "final" version of the film. Accordingly, seizing an opportunity to reshape the home video market, Hollywood studios and other DVD distributors have emphasized sales more than rentals, promoting the idea of the DVD text as a collectible commodity. Led by Warner Home Video president Warren Lieberfarb's virtual crusade to promote DVD as a purchasable format, studios moved away from the two-tier pricing system that had maintained the VHS rental market since the early 1980s, and instead introduced DVD with lower, "day-and-date" pricing.[25] This made titles directly available for purchase by consumers at the beginning of the home video window (usually a few months after its theatrical release), rather than several months or even years later, as had been the case with VHS. The list price for new feature films on DVD was typically around $25 as of 2004, but standard discounts at major retailers typically lowered the actual sales price by several dollars, putting DVDs on par with CDs at $15–20, thus sparking greater purchases. In addition, retailers also dedicated much more space to DVDs than they had to VHS tapes by the early 2000s, adding availability to the format's affordability.

This general shift to *acquisitive repetition* has certainly indicated a significant change in the consumption of film, domestic or otherwise, and is a topic itself worthy of further investigation. However, DVD has had a more profound impact on the relationship between television and home video, as the crucial issue of the physical space taken up by television-based home video objects has now been effectively solved. While space has rarely entered into the study of domestic media consumption, it is a significant consideration for home video.[26] Recorded media throughout history are always designed for optimum convenience, a quality that ideally includes not only accessibility but also *modularity*: individual units should be similar enough in dimension to others of its kind to facilitate mass production, mass retailing, and domestic storage. The mass production and circulation of publishers' libraries beginning in the late nineteenth century detailed in chapter one was only the first such expansion of industrialized culture into domestic space. Moreover, extensive media collections, so much a part of the modern domestic environment, require effective, aesthetically compatible storage. Whether the collections consist of books, LPs, CDs, VHS tapes, laserdiscs, or DVDs, users generally take care to store their media properly, ideally in some form of order. Indeed, as Bjarkman notes, the pursuit of "order," however defined, is actually one of the distinct pleasures of video collecting.[27]

Television DVD releases continue this history of modularity and efficiency. Each disk typically holds two to four episodes, thus condensing two (VHS) units into one. However, since a DVD case also takes up about half the shelf space of a VHS tape, this is actually a four-fold reduction in space. As discussed above, the DVD case also fits comfortably in existing storage systems designed for VHS tapes or CDs. Although this condensation has significantly reduced the space necessary for a large collection of titles, for television releases it still presents a considerable investment in space. For example, a complete collection of a long-running series, at a rate of two to four episodes per disc, could still result in dozens of separate cases.[28] The video industry's solution to this dilemma has been to amplify DVD's smaller dimensions, and restructure television releases around the season, rather than the individual episode. Programs are now released in this configuration as a *box set*: a single package containing several discs comprising an entire season. This practice, first effectively utilized by Fox with the release of *The X-Files: The Complete First Season* box set in 2000, has reconfigured the perception and retail prospects of television on home video.

The Box Set

Home video, like cable before it, was always premised in a large part on a marked distinction from (normal) television. However, this distinction historically applied only to the contents—the video text itself—rather than its packaging. Until the DVD era, home video objects were virtually identical, regardless of their content, once removed from their almost-as-austere protective sleeves. While packaging design has long been a critical part of book and sound recording marketing, it has only rarely been applied with as much attention to home video.[29] Since the primary revenue stream for video throughout the 1980s and 1990s was the rental trade, original packaging was most often replaced with an anonymous plastic box, with the text only indicated by a plain label on the standard black cassette. The shift to video sales prompted by DVD (i.e., as "sell-through") has necessitated a greater emphasis on packaging and overall design, enhancing the ostensible aesthetic value of an object meant for permanent ownership and domestic display rather than only temporary use. As Pierre Loubet, Warner Media Services' vice president of advanced media sales, stated in 2002, "[s]ince people are now buying these products instead of renting them, the packaging has to communicate the value of the movie's experience and the quality and the quantity of the material inside."[30] When the text in question is itself a television series, this distinction must be made even more clearly; even popular television series have had to be distanced in this way from the "stigma" of their broadcast roots. As they have with feature film releases on DVD, extra features and stylish packaging add filters of meaning to the original episodes, and function as significant texts on their own. Their inclusion further promotes the idea that a DVD set is *better* than the broadcast version, that it offers a more intensive experience than is available anywhere on mere television.

By these new standards, Fox's *X-Files* box sets are landmarks of media design, successfully reformatting a familiar brand into a new configuration, repeating the text with every audible and visual element. The seven discs included in each set are arrayed in an unfolding stack of trays, thematically resonant with the series' signature labyrinthine narrative of government intrigue and unfathomable secrets. Images and quotations from the particular season are deployed around the trays and on the discs themselves in shadowy silvers and grays on a black background, adding additional layers of textuality for users to admire, and knowing fans to decipher. The entire package is encased in a darkly reflective slipcover, with images of lead characters Fox Mulder (David Duchovny) and Dana Scully (Gillian Anderson) from that particular season, and a volume number on the spine. The set functions as an aesthetic object before it is even opened, let alone before a disc is played. It is as attractive as any well-designed hardback book, and, like the gaudy volumes of nineteenth century literature, just as striking on the aesthete's shelf.

This foregrounding of design extends from the packaging to the discs' content, which was methodically prepared for optimum distinction. In his review of the first set, videophile reviewer Bill Hunt of the popular Digital Bits website claimed he was "blown away at the quality of the image," which "puts the quality of the original network broadcasts to shame." He compares the discs' image quality to a particularly idealized exhibition space: "Unless you've visited a post production suite at Ten Thirteen Productions when one of the episodes was being edited, you've probably never seen *The X-Files* looking this good before."[31] While the image quality alone distinguishes these versions from both the earlier broadcast episodes and VHS releases, each set also includes the typical kinds of extras found on many DVD "special edition" releases, including the original Fox promotional spots; audio commentary from producers, writers, and directors; and behind-the-scenes shots. A 20-minute overview of each season, *The Truth About Season One* (*Two*, etc.), featuring new interviews with cast and crew as they recall that particular season, is also included on each set, reinforcing the concept of the season as both cultural (this particular set of stories in these characters' lives) and industrial (this particular set of episodes produced at this particular time by this particular talent), and fostering the construction of an *X-Files* heritage. Evocative animated menus, accompanied by Mark Snow's theme music, and ending in an iconic freeze frame image from the episode or feature chosen to view, complete the stylistic thread connecting all the features. Like the interstitial material on TV Land and other cable boutiques, these menus unite the themes introduced in the packaging and culminated in the program and additional features.

While feature films had already been released on DVD with attractive packaging, *The X-Files: The Complete First Season* was the first time such considerations were applied to an entire television season, and ultimately an entire series.[32] The *X-Files* sets set a high standard for television on home video, and sparked the demand for more series to be released in this configuration. Accordingly, other distributors soon adopted it, with a similar design philosophy, and similar success. By late 2001, the box set had become the standard method for releasing television series on DVD. All of the sets released since then have utilized design elements pioneered by *The X-Files* box sets, including iconic packaging and menus, enhanced audiovisual fidelity (often incorporating widescreen aspect ratios and 5.1 channel sound), and the liberal inclusion of "special features."

While critics like Hunt have hailed the product design and content quality of these sets, good design doesn't guarantee good sales. Given the uncertainty about upsetting the possible syndication of these series, the pricing and marketing of such unprecedented media products had to be carefully considered. In order to test the market for television on home video, and to assuage the anxieties of broadcast syndication divisions, distributors prioritized programs with particularly solid—if not necessarily "mass"—followings: the so-called "cult audiences" (in industry-speak) who had proven to be loyal consumers of licensed merchandize in the past. As Chapter 5 described, this kind of devotion arose with the television heritage in the 1970s, but has had very few sanctioned outlets in mainstream society. By the late 1990s, active fan cultures had grown around series ranging from *The Avengers* to *Xena: Warrior Princess*, and the video collecting "underground" described by Bjarkman had expanded alongside them. As the "ultimate" edition of a favored television text, DVD box sets represented a significant means to attract these fans, channelling their engagement to "official," industry-released products.

Although Fox was the first distributor to release a long-running series as a box set, A&E was the first to successfully gamble with a cult audience, when it began releasing *The Avengers* on DVD in 1999 (albeit in episode collections—sold in individual discs or two-disc sets—rather than box sets). The initial acclaim and success of their Diana Rigg releases prompted them to release the series' remaining episodes (as well as its 1970s sequel, *The New Avengers*). A&E subsequently issued many other "cult" titles, focusing primarily on other British imports, including *Monty Python's Flying Circus*, *The Prisoner*, *Secret Agent*, and several Gerry Anderson-produced science fiction series (e.g., *Captain Scarlet, Space: 1999, Thunderbirds*). With the exception of Monty Python, none of these series has had a high profile in the United States outside of esoteric fan circles. Indeed, most of them had had no extensive television exposure at all in this country. However, as borne out by A&E's successes with these titles, they do have just enough engaged fans to warrant carefully targeted DVD releases.[33] Moreover, A&E has advertised these releases precisely as "cult TV," dedicating an entire section of their online store under that description.

Like the "early adopters" of new high-tech products, fans can be counted on to purchase new DVDs, often as soon as they hit the market. Retailers have augmented this trend by offering large discounts for pre-orders and first-week purchases. Since most high-volume purchasing fans are also active Internet users, websites such as the Home Theater Forum, DVD File, and The Digital Bits have assumed a central role in channeling fan demands to the industry. DVD producers and studio video division representatives regularly read and even participate in these forums, attempting to understand and cater to their most ardent market.[34] Once box sets became the norm, fans pressed distributors for box set releases of their favorite shows. An entire website, tvshowsondvd.com, was even created to track television DVD releases, and help amplify fan requests. Once this fan demand was tapped, even series that had previously been released on DVD as individual discs, or in "best of" collections were reissued as season box sets.[35] A few major distributors, including Paramount, Sony and Warner Bros, even sought input directly from their potential fan consumers with online polls that gauged which of their series should be released in DVD box sets, with what additional features, and at what price. For example, while Paramount released the original *Star Trek* as individual discs (with two episodes per release) from 1999 to 2001, it shifted its strategy to season box sets for the remaining series in the franchise when overwhelming user demand for the configuration was indicated in its polling.[36] As Michael Arkin, Paramount senior VP of marketing stated in 2002, "this is how consumers are expecting to get TV series on DVD."[37]

However, even with ardent consumers on deck, product pricing has had to be carefully considered. Season box sets vary widely in price, but are typically between $60 and $100, with additional discounts of 20–40% standard on several online retailers. This is still a fairly significant investment relative to an individual feature film, and is particularly so once an entire series is purchased; a complete collection of all nine *X-Files* box sets, for example, would cost over $1000 at their original list price. However, it has apparently been a cost worth bearing for those interested in acquiring the definitive edition of their favorite television series. Indeed, despite their relatively high cost, box sets have sold much better than VHS releases of television series ever did, if not at the same levels as the typical $15–20 film release.[38] Moreover, box sets are widely available even in general retailers like Target and Wal-Mart, with a market presence television releases had never attained on VHS. Indeed, as the shift to major retailers indicates, after established success with "cult" series, distributors began to release more mainstream programs like *CSI*, *ER*, and *Friends* as box sets; even *Seinfeld* is now scheduled for a DVD box set release.[39] In only a few years, DVD box sets of television series have become as expected as DVD releases of feature films.

The success of box sets has also apparently calmed the worries of television syndicators, most of which, as the last two chapters have addressed, are more firmly integrated into the same gargantuan media corporations. Rather than only function as draws for advertisers, television programs are now seen as multi-faceted properties that can spark several complimentary revenue streams. While Fox reportedly delayed the release of the first season box set of *Buffy The Vampire Slayer* (from September 2001 to January 2002) because of concerns about interference with its syndication debut, this issue seems to have dissipated since then.[40] Indeed, *Buffy* has sold extensively on DVD while still performing relatively well in cable and local syndication. Much more telling, however, has been the move to release ongoing series in DVD box sets well *before* their syndication sale. Many popular drama series are now routinely prepared for DVD release in the midst of their network runs, a strategy that would have been inconceivable during the VHS era. Paramount had no apparent qualms about releasing the first seasons of its ultra-popular *CSI: Crime Scene Investigation* on DVD in 2003, while Fox successfully promoted the new seasons of its "real time" thriller *24* through the release of box sets of the previous seasons. As Fox Home Entertainment senior VP Peter Staddon stated in regards to *24*, "[p]eople are seeing the backend value of DVD and that there's a real revenue stream there that doesn't have to impact syndication."[41] Each of these series already function well as familiar, repeated cogs in their respective corporate machines, having run on traditional broadcast networks, and on cable networks owned by their parent corporations. Their release on home video adds another dimension to their repetition, effectively promoting the series' ongoing presence in popular culture. More significantly, such releases also call into question the nature of the "back end" in contemporary media. How long does a back end extend if it is offered almost immediately after the front end? This key question remains very open at the time of this writing.

Tangible Televisual Repetition, or, the DVD on the Shelf

In the fall of 2002, Fox chairman Peter Chernin reportedly claimed that television on DVD had generated $100 million of revenue for his studio.[42] If true, this figure is certainly large enough to indicate that a significant shift has occurred in the relationship between television programming and home video. From an industrial perspective, it may have come just in time. As analyst Paul Sweeting of *Video Business* claimed, "DVD is becoming the new after-network market, filling the void left by a disintegrating syndication market."[43] There are indeed limits to the viability of the flow model, and publishing television on DVD is clearly an effective strategy to make up for that deficit, and expand into new markets. The television series box set is now an established media configuration, and is likely to function similarly to the back catalog of a record label: as a collection of fixed recordings that can be easily reconfigured and repeated.

While this financial windfall for media corporations comes at the cost of further dents in consumers' wallets, avid viewers—including media scholars—also benefit from box sets. It is important to acknowledge the real advantages gained by acquisitive repetition. Programs can now be accessed completely at the whim of the viewer, without waiting for a rerun airing, searching through commercial breaks, or travelling to distant archives. Moreover, they can be accessed in their entirety (or "better"), with scenes long deleted for syndication added back in, and images and sounds restored to a sharper glory.[44] Accordingly, DVD box sets absorb much of the rationale for VHS collections. While the material presented is not exactly the same as the original episodes (i.e., it has often been processed more than the originals were), it is presented complete, uncut, organized, pristine, and compact: all qualities sought by VHS collectors. Moreover, box sets often contain many features not otherwise available on television, including, in the case of Artisan's *Twin Peaks* season one set, materials produced by fans themselves.

In other words, DVD box sets provide the content of television without the "noise" and limitations of the institution of television; "television" removed from television and placed upon a shelf. Accordingly, DVD box sets are perhaps the ultimate form of televisual repetition under capitalism, crystallizing the concept of the ephemeral rerun into a physical commodity. The increasingly acquisitive aspects of media experience have not been adequately explored in media studies. People have long been examined in media studies as "spectators," "viewers," and "audiences," but much less so as "users," "consumers," and "collectors." As the expansion of home video markets, the consolidation of media firms and industries, and continued technological shifts indicate, the latter categories are clearly claiming precedence in industry rhetoric and everyday experience. Media is increasingly experienced not as fleeting moments, or even only as repeated memories, but as obtainable physical (or virtual) objects in domestic (or virtual) spaces.

In the wake of innovative cultural artifacts like the *X-Files* box sets, home video has finally become, in the 2000s, a much more significant factor in televisual repetition, and the television heritage in general, than it was only a few years previously. As the television of the twenty-first century takes shape, perhaps the DVD box set is the twentieth-century medium's apotheosis. Perhaps the new flow of television—i.e., the new regime of repetition—is not only measured in time, but in commodities: in cultural objects sold to permanent media collections, alongside similarly mass-produced media artifacts (books, recordings, films on home video, etc.). As Raymond Williams argued, television is at once technology and cultural form; it should continue to be acknowledged and explored in all its variety.

Notes

1. Bernard Miège, *The Capitalization of Cultural Production* (New York: International General, 1989), 139.

2. I use the term "home video" to separate out dominant domestic applications of video technology from other functions, most notably in artworks and as surveillance tools. These latter forms have actually generated the bulk of critical thought on video technology since the early 1990s, while home video devices such as VCRs, camcorders, optical disk player/recorders, and (increasingly) home computers, have been largely taken for granted.

3. "Program" here broadly refers to audiovisual material recorded onto tangible media. This is to contrast with two additional terms, each attached to particular ends of the home video experience. I use "product" to describe programs as commodities in the market, as favored by the media industry, while "text" is used to indicate the meaning(s) constructed out of a set of signs by viewers and audiences.

4. I do not wish to over-romanticize this dichotomy. While VCRs and (especially) PVRs enable viewers to adjust the broadcast schedule to a certain degree, this certainly does not mean they "resist" television in general. Indeed, the successful use of a VCR or any other video device depends in no small part upon understanding and accepting the institution of television, e.g., in setting up to record a particular program at a particular time, or waiting until your favorite program ends before playing the movie you rented. As Frederick Wasser explains, rather than put all the power in the hands of viewers, home video technology has enabled both the media industry and viewers more flexibility in achieving their different goals. See Wasser, *Veni, Vidi, Video: The Hollywood Empire and the VCR* (Austin: University of Texas, 2001).

5. Some of the seminal works in this vein include Sean Cubitt, *Timeshift: On Video Culture* (New York: Routledge, 1991); Julia R. Dobrow, ed., *Social and Cultural Aspects of VCR Use* (Hillsdale, NJ: L. Erlbaum Associates, 1990); and Ann Gray, *Video Playtime: The Gendering of a Media Technology* (New York: Routledge, 1992). Most recently, Frederick Wasser's *Veni, Vidi, Video* has offered the first in-depth academic history of home video's role in the US film industry.

6. Miège, *The Capitalization of Cultural Production.*

7. See Wasser, *Veni Vidi Video*, 132–184.

8. Statistics from Video Software Dealers Association, "Home Video Industry Hails a \$20.3 Billion Year!," http://www.vsda.org/Resource.phx/public/press/january2003/jan09-03.htx.

9. Eileen Meehan, "Why We Don't Count: The Commodity Audience," in Patricia Mellencamp, ed., *Logics of Television* (Bloomington: Indiana University Press, 1990), 117–137.

10. Raymond Williams, *Television: Technology and Cultural Form* (New York: Schocken, 1974), 95.

11. Typical licensed products have included novelizations, comic books, posters, toys, jigsaw puzzles, lunchboxes, soundtracks, and t-shirts.

12. See Wasser, *Veni Vidi Video*, 71–80.

13. While this was a major concern of advertisers, studios, and broadcasters early on, and was presented as such in legal challenges to home video, the courts were not convinced that timeshifting produced significant harm to the flow industries. However, the more integrated and prominent timeshifting functions of PVRs have recently revived this concern. See Wasser, *Veni Vidi Video*, 82–91 on the concern over timeshifting in the 1970s and 1980s. The tension between advertisers and PVR technology is covered in many trade and lay publications of the early 2000s; see the following for highlights of this debate: Paul Bond, "PVRs could magnify woes in TV ad market," *Hollywood Reporter*, 23 January 2002; Louis Chunovic, "The PVR Revolution: Mere myth or nightmare to come?," *Electronic Media*, 18 November 2002, p. 8; Tobi Elkin, "The Biz: PVR not yet a big ad threat," *Advertising Age*, 6 May 2002, p. 55; Marlene Edmunds, "Smart TV Impact Limited," *Variety*, 1 October 2001, p. 1; "PVR Feared in Home Entertainment," *Television Digest*, 26 November 2001; Joseph Ostrow, "PVRs a real fear factor for TV's ad community," *Electronic Media*, 16 September 2002, p. 9; Chuck Ross, "Zapping the Fast Forward," *Electronic Media*, 5 March 2001, p. 1; Patti Summerfield, "PVRs won't kill the TV ad," *Strategy*, 21 October 2002, p. 1.

14. Kim Bjarkman, "To Have And To Hold: The Video Collector's Relationship With an Ethereal Medium," *Television and New Media*, forthcoming.

15. *Seinfeld* DVD box sets are in production at the time of this writing, however.

16. Blockbuster Video's name and logo (an iconic movie ticket) suggests a cinematic experience, while one of the other top video chains in the United States is actually named Hollywood Video.

17. Sam Frank, *The Buyer's Guide to Fifty Years of Television on Home Video* (Amherst, NY: Prometheus Books, 1999).

18. Almost all of these series were generally regarded as having loyal "cult" audiences, a factor that would be successfully reproduced and expanded with DVD. Paramount's *Star Trek* was the most prominent release of this nature, as all 257 episodes of the original series (1966–69) and its sequel, *Star Trek: The Next Generation* (1987–94) were released on VHS by the end of the 1990s.

19. Brian Winston, *Media Technology and Society—A History: From the Telegraph to the Internet* (New York, Routledge, 1998), 2.

20. Miège, *The Capitalization of Cultural Production*, 145.

21. "DVD Drives Video Industry to Record-Breaking Year," *Business Wire* 8 January 2004.

22. By contrast, the LP-like dimensions and attributes of laserdisc (including the necessity to "flip sides" to experience its whole program) seemed to point to the past rather than the future; the format failed to attract 95% of the U.S. home video market.

23. Aside from the enhanced navigation interface (i.e., menus) and larger storage capacity, the look, sound, and features of DVD are virtually identical to its digital predecessor, laserdisc. However, laserdisc never reached more than 5% of U.S. households. Once hardware manufacturers and software distributors started to shift production to DVD, laserdisc's fate was sealed. Although Pioneer has continued to sell a combination laserdisc-DVD player, the format officially became obsolete at the end of 1999, when the last laserdiscs were pressed.

24. These features may also actively favor particular interpretations over others, as Robert Alan Brookey and Robert Westerfelhaus argue in "Hiding Homoeroticism in Plain View: The *Fight Club* DVD as Digital Closet," *Critical Studies in Media Communication* 19 (March 2002): 21–43.

25. "Day-and-date" pricing negates the quasi-exclusive window that video rental stores enjoyed during the VHS era. While new VHS titles would be released at higher rental prices first, which were then lowered several months later, DVDs are released with only one pricing window, for both retail and rental. See Catherine Applefield Olson, "Warren Lieberfarb, The Man Who Invented An Industry," *Medialine* 12 February 2003, http://www.medialinenews.com/issues/2003/february/cover0212.shtml; Brett Sporich, "DVD is crowned sell-through king," *Hollywood Reporter*, 9 January 2002.

26. For investigation of the spatial relationships between television, domesticity, and public space and discourse, See Anna McCarthy, *Ambient Television: Visual Culture and Public Space* (Durham, NC: Duke University, 2001); and

Lynn Spigel, *Welcome to the Dreamhouse: Popular Media and Postwar Suburbs* (Durham, NC: Duke University, 2001).

27. Bjarkman, "To Have and to Hold."

28. For example, the DVD release of *I Spy* has twenty-five volumes, the original *Star Trek* forty, and *The Twilight Zone* forty-four.

29. Special Edition laserdiscs, usually necessitating three or four discs, were often packaged in somewhat portentous layers of boxes and sleeves, while occasional "collector's edition" VHS releases would come packaged with an extra tape or book, or, in the case of a 1997 special release of *Fargo*, a snowglobe.

30. Qtd. in Daniel Frankel, "They're Judging a DVD By Its Cover," *Video Business*, 16 December 2002, p. 8.

31. Bill Hunt, "*The X-Files: The Complete First Season*," DVD review, *The Digital Bits*, 12 April 2000, http://www.thedigitalbits.com/reviews/xfilesseason1.html.

32. The remaining eight seasons of *The X-Files* have since been released in box sets every six months.

33. David Bianculli, "TV Lovers Want Their DVD," *New York Daily News*, 23 April 2002, p. 35.

34. Indeed, the amount and frequency of contact between producers and users on these sites is a rare (though not unique) example of two-way interaction in mainstream textual production, a practice also worthy of further investigation. See Kurt Lancaster, *Interacting with Babylon 5: Fan Performances in a Media Universe* (Austin: University of Texas, 2001) for more discussion of this phenomenon in contemporary media production.

35. For example, both *Friends and South Park* were released in season box sets (beginning in 2002) after their "best of" collections, which sold well (over one million copies each), were criticized by fans for being too incomplete. See Thomas K. Arnold, "Home video industry makes a bunch of old 'Friends'," *USA Today*, 30 April 2002, sec. D, p. 3; Samantha Clark, ed., "Spotlight," *Video Business*, 18 February 2002, p. 20.

36. Daniel Frankel, "Next Generation Begins its DVD Trek in March," *Video Business* 14 January 2002, 4; Bill Hunt, "My Two Cents," *The Digital Bits*, 19 September 2001, http://www.thedigitalbits.com/mytwocentsa46.html. Indeed, despite the waning appeal of the franchise's latest film and television releases, demand for older *Star Trek* in this format has been high enough to warrant a reissue of the original series in box sets (in late 2004).

37. Qtd. in Jill Pesselnick, "Picture This," *Billboard*, 19 January 2002, p. 72.

38. Season sets of *Friends*, *Sex and the City*, *The Simpsons*, *The Sopranos*, *Star Trek*, and *The X-Files* have been particularly successful, with each release selling hundreds of thousands of copies. See Dave Larsen, "DVDs are on the rerun," *Toronto Star*, 11 May 2002, sec. J, p. 5; Cindy Spielvogel, "Tis the Season of Sell-Through," *Video Business*, 20 August 2001, p. 24.

39. Scott Hettrick, "Seinfeld prepping *Seinfeld*," *Video Business*, 12 May 2003, p. 6.

40. Mark A. Perigard, "On DVD," *Boston Herald*, 13 January 2002, p. 43.

41. Qtd. in Josef Adalian, "Fox out front with '24' DVD," *Variety*, 15 July 2002, p. 1.

42. Paul Sweeting, "Tune in for the next episode," *Video Business*, 23 September 2002, p. 12.

43. Sweeting, "Tune in for the next episode," p. 12.

44. Although many DVD box sets have not presented such attention to fidelity, most not only have, but have also promoted these efforts in their advertising. For example, the *Babylon 5* box sets restored the series to the widescreen aspect ratio it was originally shot in (instead of the traditional 4:3 ratio that it actually aired in), and include all episode promos. The DVD releases of the BBC series *Doctor Who* have featured an unprecedented degree of audiovisual reconstruction, to the point of digitally converting kinescopes of 1960s episodes "back" to their original videotape look.

Conclusion

Repetition has defined the production and experience of television in the United States to such a degree that even DVD box sets of television series are now taken for granted. The "old," "new," and the "newly old," continue to merge on the TV-time machine and its associated technologies and cultures, blurring the lines between past and present, forging national memory and the television heritage, driving industrial decision-making, and complicating any simple notion of contemporary culture. Moreover, like reruns themselves, elements of the history of televisual repetition continue to be, well, *repeated*. Technological innovations in distribution, such as UHF, multiplexed digital cable and satellite technology, and home video are often used not to develop entirely new forms and services but to provide additional outlets for existing texts. Similarly, as the drawn-out debates about the use of recorded media in the 1930s through 1950s and the fin-syn rules in 1970s through 1990s indicate, the industrial rhetoric of the "new" consistently masks the systemic reliance upon the "old."

However, although it is certainly dangerous to forecast general trends over several years (one reason why conclusions are much more infrequently cited than introductions), the industrial and cultural attributes of industrialized repetition described in these pages may not continue for long, at least in their current forms. While the organization, production, and consumption of the media continues to change, as it always has, the pace of such changes has accelerated since the 1990s. The consolidation of the industry around a handful of giant firms is the most crucial element of these changes, as it has fostered an increasingly greater emphasis on the immediate bottom line. Even though successful texts are still likely to be aggressively repeated throughout broadcast, cable, video, and other platforms, their typical cultural lifespan is shrinking. The rapid rise of reality genres has certainly contributed to this trend, albeit in opposite ways: narrative-heavy competition shows are never repeated (despite the fact that many of their participants remain in the fringes of the public spotlight for years), but the many "project"-based series on cable networks are repeated incessantly over several months before being completely refreshed with newer segments. However, it also affects so-called traditional "scripted" programming as well, as episodes are replayed multiple times on their "original" network runs (e.g., the dozen or so runs a "new" episode of a typical HBO series receives during its first week in release on the cable networks), double-run on both local stations and cable networks in syndication (e.g., *Friends*, which, as of this writing, airs four times a day in most markets due to its simultaneous double run on TBS), and ultimately released on DVD. Moreover, the same practices of production and distribution can also be linked to the gradual erosion of skilled and/or unionized production and management personnel. The L.A. cameraperson put out of work by a nonunion production crew is as much a victim in this scenario as the laid-off Dallas station program director whose job was reassigned to the New York corporate office.

The entire technological base of television is in flux as well, via a contentious, meandering overhaul of the U.S. broadcasting system, still slated to be complete around 2010, by which point digital television will have replaced the analog signals available now. Over 50 years of existing television, as well as over a century of film, will have to adapt to a genuinely new television aesthetic, which will provide much higher video and audio resolution, a wider aspect ratio, and limited interactive capabilities. Although this long-anticipated transition commands a great deal of attention, it is in many ways a sideshow to the more radical developments in industrial organization and cultural consumption. The sounds and images of the new television might be "crisper," and the sets themselves "sleeker," but those differences alone don't necessarily translate to any further fundamental shifts; we will all still sit around our living rooms staring at a screen. Thus, it is ultimately impossible to predict the impact that this particular change will have on the continued repetition of twentieth century media texts. That said, as the experiences with cable and home video showed, "new" media have an historic tendency to repackage "old" media.

However, on the consumption end of the cycle, and symbiotically connected to the shifts in organization and technology, are changes in the *cultures* of media technology that have already challenged the very epistemology of the repeated text. As Chapters 7 and 8 detailed, the introduction of the new, more choice-based (i.e., "push") technologies of video games, cable, and home video in the 1970s initiated the gradual unraveling of the flow model of media distribution. The publishing model has begun to surpass it, just as Miège predicted, if not in terms of total revenue (yet), but certainly in terms of the general organization of cultural production and consumption.[1] The rapid rise of DVD box sets in the logic of the industry (i.e., as a significant source of revenue), for example, indicates how the nexus point of repetition is shifting from the station (or even cable network) to the individual consumer.[2] Moreover, the abilities of acquiring and repackaging reruns are no longer the exclusive domain of media corporations: the equally swift development of multimedia-capable personal computers, portable media players, and Internet file formats and applications since the late 1990s has fostered significant new forms of repetition generated (or at least selected and recombined) primarily by users. Fans and others "grab" digitized images, sounds, video clips, and (increasingly) entire series from television and make them available online, in a wide array of forms and venues for perusal or downloading. These files, in turn, help foster web-based fan communities of message boards and chat rooms centered on particular texts and genres.[3] In the deeper recesses of the Internet, digital counterparts to Bjarkman's video collectors trade entire episodes (in the forms of high-definition MPEG, QuickTime, or DivX files) via Usenet or peer-to-peer file-sharing programs. Legal scholar Rosemary Coombe argues that the legal struggles of copyright between media corporations and these media users, who are poised precariously in an ambiguous zone, not quite "citizens" and not quite "consumers," represents the most significant future terrain in the relationship between media and society.[4] In an ongoing age of hacking, poaching, dubbing, and "ripping," the activities of such users alter the rules of repetition, and should be studied closely.

There is, however, an even larger point. While these uses' relationship to copyright is fraught with legal and ethical controversy, their continued expansion (and facilitation, given increasing access to better hardware, larger digital storage space, and high-speed networking) indicates a growing *expectation* of media-on-demand. That is, a profound shift is occurring in the normative manner of experiencing media (including "television"), from witnessing an ongoing flow to picking and choosing particular texts. Accordingly, with all due respect to Coombe's point, the much-vaunted difference between purchasing an "officially released" DVD box set, and downloading a "ripped" digital collection of the same episodes, is a relatively *minor* matter of the law (i.e., arbitrary designations of the boundaries of "property"). The very real prospect of the end of broadcast flow, as we have known it for almost a century, looms as a much more significant industrial, cultural, and ultimately social shift.

This likelihood suggests that scholars, users, and citizens simply need to better attend to matters of mediation, in contemporary as well as historical analysis. As I suggested in the introduction, such crucial questions are too often investigated at the same standard points of analysis (i.e., the text or the balance sheet), leaving larger material and cultural patterns under- or unexamined. As I have indicated throughout this study, the history of reruns on television, and the larger history of industrialized cultural repetition, have had an enormous effect on the forms, genres, practices, and experiences of mass-produced media. While theorizing such questions of culture and memory in modernity and postmodernity, *pace* Benjamin and Jameson, has certainly been fruitful, it is ultimately not enough.[5] There are, *pace* Foucault, material traces of these practices throughout the arenas of cultural production and consumption, traces that exist beyond the finished texts of television and popular culture and found instead in the accounts of industrial discourses and practices.[6] Repetition is but one underexamined facet of television; many more still remain for further investigation. I hope that this study indicates how an exploration of industrial and cultural traces can be productively linked to larger questions of cultural production.

Notes

1. Bernard Miège, *The Capitalization of Cultural Production* (New York: International General, 1989), 145.

2. Similarly, the rhetoric and experiments surrounding video-on-demand (VOD) systems point to a proposed future of content publication, rather than general broadcast flow.

3. See, for example, Television Without Pity (http://www.televisionwithoutpity. com), Ain't It Cool News (http://www.aintitcool.com), and Outpost Gallifrey (http://www.gallifreyone.com).

4. Rosemary Coombe, *The Cultural Life of Intellectual Properties: Authorship, Appropriation, and the Law* (Durham: Duke, 1998).

5. Their most seminal works are still read and consulted, for very good reason, but have unfortunately led to a focus on theory and text rather than on tracing and critiquing historical practices. For example, while Stephen Paul Miller's *The Seventies Now* is an intriguing and constructive examination of the cultures of assessment and surveillance that developed during the 1970s, his concentration on textual concerns in high art and film comes at the expense of an analysis of cultural production in other media forms that I would argue would make his point much more clearly: popular music, and (of course) television. Walter Benjamin, "The Work of Art in the Age of Mechanical Reproduction," in *Illuminations*, trans. Harry Zohn (New York: Schocken Books, 1968), 217–251; Frederic Jameson, *Postmodernism, or the Cultural Logic of Late Capitalism* (Durham, NC: Duke University Press, 1991); Stephen Paul Miller, *The Seventies Now: Culture As Surveillance* (Durham, NC: Duke University Press, 1998).

6. I am referring here to the Foucault of the episteme more than of the discursive subject, although (and I agree with Miller on this point) they can be usefully combined. Michel Foucault, *The Archaeology of Knowledge and the Discourse on Language*, trans. A. M. Sheridan Smith (New York: Pantheon, 1972).

Bibliography

For specific citations of consulted trade journal, newspaper, and magazine articles, please refer to that chapter's endnotes.

Adler, R. "Introduction: A Context For Criticism." In *Television as a Cultural Force*, edited by Richard Adler and Douglass Cater, 1–16. New York: Praeger, 1976.

Anderson, B. *Imagined Communities*. New York: Verso, 1983.

Anderson, C. *Hollywood TV: The Studio System in the Fifties*. Austin: University of Texas Press, 1994.

Anderson, K. *Television Fraud: The History and Implications of the Quiz Show Scandals*. Westport, CT: Greenwood Press, 1978.

Andrews, B. *Lucy & Ricky & Fred & Ethel: The Story of 'I Love Lucy.'* New York: E.P. Dutton, 1976.

Auslander, P. *Liveness: Performance in a Mediatized Culture*. New York: Routledge, 1999.

Baker, W. F., and Dessart, G. *Down The Tube*. New York: Basic Books, 1998.

Balio, T. "Introduction to Part I." In *Hollywood In The Age of Television*, edited by Tino Balio, 38–39. Boston: Unwin Hyman, 1990.

Barnouw, E. *Tube of Plenty: The Evolution of American Television (2nd Revised Edition)*. New York: Oxford University Press, 1990.

Baughman, J. L. "The Weakest Chain and the Strongest Link: The American Broadcasting Company and the Motion Picture Industry, 1952–60." In *Hollywood In The Age of Television*, edited by Tino Balio, 235–256. Boston: Unwin Hyman, 1990.

Benjamin, W. "The Work of Art in the Age of Mechanical Reproduction." In *Illuminations*, trans. Harry Zohn, 217–251. New York: Schocken Books, 1968.

Biel, M. J. "The Making and Use of Recordings in Broadcasting Before 1936." Ph.D. diss., Northwestern University, 1977.

Bjarkman, K. "To Have And To Hold: The Video Collector's Relationship With an Ethereal Medium," *Television and New Media*, forthcoming.

Boddy, W. "Building The World's Largest Advertising Medium: CBS and Television, 1940–60." In *Hollywood In The Age of Television*, edited by Tino Balio, 63–89. Boston: Unwin Hyman, 1990.

Boddy, W. *Fifties Television: The Industry and its Critics.* Urbana, IL: University of Illinois Press, 1990.

Boddy, W. "Loving a Nineteen-Inch Motorola: American Writing on Television." In *Regarding Television: Critical Approaches—An Anthology*, edited by E. Ann Kaplan, 1–11. Los Angeles: American Film Institute, 1983.

Brewster, B., and Jacobs, L. *Theatre To Cinema: Stage Pictorialism and the Early Feature Film.* New York: Oxford University Press, 1997.

Broadcast Music Inc., ed. *Twenty-Two Television Talks.* New York: BMI, 1953.

Broadcast Music Inc., ed. *Television Talks 1957.* New York: BMI, 1957.

Brookey, R. A., and Westerfelhaus, R. "Hiding Homoeroticism in Plain View: The *Fight Club* DVD as Digital Closet." *Critical Studies in Media Communication* 19 (March 2002): 21–43.

Brooks, T., and Marsh, E. *The Complete Directory to Prime Time Network TV Shows: 1946-Present.* New York: Ballantine, 1979.

Chandler, A. P. *The Visible Hand: The Managerial Revolution in American Business.* Cambridge, MA: Harvard University Press, 1977.

Coombe, R. *The Cultural Life of Intellectual Properties: Authorship, Appropriation, and the Law.* Durham: Duke University Press, 1998.

Cubitt, S. *Timeshift: On Video Culture.* New York: Routledge, 1991.

Davis, F. *Yearning For Yesterday: A Sociology of Nostalgia.* New York: Free Press, 1974.

Dobrow, J. R., ed. *Social and Cultural Aspects of VCR Use.* Hillsdale, NJ: L. Erlbaum Associates, 1990.

Dunlap, O. E. *The Future of Television.* New York: Harper & Brothers, 1942.

Eddy, W. C. *Television: The Eyes of Tomorrow.* New York: Prentice-Hall, 1945.

Ely, M. P. *The Adventures of Amos N Andy.* New York: Free Press, 1991.

Erickson, H. *Syndicated Television: The First Forty Years, 1947–1987.* Jefferson, NC: McFarland & Company, 1989.

Feltes, N. N. *Literary Capital and the Late Victorian Novel.* Madison: University of Wisconsin Press, 1993.

Foucault, M. *The Archaeology of Knowledge and the Discourse on Language.* Trans. A. M. Sheridan Smith. New York: Pantheon, 1972.

Glut, D. F., and Harmon, J. *The Great Television Heroes.* New York: Doubleday, 1975.

Gomery, D. *Shared Pleasures: A History of Movie Presentation in the United States*. Madison: University of Wisconsin Press, 1992.

Gray, A. *Video Playtime: The Gendering of a Media Technology*. New York: Routledge, 1992.

Gray, L. S., and Seeber, R. L. "Introduction." In *Under The Stars: Essays on Labor Relations in Arts and Entertainment*, edited by Lois S. Gray and Ronald L. Seeber, 2–6. Ithaca, NY: Cornell University Press, 1996.

Guillory, J. *Cultural Capital: The Problem of Literary Canon Formation*. Chicago: University of Chicago Press, 1993.

Gunning, T. *D.W. Griffith and the Origins of American Narrative Film: The Early Years at Biograph*. Urbana, IL: University of Illinois Press, 1991.

Harvey, R. M. *Those Wonderful, Terrible Years: George Heller and the American Federation of Television and Radio Artists*. Carbondale, IL: Southern Illinois University Press, 1996.

Hilmes, M. *Hollywood and Broadcasting: From Radio to Cable*. Urbana, IL: University of Illinois Press, 1990.

Hilmes, M. *Radio Voices: American Broadcasting, 1922–1952*. Minneapolis: University of Minnesota Press, 1997.

Hull, G. P. *The Recording Industry*. Boston: Allyn and Bacon Press, 1998.

Hutchinson, T. H. *Here Is Television, Your Window to the World*. New York: Hastings House, 1946.

Innis, H. A. *Empire and Communications*. Toronto: University of Toronto Press, 1972.

Jameson, F. *Postmodernism, or the Cultural Logic of Late Capitalism*. Durham, NC: Duke University Press, 1991.

Jenkins, H. *Textual Poachers: Television Fans and Participatory Culture*. New York: Routledge, 1992.

Kaplan, E. A. "Introduction." In *Regarding Television: Critical Approaches—An Anthology*, edited by E. Ann Kaplan. Los Angeles: American Film Institute, 1983.

Kearns, M. "The Material Melville: Shaping Readers' Horizons." In *Reading Books: Essays on the Material Text and Literature in America*, edited by Michele Moylan and Lane Stiles, 52–74. Amherst, MA: University of Massachussetts Press, 1996.

Kepley, V. Jr. "Documentary as Commodity: The Making and Marketing of *Victory At Sea*." *Film Reader* 6 (1985): 103–113.

Lafferty, W. "Feature Films on Prime-Time Television." In *Hollywood In The Age of Television*, edited by Tino Balio, 235–256. Boston: Unwin Hyman, 1990.

Manovich, L. *The Language of New Media*. Cambridge, MA: MIT Press, 2001.

McCarthy, A. *Ambient Television: Visual Culture and Public Space*. Durham, NC: Duke University, 2001.

McCrohan, D. *The Honeymooners' Companion: The Kramdens and The Nortons Revisited*. New York: Workman, 1978.

McNeil, A. *Total Television: The Comprehensive Guide to Programming From 1948 to the Present, 4th Edition*. New York: Penguin Books, 1996.

Meehan, E. "Why We Don't Count: The Commodity Audience." In *Logics of Television*, edited by Patricia Mellencamp, 117–137. Bloomington: Indiana University Press, 1990.

Miège, B. *The Capitalization of Cultural Production*. New York: International General, 1989.

Miller, S. P. *The Seventies Now: Culture As Surveillance*. Durham, NC: Duke University Press, 1998.

Moylan, M. "Materiality as Performance: The Forming of Helen Hunt Jackson's Ramona." In *Reading Books: Essays on the Material Text and Literature in America*, edited by Michele Moylan and Lane Stiles, 223–247. Amherst, MA: University of Massachussetts Press, 1996.

Mullen, M. "Surfing through 'TV Land': Notes toward a theory of 'Video Bites' and Their Function on Cable TV." *The Velvet Light Trap* 36 (Fall 1995): 60–68.

Mumford, L. S. "Stripping on the Girl Channel: Lifetime, *thirtysomething*, and Television Form." *Camera Obscura* 33–34 (Spring 1994–Winter 1995): 167–190.

Negus, K. *Music Genres and Corporate Cultures*. New York: Routledge, 1999.

Newcomb, H. "The Opening of America: Meaningful Difference in 1950s Television." In *The Other Fifties: Interrogating Midcentury American Icons*, edited by Joel Foreman, 103–123. Urbana, IL: University of Illinois Press, 1997.

Newcomb, H. *Television: The Critical View*. New York: Oxford University Press, 1976.

Newcomb, H. *TV: The Most Popular Art*. New York: Doubleday Press, 1974.

Pierce, D. "'Senile celluloid': Independent Exhibitors, the Major Studios and the Fight Over Feature Films on Television, 1939–56." *Film History* 10 (1998): 141–164.

Radway, J. *A Feeling For Books: The Book-of-the-Month Club, Literary Taste, and Middle-Class Desire*. Chapel Hill, NC: University of North Carolina Press, 1997.

Robinson, K. S. "The Performance of First-Run and Off-Network Syndicated Television Programs, 1964–1993." Ph.D. diss., Northwestern University, 1996.

Rouse, M. G. "A History of the F.W. Ziv Radio and Television Syndication Companies: 1930–1960." Ph.D. diss., University of Michigan, 1976.

Russo, A. "'Choosing Between Expediency and Refusing to See The Light of Competition': Liveness, Sound-On-Disc Recording, and the Economics of Network Broadcasting." *The Velvet Light Trap* 54 (Fall 2004).

Sanjek, R. *American Popular Music and Its Business: The First Four Hundred Years (Vol. 2, 1790–1909).* New York: Oxford University Press, 1988.

Saunders, D. *Authorship And Copyright.* New York: Routledge, 1992.

Sennett, T. *Your Show of Shows.* New York: Collier, 1977.

Settel, I., and Laas, W. *A Pictorial History of Television.* New York: Grosset & Dunlap, 1969.

Shulman, A., and Youman, R. *The Television Years.* New York: Popular Library, 1973.

Smith, R. L. *The Wired Nation.* New York: Harper Colophon, 1972.

Smith, S. B. *In All His Glory: The Life of William S. Paley, the Legendary Tycoon and His Brilliant Circle.* New York: Simon and Schuster, 1990.

Spigel, L. *Make Room For TV.* Chicago: University of Chicago Press, 1992.

Spigel, L. *Welcome to the Dreamhouse: Popular Media and Postwar Suburbs.* Durham, NC: Duke University, 2001.

Sterling, C. H., and Kittross, J. M. *Stay Tuned: A Concise History of American Broadcasting (2nd Edition).* Belmont, CA: Wadsworth Publishing, 1990.

Streeter, T. *Selling The Air: A Critique of American Commercial Broadcasting.* Chicago: University of Chicago Press, 1996.

Stiles, L. "Packaging Literature for the High Schools: From the Riverside Literature Series to *Literature and Life.*" In *Reading Books: Essays on the Material Text and Literature in America*, edited by Michele Moylan and Lane Stiles, 248–275. Amherst, MA: University of Massachussetts Press, 1996.

Tawa, N. E. *The Way to Tin Pan Alley: American Popular Song, 1866–1910.* New York: Schirmer Books, 1990.

Terrace, V. *The Complete Encyclopedia of Television Programs, 1947–1976.* New York: A.S. Barnes and Company, 1976.

Torres, S. "War and Remembrance: Televisual Narrative, National Memory, and *China Beach.*" *Camera Obscura* 33–34 (Spring 1994–Winter 1995): 147–165.

Udelson, J. H. *The Great Television Race: A History of the American Television Industry, 1925–1941.* Tuscaloosa: University of Alabama Press, 1982.

Wasser, F. *Veni, Vidi, Video: The Hollywood Empire and the VCR.* Austin: University of Texas, 2001.

Whelan, K. *How the Golden Age of Television Turned My Hair to Silver.* New York: Walker and Company, 1973.

Wilinsky, B. "First and Finest: British Films on U.S. Television in the Late 1940s." *Velvet Light Trap* 40 (Fall 1997): 18–31.

Williams, P. "Feeding Off The Past: The Evolution of the Television Rerun," *Journal of Popular Film and Television* 21:4 (Winter 1994): 162–175.

Williams, R. *Television: Technology and Cultural Form*. New York: Shocken Books, 1974.

Winston, B. *Media Technology and Society—A History: From the Telegraph to the Internet*. New York: Routledge, 1998.

Zboray, R. J. "The Ironies of Technological Innovation." In *Reading In America*, edited by Cathy N. Davidson, 180–200. Baltimore: Johns Hopkins Press, 1989.

Index

Frederick W. Ziv Company 20, 33-34, 49-50; *see also* Ziv, Frederick R., Ziv Television
The Fresh Prince of Bel-Air 145, 185
Friday the 13th: The Series 162n31
Friends xi, 70, 142, 145, 158, 166n89, 185, 195n49, 222; on home video 213, 218n35, 218n38
"fringe time" 55, 65n80, 83, 203
The Fugitive 138
Full House 144, 182
FX 187, 188, 189

The Gale Storm Show 139
game shows 70, 73, 79, 82, 91
Gangbusters 54
Gannett Communications 134, 140
Garroway, Dave 119
The Garry Moore Show 108
The George Burns and Gracie Allen Show 54
The Ghost and Mrs. Muir 140
Gillespie, Donald 143
Gilligan's Island ix, 78, 90, 104, 176, 183, 194n48
Gilmore Girls 189
Gimme A Break 136
The Girl From UNCLE 139
Gleason, Jackie 109, 112, 138
"Golden Age of Television" 104, 107, 127n25
The Golden Girls 187
Goldsmith, Alfred N. 26, 30
Gomery, Douglas 12
Gore, Al 165n77
Gould, Jack 80, 108
Gray, Gordon 46
Grayson, S.A. 49
Greenfield, Jeff 115-16
Griffith, D.W. 12
Gross-Krasne Productions 67n88
Group W 86, 87, 91, 134 *see also* Westinghouse
Guedel, John 110
Gunning, Tom 12, 13
Gunsmoke 182

Hagman, Larry 164n58
Hall, Stuart 123
Hallmark Channel 172
Hanna-Barbera 194-95n48
Happy Days 92-93, 135, 136, 137, 176, 182, 189
Hart To Hart 83, 187
Hartley, John 123
HBO (Home Box Office) 175, 176, 183, 187, 188, 189, 191n16, 195n55, 222
Hearst Broadcasting 140
Heglund, Jim 156
Hercules: The Legendary Journeys 141
Here Come The Brides 138
Highlander: The Series 141
Highway Patrol 49, 55, 66n84, 71, 72, 73, 126n19
Hogan's Heroes 87
Home Improvement 142, 145, 158, 185
The Honeymooners 54, 78, 87, 108, 109, 138, 161n19, 180, 204; fans of 124
Home Theater Forum (website) 212
home video xvii, 90, 117, 150, 190, 197-215, 216n13, 221, 222; video rental 205, 208, 209; video sales 205, 208
Homicide: Life on the Street 157, 172, 187
Hopalong Cassidy 50, 51, 64n59
horror 46, 48
The Howdy Doody Show 127n23
Hull, Geoffrey P. 18
Hundt, Reed 154-56, 165n77
Hungerford, Edward 41
Hutchinson, Thomas 41, 42, 60n8

I Dream of Jeannie 183
I Led Three Lives 49, 71
I Love Lucy 54, 70, 78, 82, 87, 93, 104, 109, 116, 142, 176, 180, 182; fans of 124
I Love The 80s 169
I Spy 218n28
independent radio stations 29